AF805710

Research on Family-School Partnerships

Series Editors

Susan M. Sheridan
Nebraska Center for Research on Children, Youth, Families and Schools
College of Education and Human Sciences
University of Nebraska-Lincoln
Lincoln, Nebraska, USA

Elizabeth Moorman Kim
Nebraska Center for Research on Children, Youth, Families and Schools
University of Nebraska-Lincoln
Lincoln, Nebraska, USA

The Research on Family-School Partnerships series carries forward work on the state-of-the-science in and critical needs of family-school partnerships research that began during the interdisciplinary conference held in Omaha, Nebraska, in September 2010. The overall objective of the book series is to set forth futuristic thinking and articulate significant directions in the area of family-school partnerships research. Each volume in the series provides analysis of the most current research by leading experts in their respective fields. Rather than merely re-presenting "state of the field" or what is already known about family-school collaboration, the primary objective of each volume is to articulate future issues, raise questions, and channel research needs and directions. The goal of the series is to focus on uncharted directions rather than past research accomplishments. The September 2010 interdisciplinary conference was co-sponsored by the National Science Foundation, the American Educational Research Association, and the Nebraska Center for Research on Children, Youth, Families and Schools. Its purpose was to develop and advance a national research agenda for family-school partnerships. The conference was organized to explore issues associated with (a) identifying research "knowns" and "unknowns" related to conditions that influence family-school continuities, partnerships, and intervention implementation; (b) determining effective mechanisms for families' and schools' engagement in partnership practices; and (c) bolstering basic and applied interdisciplinary research of the effects of specific partnership practices on the learning and development of children and adolescents. The overall objective was to advance a research agenda to enhance empirical and scientific understandings of variables and outcomes associated with family-school partnerships and enhance mutual understanding among participating researchers and stimulate research collaborations. It fostered the identification of critical research needs and methods to address research gaps and new directions. These goals were achieved through a focused effort that coalesced leading researchers and methodologists who are now developing a methodologically rigorous, comprehensive agenda and follow-up research activities on family-school partnerships. The initial four volumes in the series cover the following topical areas: • Foundational Aspects of Family-School Partnerships • Processes and Pathways of Family-School Partnerships • Family-School Partnerships in Context • Translating Family-School Partnerships Research to Practice The series volumes each have an interdisciplinary structure. Experts from a variety of disciplines (e.g., psychology, sociology, education, anthropology, methodology) contribute chapters, and the unique lens that each discipline brings to the series adds both breadth and depth and allows for cross-fertilization of knowledge, ideas, methods, and questions.

More information about this series at http://www.springer.com/series/11737

Karen L. Bierman • Susan M. Sheridan
Editors

Family-School Partnerships During the Early School Years

Advancing Science to Influence Practice

Springer

Editors
Karen L. Bierman
Department of Psychology
Child Study Center
The Pennsylvania State University
University Park, PA, USA

Susan M. Sheridan
Nebraska Center for Research on Children
Youth, Families and Schools
College of Education and Human Sciences
University of Nebraska-Lincoln
Lincoln, NE, USA

ISSN 2662-7221 ISSN 2662-723X (electronic)
Research on Family-School Partnerships
ISBN 978-3-030-74616-2 ISBN 978-3-030-74617-9 (eBook)
https://doi.org/10.1007/978-3-030-74617-9

© Springer Nature Switzerland AG 2022
This work is subject to copyright. All rights are reserved by the Publisher, whether the whole or part of the material is concerned, specifically the rights of translation, reprinting, reuse of illustrations, recitation, broadcasting, reproduction on microfilms or in any other physical way, and transmission or information storage and retrieval, electronic adaptation, computer software, or by similar or dissimilar methodology now known or hereafter developed.
The use of general descriptive names, registered names, trademarks, service marks, etc. in this publication does not imply, even in the absence of a specific statement, that such names are exempt from the relevant protective laws and regulations and therefore free for general use.
The publisher, the authors, and the editors are safe to assume that the advice and information in this book are believed to be true and accurate at the date of publication. Neither the publisher nor the authors or the editors give a warranty, expressed or implied, with respect to the material contained herein or for any errors or omissions that may have been made. The publisher remains neutral with regard to jurisdictional claims in published maps and institutional affiliations.

This Springer imprint is published by the registered company Springer Nature Switzerland AG
The registered company address is: Gewerbestrasse 11, 6330 Cham, Switzerland

Contents

About the Editors

Karen L. Bierman Ph.D., is an Evan Pugh University Professor, Professor of Psychology and Human Development and Family Studies, and Director of the Child Study Center at The Pennsylvania State University. Her more than 30-year research career has focused on social-emotional development and children at risk, with an emphasis on the design and evaluation of school-based programs that promote social-emotional competence and school readiness. She has directed several longitudinal studies evaluating the long-term impact of early school-based and family-focused preventive interventions designed to reduce aggression (Fast Track) and enhance school success (Head Start REDI). She also directs a predoctoral training program in the interdisciplinary educational sciences. Dr. Bierman's research has been funded by NICHD, IES, NIMH, Robert Wood Johnson Foundation, W.T. Grant Foundation, and W.K. Kellogg Foundation. She has served as an educational adviser to several organizations devoted to improving early education for disadvantaged children, including Head Start and Sesame Street.

Susan M. Sheridan Ph.D., is a George Holmes University Professor of Educational Psychology at the University of Nebraska-Lincoln whose research focuses on family-school partnerships and family engagement. For more than 30 years, she has been researching the efficacy of two relationally oriented, strengths-based interventions aimed at supporting parent-teacher collaboration across the early childhood (birth to age 5) and school age years (kindergarten to grade 3). The Getting Ready intervention promotes parents' competence in supporting children's early development through strategies that enhance engagement and goal-directed partnerships. Teachers and Parents as Partners (also known as conjoint behavioral consultation) supports shared responsibilities and joint problem solving among parents and teachers of elementary aged children to address challenging behaviors and promote prosocial skills. Dr. Sheridan's research has been funded by numerous grants from NIH and the U.S. Department of Education's Institute of Educational Sciences. She has authored or co-authored close to 200 refereed journal articles, books, book chapters, and research briefs on these and related topics.

Contributors

Rachel M. Abenavoli Institute of Human Development and Social Change, Steinhardt School of Culture, Education, and Human Development, New York University, New York, NY, USA

Karen L. Bierman Department of Psychology, Child Study Center, The Pennsylvania State University, University Park, PA, USA

Courtney Boise Nebraska Center for Research on Children, Youth, Families and Schools, College of Education and Human Sciences, University of Nebraska-Lincoln, Lincoln, NE, USA

Laurie Brotman NYU Grossman School of Medicine, New York University, New York, NY, USA

Esther Calzada Steve Hicks School of Social Work, University of Texas at Austin, Austin, TX, USA

Spring Dawson-McClure NYU Grossman School of Medicine, New York University, New York, NY, USA

Lauren Eales Human Capital Research Collaborative, University of Minnesota, Minneapolis, MN, USA

Kai-ama Hamer NYU Grossman School of Medicine, New York University, New York, NY, USA

Brenda S. Heinrichs Department of Psychology, Child Study Center, The Pennsylvania State University, University Park, PA, USA

Alyssa L. Kennedy Prevention Science Institute, University of Oregon, Eugene, OR, USA

Lisa L. Knoche Nebraska Center for Research on Children, Youth, Families and Schools, College of Education and Human Sciences, University of Nebraska-Lincoln, Lincoln, NE, USA

Bukky Kolawole Relationship HQ, New York, NY, USA

Sangyoo Lee Human Capital Research Collaborative, University of Minnesota, Minneapolis, MN, USA

John E. Loughlin-Presnal Child Study Center, Department of Psychology, The Pennsylvania State University, University Park, PA, USA

Katherine A. Magnuson School of Social Work, University of Wisconsin-Madison, Madison, WI, USA

Jordan M. Matulis Prevention Science Institute, University of Oregon, Eugene, OR, USA

Meghan E. McDoniel Child Study Center, Department of Psychology, The Pennsylvania State University, University Park, PA, USA

Robyn E. Metcalfe Prevention Science Institute, University of Oregon, Eugene, OR, USA

Michelle Mondesir NYU Grossman School of Medicine, New York University, New York, NY, USA

Pamela A. Morris Department of Applied Psychology, Steinhardt School of Culture, Education, and Human Development, New York University, New York, NY, USA

Robert L. Nix Human Development and Family Studies, Human Development and Relationships Institute, Universty of Wisconsin-Madison, Madison, WI, USA

Arthur J. Reynolds Institute of Child Development, University of Minnesota, Minneapolis, MN, USA

Dana Rhule NYU Grossman School of Medicine, New York University, New York, NY, USA

Katherine Rosenblatt NYU Grossman School of Medicine, New York University, New York, NY, USA

Susan M. Sheridan Nebraska Center for Research on Children, Youth, Families and Schools, College of Education and Human Sciences, University of Nebraska-Lincoln, Lincoln, NE, USA

Jessica A. Siegel Psychology and Social Intervention Program, New York University, New York, NY, USA

Nicole Smerillo Human Capital Research Collaborative, University of Minnesota, Minneapolis, MN, USA

Elizabeth A. Stormshak Prevention Science Institute, University of Oregon, Eugene, OR, USA

Nishank Varshney Human Capital Research Collaborative, University of Minnesota, Minneapolis, MN, USA

Janet A. Welsh Prevention Research Center, The Pennsylvania State University, University Park, PA, USA

Chapter 1
Family-School Partnerships at School Entry: Developmental and Conceptual Frameworks for Action

Karen L. Bierman and Susan M. Sheridan

Abstract The transition into formal schooling represents an important milestone for young children and their parents. This chapter begins with research documenting the importance of family-school partnerships as children prepare for and make the transition into elementary school. As in other key areas of development, parents influence child school adjustment and performance in unique and powerful ways because of their prominence as sources of emotional, social, and instrumental support for child development. This chapter describes the multiple aspects of family engagement that support child school success, including parent attitudes and practices at home, school and teacher attitudes toward and support for family engagement, and the quality and nature of parent-teacher partnerships. A broad conceptual framework is outlined to represent the multiple facets and features of effective family-school partnerships. One goal is to set the stage for the following chapters in this volume in which five distinct intervention models are described, each effective at fostering family engagement around the school entry transition point. A second chapter goal is to highlight a set of important conceptual and empirical questions that apply across these varied intervention approaches, including possible mechanisms of change, challenges to effective implementation, and approaches to diffusion and scaling. We conclude with a set of issues to keep in mind when considering the varied intervention approaches described in this volume that may be helpful in guiding "next steps" in areas of future research and school programming innovation.

Keywords Family engagement · Parent involvement · Kindergarten transition · School adjustment · Parenting practices · Parent-teacher relationships · Family-school partnerships · Implementation · Intervention diffusion

K. L. Bierman (✉)
Department of Psychology, Child Study Center, The Pennsylvania State University, University Park, PA, USA
e-mail: kb2@psu.edu

S. M. Sheridan
Nebraska Center for Research on Children, Youth, Families and Schools, College of Education and Human Sciences, University of Nebraska-Lincoln, Lincoln, NE, USA
e-mail: ssheridan2@unl.edu

© Springer Nature Switzerland AG 2022

K. L. Bierman, S. M. Sheridan (eds.), *Family-School Partnerships During the Early School Years*, Research on Family-School Partnerships,
https://doi.org/10.1007/978-3-030-74617-9_1

1.1 Introduction

The transition into kindergarten represents an important developmental milestone for young children and their parents. The social-emotional and cognitive skills that children display as they enter kindergarten set the stage for their future school success, predicting their later school performance and long-term education and employment outcomes (Ryan et al., 2006). A growing body of research suggests that family-school partnerships play a unique and critical role in supporting child readiness and adjustment as children enter formal schooling (Rimm-Kaufman & Pianta, 1999; Stormshak et al., 2002). Family engagement appears especially helpful to children growing up in economically disadvantaged and under-resourced families (Miedel & Reynolds, 1999), where access to early educational supports is limited and children are often exposed to adversities that reduce their school readiness. We begin this chapter by considering the various factors that contribute to effective family-school partnerships, along with evidence of their developmental importance at school entry.

1.2 Parent Engagement and Family-School Partnerships

Across studies and programs, parent engagement and family-school partnerships have been defined and operationalized in a variety of ways. The model guiding this volume recognizes the multidimensional nature and varied processes that contribute to effective family-school partnerships. These include processes that occur at home and processes that occur at school, roles played by parents and those played by teachers and schools, and supports that derive from behaviors and activities, attitudes and expectations, and the dynamic qualities of teacher-parent relationships (see also Christenson & Sheridan, 2001). Much of the original research on this topic focused on the construct of parent involvement, identifying what parents were doing to get involved with and support their child's schooling. More recently, the term "involvement" has been replaced with the term "engagement" in recognition of the important role that schools and teachers play in the process. That is, whereas involvement is a term that focuses on parent behaviors, engagement is a term that reflects the joint influences of parents and schools and the collaborative efforts of parents and teachers working in alignment to support child school success. The term "family-school partnerships" underscores the breadth of this domain, recognizing the contributions made by parents, teachers/schools, and the quality of their partnership and collaboration (Sheridan & Kim, 2015).

In terms of parent contributions to this partnership, past research has identified several important dimensions of parent involvement that are associated in differential ways with child school readiness and school functioning. Studying these factors in a large sample of low-income families, Fantuzzo, Tighe, and Perry (2000) identified three dimensions of parent involvement, validated cross-sectionally in prekindergarten, kindergarten, and first grade: home-based involvement, school-based involvement, and parent-teacher conferencing. Home-based involvement included parent support for learning outside of the school setting, reflected by parent-child reading, working on learning activities at home, and parent-child conversations about school. School-based involvement included activities and behaviors that occurred at school in support of child learning, such as volunteering in the classroom, going on school trips, and attending school events. Home-school conferencing was defined by communications between parents and school personnel focused on child learning, such as talking with the teacher about school progress, problem-solving about child problems at school, and discussing parent activities that might support child learning. In a subsequent longitudinal study, Fantuzzo, McWayne, Perry, and Childs (2004) found that all three dimensions of parent involvement were associated with child adjustment and performance at school, including fewer behavior problems, higher levels of social competence and motivation, and larger vocabularies. When considered together, home-based involvement emerged as the best unique predictor of reduced behavior problems, adaptive approaches to learning, and vocabulary. School-based involvement and home-school conferencing also predicted positive school outcomes, but their contributions were not significant once the association with home-based involvement was taken into account. The researchers speculated that school-based parent involvement and parent-teacher conferencing were less uniquely predictive of child outcomes because the impact of these forms of engagement may depend heavily on the quality of interactions that parents experience with teachers and at schools (Fantuzzo et al., 2004). Such speculations open the door for more family-school research focusing on the quality of interpersonal dynamics between parents and teachers (i.e., how they interact) and not simply structural features of the interaction (i.e., what they do). Additional research has identified factors underlying and complementing parent involvement behaviors, including attitudes and beliefs about parental roles, motivation and self-efficacy, as well as academic expectations for child performance that contribute to the impact of parent involvement on child school success (Martini & Senechal, 2012; Whitaker, 2018).

Whereas studies of parent involvement focus on parent attitudes and behaviors, researchers have noted that these parent attitudes and behaviors are affected by features embedded in the school context, including the quality of parents' interpersonal relationships with teachers and school personnel (Fantuzzo et al., 2004) and the school practices and teacher attitudes and behaviors that invite and support parent engagement (Green et at., 2007). For example, among families participating in Early Head Start (serving children 0–3 years of age), Elicker and colleagues, (2013) found that the quality of teacher-parent relationships (reflecting warmth and collaboration) was a significant predictor of positive parenting and of child social competence and early learning. Broad factors such as school climate as well as specific suggestions and invitations may affect parent perceptions of opportunities for school-based engagement and parent decisions regarding participation (Green et al., 2007).

Beyond opportunities for parents to visit and support their children at school, the degree to which teachers and parents are able to work collaboratively and in alignment also appears important. Collaborative practices between parents and teachers include aligning assessments of child needs and educational goals and developing and implementing coordinated home-school plans (Sheridan & Kratochwill, 2008). This kind of home-school coordination may be especially beneficial for children from economically disadvantaged or culturally diverse backgrounds, particularly when school personnel make efforts to reach out and establish partnerships that respect the parent's perspective (Clarke et al., 2017; Raffaele & Knoff, 1999). A strength-based orientation that invites parents' input regarding goals and aspirations reinforces their skills and knowledge and respects their time and resources for involvement, enhancing parental self-efficacy and practices (Dunst et al., 2007; Green et al., 2007). Factors at the school level, such as a positive school-wide climate and welcoming attitude, along with specific invitations, have emerged as important facilitators of parent engagement (Green et al., 2007).

1.3 Family-School Partnerships at the Transition into Formal Schooling

The transition into formal schooling represents an important developmental milestone for young children and their parents. Longitudinal studies document academic gains for children when parents increase their support for learning at home as children transition into and through kindergarten (Powell et al., 2012). Children also show higher levels of social competence and fewer behavior problems at school when their parents maintain high levels of parent involvement as they enter and continue through elementary school (El Nokali e tal., 2010).

The importance of strong family-school partnerships at this transition point likely reflects several factors. First, as children transition into kindergarten, they are faced with an increase in behavioral and cognitive demands, creating new challenges for self-regulation, attentional focus, and interpersonal interaction (Bassok et al., 2016). Parents can provide an invaluable source of support to help children cope with these challenges in the behavioral domain (by setting up routines, positive expectations, and using positive management strategies), in the social-emotional domain (by talking with children, planning, and problem-solving), and in the cognitive domain (by reinforcing skill acquisition with home reading and learning games). Second, this transition to school takes place during a period of active neurodevelopment, when the prefrontal cortex that supports self-regulation, emotion coping, and attentional control is undergoing rapid growth. Parents and schools can facilitate growth in the neural architecture supporting these competencies by providing safe, secure, predictable, and cognitively stimulating contexts for development (Blair & Raver, 2015). Third, the quality of family-school partnerships formed at school entry sets the stage for and predicts levels of parent engagement and partnership quality in future school years (Hayakawa et al., 2013). The value of family-school partnerships at school entry is exemplified in a study by Sheridan and colleagues (Sheridan et al., 2020), who found that family-school connections in prekindergarten predicted children's social skills, behavior problems, and academic (math achievement) through first grade.

Despite the value of strong family-school partnerships during this important transition period, research documents normative declines in parent engagement when children enter elementary school. Parents' active involvement in their children's learning at home declines, with rates decreasing as children move from prekindergarten into kindergarten and then decreasing more as children move from kindergarten into first grade (Powell et al., 2012). In addition, teacher-family contact decreases over time as children move from preschool into kindergarten and the nature of teacher-family communication shifts. Compared with preschool, elementary school communications are more likely to be initiated by school personnel (rather than by parents) and the communications are more frequently negative rather than informational or positive in content (Rimm-Kaufmann & Pianta, 1999).

These data reflect the major dilemma facing schools today. On the one hand, the value of engaging families at school entry is widely acknowledged; a majority of states (40) have regulations requiring schools to implement family engagement policies (USDE, 2013). Yet, on the other hand, current practices are woefully underperforming (Weiss et al., 2011), with family engagement identified as the weakest area of compliance for schools receiving Title I funding (USDE, 2008) and named by teachers and principals as one of the most challenging aspects of their work (Markow et al., 2012).

The need to strengthen family-school partnerships is most acute when schools serve a high proportion of children from low-income families. Children who grow up in poverty are at increased risk for exposure to a host of adverse events that undermine healthy development during the early years and reduce school readiness (Blair & Raver, 2015). These include heightened levels of family instability, crowded and chaotic living conditions, limited access to educational materials and high-quality early educational supports, and parenting support diminished by chronic stress and maternal depression (Ryan et al., 2006). Harnessing the power of strong family-school partnerships represents a potentially robust and underutilized strategy for supporting child school success; it may also represent a critical strategy for reducing the socioeconomic gap in early development and school readiness that is evident at school entry and continues through the school years (Duncan et al., 2012). Consistent with this perspective, Crosnoe, Leventhal, Wirth, and Pierce (14) followed a large sample of American children making the transition into school and demonstrated that child math and reading achievement scores in first grade reflected the cumulative quality of learning support they received across preschool and home settings, with the benefits of home learning support amplified for children from low-income families.

1.4 Implications for Effective Intervention

Clearly, new approaches are needed as schools reach out to improve family-school partnerships and more effectively engage parents in ways that will benefit their children at school entry and during the early elementary years. This volume describes five distinct intervention programs designed to promote family-school partnerships that have undergone rigorous evaluation and have demonstrated positive effects for parents and children. Interestingly, the programs are quite varied in approach, demonstrating both overlapping and unique features that emphasize different levers of change. Given the multidimensional nature of family-school partnerships, intervention programs may emphasize change in some dimensions more than others. As noted earlier, typologies of parent involvement have differentiated three types – school-based involvement, home-based involvement, and parent-teacher communications (Fantuzzo et al., 2000). In general, school-based involvement has not proven to be a useful focus of intervention, as it has little impact on child adjustment or attainment (see meta-analyses by Sheridan et al., 2019 and Smith et al., 2019). The value of intervention approaches that target home-based support for learning and parent-teacher communication and collaboration have been documented, however, and building trusting relationships between schools and parents also appears central to engaging diverse families (Sheridan et al., 2019; Smith et al., 2019). These different foci are apparent to differing degrees in the effective programs described in this volume (see Fig. 1.1).

Next, we briefly describe the intervention models that are featured in the following chapters, highlighting the primary and secondary areas of focus of each

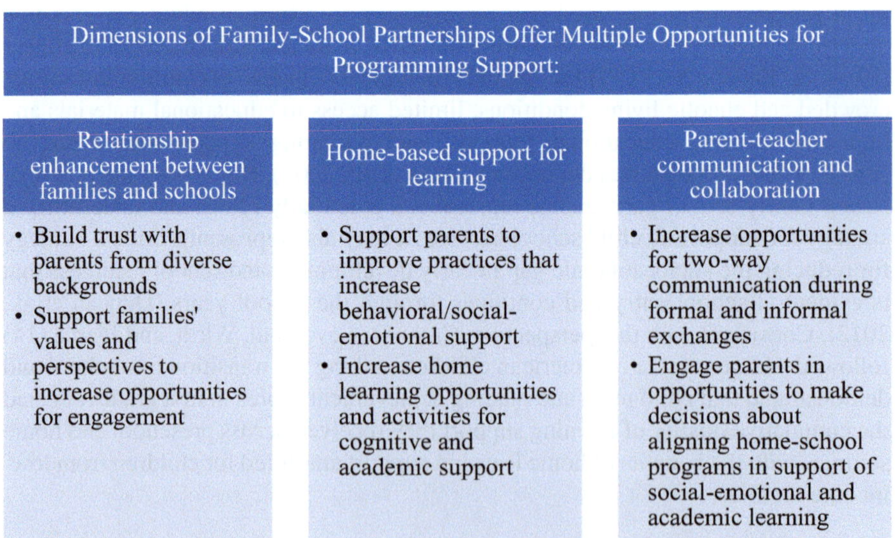

Fig. 1.1 Dimensions of family-school partnerships and intervention opportunities

approach. Our goal is not to determine which approach is best, but rather to illustrate the ways in which different approaches have proven effective at supporting parents and fostering child success at school.

Two of the school-based intervention models focus primarily on the provision of outreach activities that help parents support their child's school success at home. The Family Check-Up (FCU) is a universal intervention offered to all families of incoming kindergarten children (Stormshak et al., this volume). It begins with a three-session process, including an initial interview, brief school readiness assessment, and feedback session for families. At the feedback session, motivational interviewing strategies are used to promote parent self-reflection, help parents identify areas of strength and areas for growth, and motivate active engagement in supporting the child's development and school adjustment. Depending upon their needs and interests, additional intervention is available. In terms of process, the primary emphasis of this intervention is on fostering parent self-reflection, goal-setting, and motivation to act in behalf of child school readiness. In terms of content, the primary focus is on strengthening positive family management strategies, including the use of routines, positive support, and parent-child interaction in order to foster child self-regulation skills, behavioral control, and social skills. A related goal is to increase home support for child reading and learning.

The Research-based, Developmentally-Informed Parent (REDI-P) program also emphasizes parent support for learning at home (Bierman, Nix, Welsh, Henirichs, Loughlin-Presnal & McDoniel, this volume). The program is delivered via a series of home visits (10 in the prekindergarten year prior to transition; 6 in kindergarten post-transition). Parents are provided with learning materials to use at home and are coached in parenting strategies that support child language and social-emotional skill development. REDI-P helps parents implement a developmentally sequenced home learning curriculum designed to foster child self-regulation and language/literacy skills. There is a secondary focus on improving parenting practices with an emphasis on enriching parent language use and parent-child conversations, along with parent-child joint planning and problem solving.

Whereas FCU-Kindergarten and REDI-P both emphasize the promotion of parent engagement in home learning, they differ in the relative emphasis given different parenting skills (e.g., those boosting behavioral vs. cognitive support for learning) as well as in the design and delivery of the intervention process. FCU-Kindergarten takes an individualized approach, with personalized assessments/feedback and intervention components tailored to the families' needs and interests. In this way, FCU-Kindergarten can be quite efficient, adjusting the intensity of intervention support to the needs of participating families. In contrast, REDI-P is a manualized program, which delivers a standard developmentally sequenced home learning curriculum to all families (with difficulty level adjusted based on child skills) and which presents a similar set of parenting ideas to all participating families (with personalized applications discussed in home visits). In the REDI-P logic model, the home learning curriculum is anticipated to have direct effects boosting child school readiness, in addition to the more indirect effects on child readiness of the parenting practices targeted in the intervention. Relative to an individualized approach tailored to each family, the logic behind this kind of standard intervention is that it can more easily incorporate learning activities that follow a developmental scope and sequence and assure coverage of domains with documented importance for school success.

In contrast to these two interventions that involve individual work with families, the ParentCorps program (Dawson-McClure et al., this volume) uses a group intervention model, with families attending group sessions at their child's school. ParentCorps is designed to enrich prekindergarten programs serving children from low-income families and to strengthen family-school partnerships and foster practices that help parents and teachers collaboratively support foundational social, emotional, and behavior regulation skills. Families of all prekindergarten children in participating schools are invited to attend a series of 14 2-hour school-based group meetings. These discussion groups are designed to create connections among parents and between parents and school staff, to increase school bonding, and to share information about positive parenting practices that support child school success. Parallel group meetings for children provide direct coaching in the social-emotional skills that foster school adjustment. In terms of content, ParentCorps focuses especially on positive family management strategies that support child self-regulation and behavioral adjustment to school, with a secondary focus on supporting child learning at home and in this way is similar to FCU-Kindergarten. During group meetings, leaders follow a manualized curriculum to present parenting ideas and encourage group discussion and sharing regarding parent experiences and input. ParentCorps also includes separate professional learning workshops for teachers, designed to build their skills at understanding, communicating with, and collaborating with families. By holding parent group meetings at school and working with teachers on partnership skills, ParentCorps seeks to strengthen parent's school-based engagement, increase home positive behavioral support, and improve parent-teacher partnerships.

The Getting Ready (GR) intervention is distinguished by its primary focus on strengthening the parent-teacher partnership and enhancing the degree to which parents and teachers share perspectives, plan together, and collaborate in aligned home-school programming goals and activities to support child development (Sheridan et al., this volume). GR involves coaching early childhood educators to utilize a set of eight strategies designed to build parents' competencies and strengthen relationships. The logic model emphasizes the teachers' use of these partnership strategies during formal sessions with parents (home visits and conferences) as well as during more informal teacher-parent contacts. These parent-teacher communications provide the central lever of change, directly boosting parenting practices, enhancing parent-teacher relationships, and creating home/school program alignment which, in turn, may enhance child school readiness skills. Like FCU-Kindergarten, GR provides individualized support to parents rather than following a standard or manualized intervention program. Parallel to REDI-P, GR includes home visits (6 per year for two years), but in the case of GR, the teacher makes the home visits in order to support a strong partnership with each parent and provide a foundation for collaborative planning.

The Child-Parent Centers (CPC) program is a family-centered early childhood preschool model. Rather than providing a specific program or set of intervention strategies, it is distinguished from other interventions described in this volume by a focus on structural changes in school design and staffing to support programming that enhances family engagement and positive family-school partnerships. CPC programs are implemented by a collaborative team that includes two staff members (in addition to the classroom teacher) who are focused on supporting families – a parent resource teacher and a school-community representative. The parent resource teacher provides parent workshops in six areas, providing information about parenting and child development, suggestions for supporting academic learning at home, descriptions of community resources, as well as information about how to be an advocate for your child. The parent resource teacher also supports parent visits to the school to promote home-school connections and align home learning support with the classroom curriculum. The school community representative makes home visits, helps families connect with appropriate community resources, and supports enrollment and attendance. Specific program activities may vary across classrooms and families, tailored by the collaborative teaching team. Parent involvement is encouraged and reinforced by contracts in which they commit to invest 2.5 hours per week to family-school partnership activities.

1.5 Crosscutting Issues and Questions

A key goal of this volume is to illustrate the commonalities and differences that characterize these five evidence-based approaches to promoting family-school partnerships. The general descriptions of the various programs provided in this chapter do not do justice to the complexity and nuances in each of the models and the reader is directed to the subsequent chapters for more detail. However, it is helpful to recognize the broad-brush commonalities and differences in the approaches, as they highlight the need for additional research focused on understanding how different programs achieve their benefits and addressing the question of what works best for whom under what conditions. These similarities and differences in program content, process, delivery system, and focus are summarized in Table 1.1. Each of these programs has strong evidence of positive impact, but there may be variations across programs in the outcomes they affect, the types of families they serve best, or the school and community contexts in which they best fit.

In all cases, the programs described in this volume represent model programs that will need adaptations to diffuse widely and scale up to broad use. A consideration of the crosscutting issues and questions that each of these programs must face as they consider scaling up may be helpful in guiding "next steps" in the general area of future research on school-family partnerships and school programming innovation. The last two chapters of this volume provide commentary on the programs and situate this research in the larger context of programs and policies designed to reduce educational disparities and foster school success for all children.

Table 1.1 Comparing model interventions fostering effective family-school partnerships

	Intervention program				
Dimensions of variation	FCU-Kindergarten	REDI-P	ParentCorps	GR	CPC
Intervention process					
Manualized program		X	X		
Individualized program	X			X	X
Parenting skill focus					
Behavioral supports	X		X	X	
Cognitive supports		X		X	
Locus of delivery					
Individual visits	X	X		X	X
Group meetings			X		X
Type of engagement targeted					
Engagement at home	X	X	X		X
Engagement at school			X		X
Parent-teacher partnership			X	X	

Note: Only the **primary** emphasis of each program is shown. Many of these programs have secondary areas of focus as well. *FCU-Kindergarten* Family Check-up Kindergarten, *REDI-P* *R*esearch-based, *D*evelopmentally-*i*nformed Parent program; *GR* Getting Ready, *CPC* Chicago Parent-Child Centers

Here, we briefly raise a set of key issues to consider as we move forward to bridge the gap between current typical family-school partnership practices and the potential power evident in these more intensive and extensive model programs.

Understanding Mechanisms of Action Each of the programs featured in this volume has evidence of impact; however less is known about how they each achieve this impact. Although developmental studies have identified facets of family-school engagement that are linked with child school success, these associations are not necessarily causal. In addition, even when causal links are understood, the contributions of various intervention strategies to programs' overall efficacy at changing targeted constructs must be tested. Increasingly, researchers are calling for more intensive study of the potential change processes that underlie effective family-focused interventions (Patel et al., 2017). To do so, it is critical to have a clearly articulated logic model that specifies the features of the intervention hypothesized to play a role in the change process and to include measures of those features over time. This kind of framework and measurement allows for tests of questions attempting to verify the change model – for example, did the intervention increase the intended parenting skill or improve the targeted parent-teacher relationship, and did skill or relationship improvements then lead to child skill acquisition? Methodological advances provide a basis for testing mediation (Patel et al., 2017). These kinds of models that "unpack" an intervention often involve within-group comparisons and are therefore, like developmental research, associative. Without randomization to different intervention components or processes, mediation models cannot confirm causal associations, but they can illuminate associations that are consistent with or at odds with expectations. Mediation findings can thus reinforce certain aspects of an intervention design or suggest changes in the intervention design that might strengthen impact.

Understanding Variation in Intervention Response Interventions may also work differently in different school/community contexts or for different families, and understanding these variations is important. A better understanding of school or community factors associated with the successful implementation of various intervention approaches and more optimal family engagement levels could inform intervention design and facilitate optimal decision-making regarding intervention options by different school districts or communities. For example, meta-analyses suggest larger effects of family-school interventions on some aspects of children's social-emotional functioning have been found in nonurban/rural settings relative to urban settings (Sheridan et al., 2019), suggesting that programs supporting family engagement may provide an important resource in small schools or geographically remote communities. More research pinpointing the role of contextual features on intervention uptake is necessary.

Moderation studies that identify characteristics of parents or children that improve or impede engagement in and response to different intervention approaches can provide a foundation for tailoring or personalizing interventions for different families in ways that might increase impact. In a meta-analysis evaluating the efficacy of family-school interventions on students' social-emotional functioning, Sheridan et al. (2019) found the effects to be greatest at enhancing mental health outcomes for Black students, relative to White and Latinx children. Moderation analyses can also illuminate potential variations in the benefits different families or children experience when engaged in the same intervention or exposed to similar intervention components. For example, Mathis and Bierman (2015) found that children acquired more literacy skills in a home learning program when participating parents were high in sensitive-responsiveness at baseline; however parents participating in the same program showed greater increases in the acquisition of sensitive-responsive behavior when they were low at baseline. In other words, different families benefitted in different ways from the same program.

Moderation can also occur when children or families with certain characteristics respond differently to the same intervention. For example, Smith, Sheridan, Kim, Park, and Beretvas (2019) found that the efficacy of certain components implemented in family-school partnership interventions (i.e., bidirectional communication, behavioral support) was moderated by student grade which ranged from early childhood through high school, such that they were more effective for older students. Whereas this line of work provides useful information on general family-school intervention components related to positive student outcomes, it is necessary to understand the manner in which they function within the context of specific interventions (e.g., Family Check Up, REDI-P, Getting Ready, ParentCorps).

Identifying Efficacious, Culturally Relevant Practices A particularly important area that requires more exploration is the degree to which adaptation or tailoring of intervention approaches is necessary to respond to varying cultural norms or expectations. Research intended to establish an evidence base for family-school partnerships in the early years has recognized that there is no standard approach that is accessible or efficacious for all. Families' ethnic or cultural experiences, values, and perspectives influence their interactions with educators and may necessitate unique approaches or actions vis à vis partnership practices. It has been long known that diverse families face significant barriers to participation (De Luigi & Martelli, 2015). For example, typical family engagement strategies that involve school events, parent-teacher conferences, and volunteer opportunities (de Carvalho, 2001) are most likely to be accessible to and attract white families of higher sociometric status (SES) rather than lower SES and ethnic/racial minority families (Abrams & Gibbs, 2002; Turney & Kao, 2009; Weiss et al., 2011). In addition to practical challenges (transportation, work schedule inflexibility), lower-SES families identify discomfort or distrust of schools, low self-efficacy regarding their capacity to help, and cultural beliefs about their role as barriers to participation to these kinds of formal school events (Bolivar & Chrispeels, 2010). Although many schools rely on formal school-based activities to engage parents, schools that use a wider array of parent engagement strategies, including opportunities to support learning at home successfully engage a larger proportion of families, especially Black and Latinx families (Marschall & Shah, 2016).

Bridging the Gap from Experimental Trials to "Real World" Implementation In addition to understanding how model programs attain their gains and who benefits the most, it is important to consider factors that must be addressed to scale up model programs for wide diffusion. Currently, there is a sizeable gap between typical family engagement practices used by schools and the kinds of programming used in the model programs described here. Better understandings of the implementation and efficacy of existing practices, such as parent-teacher conferencing, volunteering opportunities, and homework support, are necessary. Unfortunately, little is known about the efficacy of family engagement practices that appear to be most practical and thus common in schools. One recent large-scale meta-analysis of family-school interventions found that two common approaches to family-school involvement (i.e., support for homework and parents' involvement at school) were minimally effective at supporting children's social-emotional functioning (Sheridan et al., 2019). Specifically, homework was not significantly related to children's gains in either social-behavioral competence or mental health, and parents' involvement at school was related to social-behavioral competence only. Other components demonstrating greater efficacy require more resources, including communication, parent-teacher collaboration, home-based involvement, and tangible behavioral supports. There is a need to better understand methods to bolster the effects of typical practices for maximal student benefit and to adapt effective interventions to ensure fit in school-based practices.

In each of the following intervention chapters, the authors consider factors that may require modification to expand the diffusion of their intervention approaches, including reducing the intensity or dose of the intervention, simplifying the measures and methods, engaging parents in new ways (such as online, Stormshak et al., this volume), and streamlining professional development and training supports. Unpacking the elements of interventions that are both efficacious and feasible for school implementation may be a first step in bridging the gap from experimentation to real-world uptake. In all cases, the challenge will be to make modifications that reduce the resources needed to mount and sustain the intervention while maintaining the intervention impact.

The model programs featured in this volume demonstrate that low-income and culturally and racially diverse families are interested in helping their children succeed in school and can be effective partners in their child's education with the right intervention resources and approach. The key question is whether and how the intensive effective programs featured here can be scaled for broad diffusion and retain their efficacy and positive impact.

Fostering Institutionalization and Sustainability The commentary chapters included in this volume introduce a host of factors that are important to consider in light of the goal of scaling up and sustaining high-quality, high-impact family-school partnership interventions. These include factors such as the cost of the intervention, the resources needed for successful implementation and sustained high-quality implementation, and the development of policies and institutional supports that motivate and enable sustained programming. To reach the broad goal of improving the kinds of family engagement programming used in the "real world" and increase the participation of the low-income families who have the most to gain from this programming, it will be important to identify and implement policy-relevant research to support the scaling and broad diffusion of evidence-based family-school partnership models. This will include a consideration of the costs and resources involved, governance structures needed, professional development supports required, and implementation monitoring and continuous improvement plans needed to incorporate effective family-school partnership programs into school practice.

We hope this volume illuminates the tremendous potential of effective family-school partnership interventions to enhance the well-being of families and promote the school success of children, particularly those most vulnerable to underachievement. We also hope it identifies key areas for future intervention design and research, with the goal of moving toward wide-scale implementation of effective programming that can more effectively harness the power of family-school partnerships and thereby reduce the socioeconomic gap in educational attainment.

References

Abrams, L. S., & Gibbs, J. T. (2002). Disrupting the logic of home-school relations: Parent involvement strategies and practices of inclusion and exclusion. *Urban Education, 37*, 384–407.

Bassok, D., Lathan, S., & Rorem, A. (2016). Is kindergarten the new first grade? *AERA Open, 1*(4), 1–31.

Blair, C., & Raver, C. C. (2015). School readiness and self-regulation: A developmental psychobiological approach. *Annual Review of Psychology, 66*, 711–731.

Bolivar, J. M., & Chrispeels, J. H. (2010). Enhancing parent leadership through building social and intellectual capital. *American Educational Research Journal, 48*, 4–38.
Christenson, S. L., & Sheridan, S. M. (2001). *Schools and families: Creating essential connections for learning*. New York: Guilford.
Clarke, B. L., Wheeler, L. A., Sheridan, S. M., Sommerhalder, M. S., & Witte, A. L. (2017). Supporting Latinx student success via family–school partnerships: Preliminary effects of conjoint behavioral consultation on student and parent outcomes. *Journal of Educational & Psychological Consultation, 27* (3), 317–343.
de Carvalho, M. E. P. (2001). *Rethinking family-school relations: A critique of parental involvement in schooling*. Mahwah: Lawrence Erlbaum.
De Luigi, N., & Martelli, A. (2015). Attitudes and practices of parents: Disadvantage and access to education. *European Education, 47*, 46–60.
Dunst, C. J., Trivette, C. M., & Hamby, D. W. (2007). Meta-analysis of family-centered helpgiving practices research. *Mental Retardation and Development Disabilities Research Reviews, 13*, 370–378.
Duncan, G.J., Magnuson, K., Kalil, A., & Ziol-Guest, K. (2012). The importance of early childhood poverty. *Social Indicators Research, 108*, 87–98.
El Nokali, N. E., Bachman, H. J., & Votruba-Drzal, E. (2010). Parent involvement and children's academic and social development in elementary school. *Child Development, 81*, 988–1005.
Elicker, J., Wen, X., Kwon, K., & Sprague, J. B. (2013). Early Head Start relationships: Association with program outcomes. *Early Education and Development, 24*, 491–516.
Fantuzzo, J., Tighe, E., & Childs, S. (2000). Family involvement questionnaire: A multivariate assessment of family participation in early childhood education. *Journal of Educational Psychology, 92*, 367–376.
Fantuzzo, J., McWayne, C., Perry, M. A., & Childs, S. (2004). Multiple dimensions of family involvement and their relations to behavioral and learning competencies for urban, low-income children. *School Psychology Review, 33*, 467–480.
Green, C. L., Walker, J. M., Hoover-Dempsey, K. V., & Sandler, H. M. (2007). Parents' motivations for involvement in children's education: An empirical test of a theoretical model of parental involvement. *Journal of Educational Psychology, 99*, 532–544.
Hayakawa, M., Englund, M. M., Warner-Richter, M. N., & Reynolds, A. J. (2013). The longitudinal process of early parent involvement on student achievement: A path analysis. *NHSA Dialog, 16*, 103–126.
Markow, D., Macia, L., & Lee, H. (2012). *The MetLife survey of the American teacher: Challenges for School Leadership*. New York: MetLife.
Marschall, M. J., & Shah, P. R. (2016). Linking the process and outcomes of parent involvement policy to the parent involvement gap. *Urban Education, 55*, 1–16.
Martini, F., & Senechal, M. (2012). Learning literacy skills at home: Parent teaching, expectations, and child interest. *Canadian Journal of Behavioural Science, 44*, 210–221.
Mathis, E. T. B., & Bierman, K. L. (2015). Effects of parent and child pre-intervention characteristics on child skill acquisition during a school readiness intervention. *Early Childhood Research Quarterly, 33*, 87–97.
Miedel, W. T., & Reynolds, A. J. (1999). Parent involvement in early intervention for disadvantaged children: Does it matter? *Journal of School Psychology, 37*, 379–402.
Patel, C. C., Fairchild, A. J., & Prinz, R. J. (2017). Potential mediators in parenting and family intervention: Quality of mediation analyses. *Clinical Child and Family Psychology Review, 20*, 127–145.
Powell, D. R., Son, S., File, N., & Froiland, J. M. (2012). Changes in parent involvement across the transition from public school prekindergarten to first grade and children's academic outcomes. *The Elementary School Journal, 113*, 276–300.
Raffaele, L. M., & Knoff, H. M. (1999). Improving home-school collaboration with disadvantaged families: Organizational principles, perspectives, and approaches. *School Psychology Review, 28*, 448–466.

Rimm-Kaufman, S. E., & Pianta, R. C. (1999). Patterns of family-school contact in preschool and kindergarten. *School Psychology Review, 28*, 426–438.

Ryan, R. M., Fauth, R. C., & Brooks-Gunn, J. (2006). Childhood poverty: Implications for school readiness and early childhood education. In B. Spodek & O. N. Saracho (Eds.), *Handbook of research on the education of children* (2nd ed., pp. 323–346). Mahwah: Erlbaum Associates.

Sheridan, S. M., & Kim, E. M. (Eds.). (2015). *Research on family-school partnerships: An interdisciplinary examination of state of the science and critical needs (Vol. II: Processes and pathways of family–school partnerships)*. New York: Springer.

Sheridan, S. M., & Kratochwill, T. R. (2008). *Conjoint behavioral consultation: Promoting family-school connections and interventions*. New York: Springer.

Sheridan, S. M., Smith, T. E., Kim, E. M., Beretvas, S. N., & Park, S. (2019). A meta-analysis of family-school interventions and children's social-emotional functioning: Moderators and components of efficacy. *Review of Educational Research, 89*, 296–332.

Sheridan, S. M., Knoche, L. L., Boise, C., Witte, A., Koziol, N., Prokasky, A., Schumacher, R., & Kerby, H. (2020). Relationships as malleable factors for children's social-behavioral skills: Concurrent, lagged, and sustained associations for children of low income from preschool to grade 1. Unpublished manuscript.

Smith, T.E., Sheridan, S.M., Kim, E.M., Park, S., & Beretvas, N. (2019). The effects of family-school partnership interventions on academic and social-emotional functioning: A metaanalysis exploring what works for whom. Moderators and components of efficacy. *Educational Psychology Review, 32*, 511-544.

Stormshak, E. A., Kaminski, R., & Goodman, M. R. (2002). Enhancing the parenting skills of Head Start families during the transition to kindergarten. *Prevention Science, 3*, 223–234.

Turney, K., & Kao, G. (2009). Barriers to school involvement: Are immigrant parents disadvantaged? *The Journal of Educational Research, 102*, 257–271.

U.S. Department of Education. (2008). *2003–2006 monitoring cycle report.* Office of Elementary and Secondary Education, Student Achievement and School Accountability Programs. Retrieved from http://www.ed.gov/admins/lead/account/monitoring/monitoringcyclerpt1008.pdf

U.S. Department of Education (2013). *Partners in education: A dual capacity-building framework for family-school partnerships.* Retrieved from https://www2.ed.gov/documents/family-community/partners-education.pdf

Weiss, H. B., Lopez, M. E., & Rosenberg, H. (2011). *Beyond random acts: Family, school, and community engagement as an integral part of education reform.* Cambridge, MA: Harvard Family Research Project. Retrieved from http://www.nationalpirc.org/engagement_forum/beyond_random_acts.pdf.

Whitaker, M. C. (2018). The Hoover-Dempsey and Sandler model of the parent involvement process. In S. B. Sheldon & T. A. Turner-Vorbeck (Eds.), *The Wiley handbook of family, school, and community relationships in education* (pp. 419–443). New York: Wiley.

Chapter 2
Getting Ready: A Relationship-Based Approach to Parent Engagement in Early Childhood Education Settings

Susan M. Sheridan, Lisa L. Knoche, and Courtney Boise

Abstract Relationships are important to the developmental success of young children. Specifically, strong relationships between parents and their young children provide a foundation for lifelong healthy growth and development. Furthermore, partnerships between parents and other adults, including educators, who are actively involved in children's lives also support positive developmental trajectories. Distinct from programming focused on parent involvement, partnership-based interventions encourage active connection and collaboration between parents and educators. Getting Ready is one such early childhood parent engagement intervention that promotes children's learning and development by enhancing relationships and strengthening partnerships among families and early childhood educators.

This chapter describes the evidence-based Getting Ready intervention, including the eight Getting Ready strategies and collaborative process used by educators in their interactions with families. Research evidence highlighting the intervention's effectiveness on child, parent, and teacher outcomes is included. Though evidence of effectiveness has been established, there remains much to be learned about mechanisms contributing to intervention effects, issues that influence its uptake, challenges associated with implementation and cost, and a host of other important variables that have potential to impact how it is received and maintained. The chapter concludes with a research agenda to guide future investigations of the Getting Ready intervention and support scale-up and use in new settings and programs.

Keywords Family engagement · Home-school partnerships · Parent · Educator relationships · Getting Ready · Ecological intervention · Collaborative partnerships · Early childhood intervention

---

S. M. Sheridan (✉) · L. L. Knoche · C. Boise
Nebraska Center for Research on Children, Youth, Families and Schools, College of Education and Human Sciences, University of Nebraska-Lincoln, Lincoln, NE, USA
e-mail: ssheridan2@unl.edu; lknoche2@unl.edu; cboise2@unl.edu

© Springer Nature Switzerland AG 2022

K. L. Bierman, S. M. Sheridan (eds.), *Family-School Partnerships During the Early School Years*, Research on Family-School Partnerships,
https://doi.org/10.1007/978-3-030-74617-9_2

2.1 Introduction to the Getting Ready Approach

From the beginning of life, children are inherently relationship seeking. Relationships early in a child's life create a system of supports that facilitates healthy growth and development. Of all relationships, perhaps the one most important is the relationship a child has with a parent. Parents provide nurturance, security, and opportunities for stimulation. In ideal circumstances, parents help their children explore their environments and make sense of their world. They are their children's first social agents, interacting in responsive and reciprocal ways and guiding their children as they learn to interact with others. Parents who are warm and sensitive, support their children's emerging autonomy, and participate actively in their children's learning – i.e., *engaged parents* – provide the context for an optimal early developmental trajectory. Thus, the focus of many family interventions in early childhood contexts is to promote parental engagement with their child to enhance learning and development.

Relationships with parents are not the only relationships that are important in young children's lives. As children grow and develop, the responsibility for their learning becomes dispersed among a network of adults within and outside of the family system. Relationships among caregivers who are part of children's broadened (i.e., cross-system) support network become important.

Family-school partnership approaches emphasize the bidirectional relationship between families and schools and enrich children's outcomes through coordinated, cross-system supports (Downer & Myers, 2010; Lines et al., 2011). Distinct from parental involvement practices that emphasize parents' parallel efforts to augment what educators do to promote learning, collaborative partnership practices focus on building positive working relationships between families and educators to promote children's social, emotional, behavioral, and academic development.

Getting Ready is a parent engagement intervention that promotes children's learning and development by enhancing relationships and strengthening partnerships among families and early childhood educators (ECEs). Foundationally, it is based on two research-based interventions in the field of early childhood and education: triadic (McCollum & Yates, 1994) and conjoint (i.e., parent-educator; Sheridan & Kratochwill, 2008) consultation. Its goals are to promote young children's development by (a) engaging parents in meaningful ways; (b) enhancing relationships between parents and children, and between parents and ECEs; (c) building parents' competencies at supporting children's learning; and (d) strengthening collaborative partnerships between parents and ECEs. These goals are achieved through interactions between parents and educators that are characterized by reciprocity, trust, and shared responsibility for children's learning and healthy development.

Getting Ready Strategies Getting Ready supports ECEs in the flexible and responsive use of a series of eight strategies when interacting with parents. These strategies are used to support parents' engagement; that is, they are intended to enhance parents' relationships with their child and strengthen their role as partners. When used flexibly and effectively by ECEs, the strategies provide opportunities to support positive parent–child interactions, bolster parents' confidence regarding their parenting practices, gently guide parents in methods for scaffolding their child's learning, and ensure parents have input on how their child's learning can best be encouraged at home and in other settings.

Table 2.1 outlines and defines each of the strategies. The Getting Ready strategies work in unison to support parents and children; they are not intended to be practiced in a rigid sequence or order. Collectively, the strategies are used to both strengthen relationships (e.g., communicate openly and clearly, encourage parent-child interaction, affirm parents' competencies, make mutual decisions) and build parents' competencies (e.g., focus parent's attention, use observations and data, share information and resources, model and suggest new practices).

Implementation Contexts Because the Getting Ready strategies are used in fluid and responsive ways, they can be integrated effectively into any situation wherein parents and educators have the opportunity to communicate about children's learning and development. The myriad contexts within which Getting Ready strategies are used include those that are structured and unstructured, as depicted in Fig. 2.1.

Table 2.1 Getting Ready strategies: ECE practices to enhance relationships and strengthen partnerships

Strategy	Definition
Communicate openly and clearly	Parents and early childhood educators are fully engaged in a two-way exchange in which each participant's input is valued. ECE interacts with parents in ways that promote two-way exchange of information that is focused and intentional
Facilitate connection between parent and child	Elements of the environment are intentionally and actively arranged or rearranged to increase the probability of developmentally matched, mutually enjoyable parent–child interaction
Affirm parent's competencies	Parent's strengths at using effective parent–child interaction practices are identified, recognized, and built upon
Focus attention on child's development	Parent's attention is oriented toward their child's specific developmental strengths and needs in either subtle or more overt ways as an opportunity to help parents understand their child's development
Use observations and data	Discussions of objective information about the child, including the child's skill levels and progress toward developmental goals occur between the parent and ECE
Make mutual, joint decisions	Parents and early childhood educators have conversations as co-equal participants wherein they agree on goals, priorities, plans, and plan steps regarding the child's learning and development
Share information and resources	ECE asks about or labels, interprets, or explains the developmental significance of the child's observed social-emotional, cognitive, language, and physical development
Model and make suggestions	*Model:* ECE uses a teaching technique with a child while the parent observes and then invites the parent to use the technique in the moment, during a parent–child–educator interaction *Make suggestions:* ECE makes explicit statements to parent about behaviors to support child's development and parent–child interactions

Fig. 2.1 A schemata of the Getting Ready approach

Structured contexts, or settings, are those where formal educational discussions and planning occurs between an educator and parent. In early childhood programs, structured settings include 60-minute home visits and parent–ECE conferences conducted with at least one parent, the ECE, and the child. As part of the Getting Ready approach, ECEs complete 12 structured contacts over two study years (i.e., six contacts annually). Contacts that take place in structured contexts are extended, regular opportunities for parents and educators to partner about a child's learning.

One of the ways that a partnership between parents and educators can be maximized is through a collaborative planning process wherein the unique perspectives and expertise of both parties come together. Many important topics can be explored through a structured, collaborative process, including individual child strengths, goals shared by parents and ECEs, plans for helping the child realize her/his potential across home and school, and assessments about whether a child is meeting important goals. Specific situations where a collaborative planning process provides important structure in a constructive and mutually respectful way are home visits, parent–educator conferences, and Individualized Family Service Plan (IFSP) or Individualized Education Plan (IEP) meetings.

During structured contacts, a collaborative process provides a method for planning, supporting, and monitoring mutually determined developmental goals and targets. The collaborative planning process creates a formal opportunity for parents and educators to assume mutual responsibility for a child's learning and development. The process is strength-based, capitalizing not only on a child's strengths but also the strengths of ECEs and parents given their unique sources of expertise when it comes to supporting a child. Essentially, this structured partnership creates a safety net for children, ensuring that parents and educators are working together in consistent and intentional ways.

The collaborative planning process used in structured Getting Ready parent–educator contacts is depicted in Fig. 2.2. It is comprised of six steps that are practiced in a cyclical, goal-directed manner: (1) establish/reestablish a partnership with parents; (2) discuss child strengths and concerns; (3) select or review/revise goals; (4) develop a partnership plan; (5) engage parent and child in an interactive activity; and (6) reflect and specify action steps. As an ECE guides parents through the collaborative planning process, she/he uses the Getting Ready strategies (e.g., open communication, affirm parents' strengths, make mutual decisions; see Table 2.1) in an intentional way to enhance relationships, build parent competencies, and strengthen partnerships with parents.

In addition to structured settings such as home visits and conferences, Getting Ready strategies are relevant and useful in any parent–educator interaction.

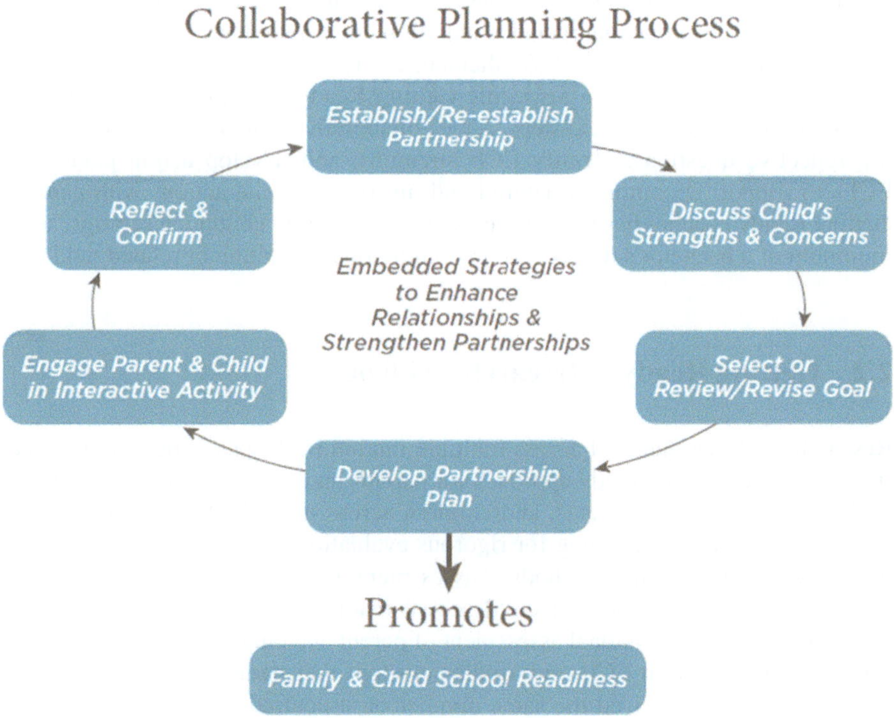

Fig. 2.2 The Getting Ready collaborative planning process

Unstructured situations include all brief encounters between educators and parents during daily and weekly routines, as well as during school- or agency-sponsored family activities. Unstructured contexts occur naturally and "on the spot" when interacting with parents. Examples include conversations when a mother drops her child off at a childcare center or picks her up at the end of the day, during family fun nights, via phone calls, and in email or text messages. Some unstructured opportunities occur incidentally, without extensive preplanning (such as at child drop off); others can be organized with advance thought (such as a daily information-sharing sheet written to update a parent about her child's day). Although brief and unstructured, these exchanges with parents are practiced by educators with intention. They represent potentially powerful opportunities to affirm a parent, focus his attention, check in on progress at home, and engage in a host of other practices that build relationships and enhance a parent's competency.

Getting Ready Training and Support In Getting Ready, ECEs participate in a one-day training institute where they receive information about the Getting Ready strategies and collaborative planning. Exposure to the goals, strategies, and implementation contexts (e.g., structured and unstructured interactions with parents) occurs via formal presentations, video exemplars, practice-friendly materials, and discussion. Following the training institute, ECEs are supported in their delivery of the Getting Ready intervention with families through 90-minute individualized and small group coaching delivered bimonthly by an early childhood coach. Coaching sessions follow a format that includes initiation, observation/action, joint planning, reflection, and evaluation (Rush & Shelden, 2011). The agenda for each coaching session focuses primarily on a specific Getting Ready strategy, its use with individual families and ECEs, and steps in the collaborative planning process. Coaches use reflective questions, identify ECE strengths, and develop action plans with ECEs to support upcoming structured and unstructured interactions with parents. Getting Ready coaches have extensive experience in early childhood settings, and a minimum of a bachelor's degree in Early Childhood Education or related field.

2.2 Getting Ready's Research Evidence

Research evidence gathered across multiple randomized trials indicates the effectiveness of the Getting Ready approach for parents and children. These randomized trials follow educators, parents, and children across the entirety of their two-year preschool experience, allowing for rigorous evaluation of Getting Ready's impact over time through multiple methods of assessment. In each trial, data have been collected via direct assessment of child school readiness competencies, parent and ECE report, and observational assessment of parent and child behaviors. To control for time spent with an ECE, our studies ensured that treatment and comparison group participants received the same number of structured contacts with families over their 2 years in preschool. Further, an observational tool was developed for fidelity evaluation of Getting Ready strategy use by ECEs during structured contacts with families. Following a lengthy training protocol to establish reliability to a gold standard, observers used partial interval coding to record use of Getting Ready strategies during 1-minute intervals across home visits. Trained observers also recorded interactions and evaluated parent engagement and ECE effectiveness during these structured contacts. Fidelity data were collected for both treatment and comparison group allowing for stringent evaluation of ECE use of Getting Ready strategies during structured contacts and to uncover practices of both the Getting Ready and control group participants (Knoche et al., 2010).

In a randomized controlled trial of 220 typically developing preschool children attending publicly funded preschool programs, results indicated positive contributions to children's school readiness as well as parental engagement. As compared to children in the comparison condition, children involved in the Getting Ready approach experienced significant, positive gains in school readiness skills including social-emotional, language, and early literacy readiness. Educators reported significant gains in children's attachment with adults and initiative, as well as a reduction in their levels of anxiety and withdrawal (effect size range = 0.56–0.75; Sheridan et al., 2010). Similarly, relative to comparison group children, those whose ECEs were part of the Getting Ready intervention group showed significant decreases in overactive behaviors (e.g., disruptive, dysregulated play behaviors) when observed interacting with their parents (effect size = −0.71; Sheridan et al., 2014). Teachers' reports of children's language use, reading, and writing skills also were enhanced after participating in Getting Ready (effect sizes = 1.11, 1.25, and 0.93, respectively; Sheridan et al., 2011).

Parents also experienced gains as a result of their participation in Getting Ready. Parents in the programs who experienced the Getting Ready intervention were observed to be significantly more warm and sensitive in interactions with their children and supportive of their children's autonomy and offered more developmentally appropriate guidance, directives, and learning supports as compared to parents in the "business as usual" control group (effect sizes = 0.67–1.23; Knoche et al., 2012). They also reported greater levels of self-efficacy, including enhanced beliefs and confidence in their abilities to interact with their children (Knoche et al., 2020).

It is worthwhile to explore for whom Getting Ready is most effective by investigating child- and family-level moderators that may be associated with differential treatment effects. Exploring moderation helps to illuminate intervention strengths and limitations, thereby guiding future refinements and applications as the intervention transitions outside of research to real-world contexts. Moderation analyses revealed that Getting Ready was most effective at improving the expressive communication, language use, early reading, and writing skills of children with a developmental concern at the beginning of preschool. That is, children in Getting Ready demonstrated the largest gain in language and literacy outcomes when a developmental concern was evident upon entry into preschool (Sheridan et al., 2011). Children's home language was another significant moderator of language and literacy outcomes. The effect of Getting Ready on children's language use was greatest for children whose parents indicated their child's language as other than English upon entry into preschool (Sheridan et al., 2011).

Getting Ready requires the active participation of families; therefore, family characteristics may also moderate intervention effects. Indeed, family characteristics (e.g., education, household composition, health) interacted with the Getting Ready intervention in important ways to impact children's development (Sheridan et al., 2011). When parents had less than a high school education or GED, there was significantly less improvement in children's expressive language as a function of Getting Ready. In addition, when parents reported more health concerns, children made fewer language gains in the Getting Ready intervention. Parent mental health also moderated intervention effects, such that parents who reported more depressive symptomatology but were involved in Getting Ready had children who showed greater improvements on their positive affect and verbal behaviors (Sheridan et al., 2014). Household composition was another moderating factor; the number of adults in the home moderated the effects of Getting Ready on children's language outcomes. It is possible that greater improvements in children's language were noted when more adults were residing in the home; alternatively, it is possible that children in single parent households responded less favorably. More research is needed to disentangle the influence of number of adults in either amplifying or lessening Getting Ready's effects.

To further advance our understanding of the effects of the Getting Ready intervention, we assessed effectiveness in a second randomized trial, focusing on a group of children exclusively at educational risk, defined by measured delays in performance. This study included 267 preschool-aged children and their parents. Results were consistent with findings generated from the first study, including positive intervention effects on children's relationships and language skills. Specifically, when parents and educators were engaged in Getting Ready, children showed enhanced social skills across the two-year preschool period and improved relationships with their educators, relative to the comparison group, based on educator report (effect sizes = 0.24–0.33; Sheridan et al., 2019). Additionally, educators involved in Getting Ready reported significant gains in their relationships with parents relative to their peers who did not participate (effect size = 0.36).

2.3 Implications of Getting Ready Findings for Future Intervention Design and Research

Despite the increasing empirical support for the efficacy of the Getting Ready approach, important research questions remain. In this section, we explore directions in need of further empirical investigation. A current agenda for Getting Ready research, presented below, includes identifying (a) core intervention components, (b) mechanisms of change, (c) long-term effects, (d) the role of provider variables and support, (e) cost, (f) adaptations and scalability, (g) contextual influences, and (h) the role of language.

Core Intervention Components Many Getting Ready studies have explored its effects as a multidimensional intervention comprised of strategies delivered by ECEs, across structured and unstructured situations, with the support of an early childhood coach. Much more research is necessary to pinpoint components of the intervention that contribute significantly to observed effects. Core components, or "kernels" of the Getting Ready intervention, are those elements that have a reliable effect on one or more desired outcomes and that are necessary to observe the effect (Embry & Biglan, 2008). This type of empirical approach to operationalizing the intervention will aid our understanding of the essential features of Getting Ready, and their role in promoting positive effects.

Mechanisms of Change Getting Ready research has focused primarily on its effect on children's developmental outcomes, with much less attention to variables that are responsible for or influence its efficacy. By definition, Getting Ready is comprised of collaborative strategies led by an ECE during all interactions with parents, with the primary goal of supporting children's positive growth. To date, no research has been conducted exploring the pathways (i.e., mediators) by which the primary goal is achieved.

Extant discussions of Getting Ready have presumed select inputs (i.e., implementing the eight GR strategies in structured and unstructured situations, engaging in a collaborative planning process) are responsible for its positive outcomes. As an indirect model, however, it is implied that Getting Ready operates through other mechanisms (e.g., ECE-parent partnership, parent-child relationship) to effect change in children's learning and behavior. Because parents are the direct recipients of the intervention, we assume these inputs (strategy use, collaborative planning) are associated with proximal change in parents' behaviors (i.e., increased parent engagement, defined in terms of enhanced parent-child interactions) and subsequent child outcomes. There are several mechanisms, however, that may facilitate or enhance the effects of the inputs on parent behavior change and are worthy of investigation. Collaboration and partnership between parents and ECE professionals may result in uptake of parents' skills to the extent that the partnership yields action steps for practices at home, engenders trust, and builds parental self-efficacy and confidence. In turn, parent engagement is expected to directly modify child outcomes. Parent-child interactions that are nurturing and stimulating, continuity in practices between home and classroom/center, and enhanced relationships between parents and ECEs are all possible mediators of Getting Ready on child outcomes. It is also possible that some of these same variables (e.g., collaboration, partnership) amplify or moderate the effects of the Getting Ready inputs on parent engagement practices. Further studies that verify mediating and moderating variables that influence proximal and distal outcomes of Getting Ready are needed.

Long-Term Effects Longitudinal follow-up data are needed to determine if Getting Ready's effects on parents' practices to support their child's learning, and partnerships formed between parents and educators who work with their child in later grades, will have downstream effects on child skills in future years. That is, it is possible that parents who received Getting Ready in preschool will bring their enhanced skills and expectations with them to relationships with new educators as their children progress through the elementary years. Likewise, educators they encounter over time vary greatly in their perspectives and practices vis-à-vis parent engagement. Given that the Getting Ready approach effectively improves relationships between parents and their child's ECE during preschool, it is important to understand how future interactions unfold.

Role of Provider Variables and Support Importantly, the Getting Ready intervention has been used by ECEs of varying educational backgrounds and levels of experience. In our studies to date, the educational backgrounds of educators have ranged from those with high school diplomas through advanced post-baccalaureate degrees. The early childhood knowledge of educators varies with some ECEs having teaching certificates, early childhood endorsements, or other specialized training. Furthermore, educators have varying years of experience working with children and families as well as differing levels of tenure within agencies or programs. To date, we have not explored how these educator variables contribute to educators' abilities to deliver the Getting Ready intervention and the subsequent effectiveness of Getting Ready strategies with families. A question for future research is whether any adaptations in the Getting Ready training model are needed to accommodate ECEs based on prior education, experience, or skillsets.

Professional development via a coaching model appears to be essential to educators' uptake of the Getting Ready approach and is ideally suited to handle the unique background characteristics and experiences of ECEs. We currently provide coaching across one full year of implementation. In our coaching model, a Getting Ready coach and early childhood educator co-implement meetings with parents; the coach provides modeling, encourages reflective practice, helps educators set implementation goals, and scaffolds new skill development. In the second year, that level of support is weaned and educators assume responsibility for implementing Getting Ready with parents. This method of coaching has been useful in supporting educators in their use of Getting Ready; however, we need to understand if there are other, more efficient ways of preparing ECEs in implementing Getting Ready at high levels of fidelity. We also need to identify how specific coaching supports interact with educator characteristics. For example, whether educators with differing levels of education require a tailored approach to coaching (e.g., varying by characteristics such as frequency of contact, planning time with a coach) to implement Getting Ready is not currently known. It is possible that ECEs will vary in the amount of support needed (i.e., some may not require a full year of implementation support) to achieve fidelity in the Getting Ready model. These types of analyses will allow us to tailor professional development offerings and increase efficiency and cost-effectiveness of the intervention.

Cost Once established, Getting Ready is conceptualized as a "way of doing business" and not a curriculum with prescribed lessons. Likewise, it is time insensitive, meaning that it is not constrained with a starting and ending point. Thus, once the Getting Ready skills are successfully embedded within the ECEs everyday practices, there are no incremental costs to maintaining the intervention (or very minimal costs that might be associated with periodic professional development booster sessions). That is, as a professional approach that defines the manner in which ECEs interact with children and parents in the naturalistic setting of classrooms and home visits, there are no "extra" costs in daily operations. Likewise, the intent is that ECEs and parents can use materials that are already available in the classroom or home setting; thus, there is no need to purchase additional curricular materials or teaching or learning tools.

Hence, the major costs of the Getting Ready intervention involve the initial training and supporting ECEs through individualized or small group coaching. Research is needed to quantify the costs associated with training and supporting ECEs as they learn to engage parents actively as partners and as they acquire skills associated with the Getting Ready strategies, contexts, and collaborative planning elements. In addition, research is needed to determine whether the Getting Ready skills are sustained in the daily practice of trained ECEs or whether some level of ongoing supervision, monitoring, or periodic professional development support is needed to sustain high-fidelity implementation of the Getting Ready strategies.

Adaptations and Scalability Ultimately, a goal for early childhood intervention researchers is to develop an evidence-based product that supports and improves developmental outcomes for young children. A related challenge is moving that product from a research context to an authentic practice environment. The process of translating an evidence-based approach to the real world is guided by an implementation science framework (Metz et al., 2015). Using this framework, we will approach scale-up of Getting Ready through stage-based implementation including exploration, installation, initial implementation, and, ultimately, full implementation. Data and feedback loops, including rapid-cycle problem solving, will be a priority implementation component as we move forward to provide assessment of need, infrastructure, and usability. To prepare Getting Ready for a move to scale, we must first understand modifications and adaptations that may produce strong treatment effects with greater efficiency, thus facilitating scalability. Specifically, we are interested in exploring the duration and intensity of the intervention and professional development, as well as user-friendly methods for measuring fidelity.

Getting Ready has been operationalized and evaluated as a two-year intervention. This requires implementation across 2 years of preschool or 2 years of infant/toddler programs. The duration was intentionally selected to align with the partnership focus of the intervention based on the recognition that relationships would need time to evolve. The professional development model as previously described includes 1 year (six visits) of co-facilitation between coach and educator with a reduction in support during the second year. While this duration and intensity have produced significant gains, there are limitations when considering a move to authentic early childhood programs. Given typical programmatic resources, the length and cost of a two-year coaching model with an exclusive focus on family engagement may be a barrier to wide dissemination. Additionally, many children are enrolled in pre-K settings for only 1 year before kindergarten, yet we want this model to be effective for all children and families and not just those enrolled for 2 years of programming. Thus, we may improve the scalability of the program if we can identify methods for increasing intervention intensity over a shorter period of time (i.e., one academic year or less). Furthermore, our current approach for measuring fidelity has been designed through a research lens. As previously discussed, a more efficient and less complex tool for monitoring fidelity needs to be developed and tested. With these adaptations to duration, intensity, and measurement, our partnership intervention could move more readily to real-world early childhood settings.

Contextual Influences Most of the research on Getting Ready has taken place in the Midwest, namely, one state (Nebraska) that is comprised of two urban areas and many remote rural communities. Our research has not sufficiently explored the effect of geographic locale on the uptake and effects of Getting Ready. For example, services in rural communities may be situated in unique settings relative to those offered in urban contexts. Differences between settings in personnel (education, training, experience, availability), connections with other early childhood professionals, opportunities for professional development, financial resources, and external community supports for families may influence how the Getting Ready or other family engagement interventions function. Though we have not explored the impact of geographic or similar contextual variations on the implementation and efficacy of Getting Ready intentionally, it has been effectively implemented in communities of varying population size and demographics and in programs experiencing a range of internal and external resources. We have reason to believe it could generalize given our experience in various communities to date; however, because our research has been relatively confined to the Midwest, we simply do not know how geographic factors interact with the Getting Ready approach and its effects.

Over several years, we have worked in various program contexts, such as Early Head Start, Head Start, Part C programming, and other publicly funded programs. Variability in policies, services, personnel, support staff, agency resources, and other contextual factors that may influence uptake and sustainability need to be considered in future research. Different practice settings provide very different delivery mechanisms and opportunities for parents and ECEs to interact. For example, we recognize that our specification of six meaningful contacts taking place in home visits or conferences may not be plausible in all settings. Contrarily, in some situations and within some early childhood agencies, services are delivered entirely via a home-based approach with few opportunities for unstructured, incidental interactions between parents and ECEs. The intent is for Getting Ready implementation to become integrated seamlessly into existing service structures; thus, we need to explore carefully interactions between structural features of Getting Ready and contextual variations within which it is implemented to determine the feasibility and impact of varying implementation formats.

Role of Language Little is known about practice implications and outcomes for children and families for whom English is not their first language. Whereas our prior evaluation of the Getting Ready intervention demonstrated greater effects on children's expressive language skills when children did not speak English at preschool entry, there is still much to be learned about how this intervention works with non-English-speaking families. There may be added factors to consider when building collaborative partnerships with non-English-speaking families. The degree to which there is a match between parent and ECE in cultural expectations and spoken language may impact child and family outcomes of the intervention (Good et al., 2010).

A related area for future research involves the exploration of the role of interpreters when working with families for whom English is not their first language. To date the Getting Ready approach has been conducted with both English- and Spanish-speaking families. With English-speaking coaches and educators, the intervention has relied on the use of interpreters during structured contacts with Spanish-speaking families. While we have seen positive effects on outcomes for all families receiving the Getting Ready intervention, the role of the interpreter in intervention services delivered to non-English-speaking families remains underexplored. Beyond simply offering word-for-word translation, interpreters serve as cultural and linguistic brokers during structured contacts as they attempt to relay the meaning behind the words expressed by both teachers and parents (Cheatham, 2011; Davitti, 2013). This suggests that interpreter level characteristics, such as years of experience in early childhood, knowledge of the family, and familiarity with the Getting Ready intervention, may impact the interpreter's ability to both accurately relay information and assist in the promotion of a collaborative partnership between educator and parent. As interpreters working with the Getting Ready intervention have ranged from family members or family friends to project or agency staff, the impact of these characteristics warrants investigation. Further, observational assessments have shown that factors such as positioning of the interpreter, eye contact between conversational partners, and interpreter's use of gesturing impact parent engagement during parent-teacher interactions (Davitti & Pasquandrea, 2017). Future research should assess the impact of these factors on parent engagement in the intervention.

Additionally, the linguistic needs of early childhood programs continue to grow more diverse as programs have increasing numbers of English language learners who are part of many diverse language groups. Future work should focus on how to scale up Getting Ready to meet these varied needs, as the intervention to date has exclusively focused on working with English- and Spanish-speaking families. A first step may be examining the feasibility and impact of providing all written materials translated into the parent's first language for families with a first language other than English or Spanish (Ma et al., 2014).

2.4 Conclusions

The Getting Ready intervention has been developed and tested in several randomized controlled trials over the past two decades. We have found routinely that it is efficacious for producing important outcomes for children and parents and that with training and intentional professional support, ECEs can implement the intervention in ways that improve quality of engagement relative to comparison participants. Much is now known about child and family characteristics that moderate certain effects. However, there is a plethora of research questions still to be addressed, including those associated with mediation (how the Getting Ready operates to produce certain effects), cost, fidelity and uptake, scalability, role of providers' personal and professional characteristics, contexts, and influence of family language, to name a few. These and related issues provide a robust research agenda moving forward.

References

Cheatham, G. A. (2011). Language interpretation, parent participation, and young children with disabilities. *Topics in Early Childhood Special Education, 31*, 78–88. https://doi.org/10.1177/0271121410377120.

Davitti, E. (2013). Dialogue interpreting as intercultural mediation: Interpreters' use of upgrading moves in parent–teacher meetings. *Interpreting, 15*, 168–199. https://doi.org/10.1075/intp.15.2.02dav.

Davitti, E., & Pasquandrea, S. (2017). Embodied participation: What multimodal analysis can tell us about interpreter-mediated encounters in pedagogical settings. *Journal of Pragmatics, 107*, 105–128. https://doi.org/10.1016/j.pragma.2016.04.008.

Downer, J. T., & Myers, S. S. (2010). Application of a developmental/ecological model to family–school partnerships. In S. L. Christenson & A. L. Reschly (Eds.), *Handbook of school–family partnerships* (pp. 3–29). New York: Routledge/Taylor & Francis.

Embry, D. D., & Biglan, A. (2008). Evidence-based kernels: Fundamental units of behavioral influence. *Clinical Child and Family Psychology Review, 11*, 75–113. https://doi.org/10.1007/s10567-008-0036-x.

Good, M., Masewicz, S., & Vogel, L. (2010). Latino English language learners: Bridging achievement and culture gaps between schools and families. *Journal of Latinos and Education, 9*, 321–339.

Knoche, L. L., Sheridan, S. M., Edwards, C. P., & Osborn, A. Q. (2010). Implementation of a relationship-based school readiness intervention: A multidimensional approach to fidelity measurement for early childhood. *Early Childhood Research Quarterly, 25*, 299–313. https://doi.org/10.1016/j.ecresq.2009.05.003.

Knoche, L. L., Edwards, C. P., Sheridan, S. M., Kupzyk, K. A., Marvin, C. A., Cline, K. D., & Clarke, B. L. (2012). Getting ready: Results of a randomized trial of a relationship-focused intervention on parent engagement in rural early head start. *Infant Mental Health Journal, 33*, 439–458. https://doi.org/10.1002/imhj.21320.

Knoche, L. L., Sheridan, S.M., Boise, C.E., Prokasky, A.A., Scruggs, S.L. & Hechtner-Galvin, T.S. (2020). Creating connections between infant/toddler educators and families: Effects of the Getting Ready 0-3 approach. In K. Dwyer (Chair), Targeting parents and teachers to support infant and toddler development: Initial findings from the Early Head Start Parent-

Teacher Intervention Consortium. Paper symposium presented at the 2020 National Research Conference on Early Childhood, Washington, DC, United States.

Lines, C., Miller, G. E., & Arthur-Stanley, A. (2011). *The power of family–school partnering (FSP): A practical guide for school mental health professionals and educators*. New York: Routledge/Taylor & Francis.

Ma, X., Shen, J., & Krenn, H. Y. (2014). The relationship between parental involvement and adequate yearly progress among urban, suburban, and rural schools. *School Effectiveness and School Improvement, 25*, 629–650. https://doi.org/10.1080/092433453.2013.862281.

McCollum, J. A., & Yates, T. J. (1994). Technical assistance for meeting early intervention personnel standards: Statewide processes based on peer review. *Topics in Early Childhood Special Education, 14*, 295–310. https://doi.org/10.1177/027112149401400303.

Metz, A., Naoom, S. F., Halle, T., & Bartley, L. (2015). *An integrated stage-based framework for implementation of early childhood programs and systems* (Research Brief OPRE 2015–48). Washington, DC: U.S. Department of Health and Human Services, Administration for Children and Families, Office of Planning, Research and Evaluation.

Rush, D. D., & Shelden, M. L. (2011). *The early childhood coaching handbook*. Baltimore: Brookes.

Sheridan, S. M., & Kratochwill, T. R. (2008). *Conjoint behavioral consultation: Promoting family–school connections and interventions*. New York: Springer.

Sheridan, S. M., Knoche, L. L., Edwards, C. P., Bovaird, J. A., & Kupzyk, K. A. (2010). Parent engagement and school readiness: Effects of the getting ready intervention on preschool children's social–emotional competencies. *Early Education and Development, 21*, 125–156. https://doi.org/10.1080/10409280902783517.

Sheridan, S. M., Knoche, L. L., Kupzyk, K. A., Edwards, C. P., & Marvin, C. A. (2011). A randomized trial examining the effects of parent engagement on early language and literacy: The getting ready intervention. *Journal of School Psychology, 49*, 361–383. https://doi.org/10.1016/j.jsp.2011.03.001.

Sheridan, S. M., Knoche, L. L., Edwards, C. P., Kupzyk, K. A., Clarke, B. L., & Kim, E. M. (2014). Efficacy of the getting ready intervention and the role of parental depression. *Early Education and Development, 25*, 746–769. https://doi.org/10.1080/10409289.2014.862146.

Sheridan, S. M., Knoche, L. L., Boise, C. E., Moen, A. L., Lester, H., Edwards, C. P., Meisinger, R. E., & Cheng, K. (2019). Supporting preschool children with developmental concerns: Effects of the getting ready intervention on school-based social competencies and relationships. *Early Childhood Research Quarterly, 48*, 303–316. https://doi.org/10.1016/j.ecresq.2019.03.008.

Chapter 3
The REDI-Parent Program: Enhancing the School Success of Children from Low-Income Families

Karen L. Bierman, Robert L. Nix, Janet A. Welsh, Brenda S. Heinrichs, John E. Loughlin-Presnal, and Meghan E. McDoniel

Abstract This chapter describes the Research-based, Developmentally Informed Parent (REDI-P) home visiting program that was designed to support families of 4-year-old children attending Head Start through the transition into kindergarten. In REDI-P parents are provided with learning materials to use at home and coached in strategies to support child skill development in the dual domains of language-emergent literacy skills and social-emotional learning. A randomized trial documented significant benefits for children in kindergarten in areas of academic performance and social competence, and these benefits were sustained through third grade. Parents increased positive interactions and conversations with their children and reported higher academic expectations. By third grade, parents reported fewer child problems at home and less parenting stress. In addition to describing the program and its outcomes, this chapter describes links between initial program response (program engagement and intervention-related improvements in targeted competencies in kindergarten) and sustained benefits evident 2–4 years later, revealing the potential mechanisms of action

K. L. Bierman (✉) · B. S. Heinrichs
Department of Psychology, Child Study Center, The Pennsylvania State University, University Park, PA, USA
e-mail: kb2@psu.edu; ibc@psu.edu

R. L. Nix
Human Development and Family Studies, Human Development and Relationships Institute, Universty of Wisconsin-Madison, Madison, WI, USA
e-mail: robert.nix@wisc.edu

J. A. Welsh
Prevention Research Center, The Pennsylvania State University, University Park, PA, USA
e-mail: jaw900@psu.edu

J. E. Loughlin-Presnal · M. E. McDoniel
Child Study Center, Department of Psychology, The Pennsylvania State University, University Park, PA, USA

© Springer Nature Switzerland AG 2022

K. L. Bierman, S. M. Sheridan (eds.), *Family-School Partnerships During the Early School Years*, Research on Family-School Partnerships,
https://doi.org/10.1007/978-3-030-74617-9_3

and key factors that may account for the long-term benefits of parent engagement efforts at school entry. Implications of this research for the scaling of REDI-P and future design of similar family engagement programs are described, along with recommendations for next steps in this important area of research.

Keywords Family engagement · Home visiting · School readiness · Preschool intervention · Parenting practices · Kindergarten transition · Academic performance · Social-emotional learning · Socioeconomic disadvantage · Home learning

Approximately four million children start kindergarten in the United States each year, and many of them are not ready socially, emotionally, or cognitively for the challenges they will face at school. Children from low-income families are particularly vulnerable; fewer than half (48 percent) enter kindergarten with adequate readiness, compared to 75% of children from more economically advantaged families (Isaacs, 2012). In fact, on average, children growing up in poverty start kindergarten with language and emergent literacy skills that are more than a full year behind their more advantaged peers (Committee on Integrating the Science of Early Childhood Development, 2000). Starting kindergarten with low readiness predicts elevated rates of later learning difficulties and behavior problems and an ongoing trajectory of low achievement (Ryan et al., 2006), creating a socioeconomic gap in school attainment that is now almost twice as large as the racial achievement gap (Reardon, 2011).

Based upon evidence that attending a high-quality preschool reduces the socioeconomic gap in school readiness, public investment in preschool programs has increased substantially over the past two decades, with a primary goal of enriching early learning opportunities for economically disadvantaged children (Yoshikawa et al., 2013). At the same time, long-term benefits are disappointing; a recent review of 67 high-quality early childhood interventions showed academic benefits fading over time, with half of the preliteracy and early math benefits associated with preschool attendance fading within a year of elementary school entry and another half of the benefits fading again 2 years later (Bailey et al., 2017).

This chapter describes the Research-based, Developmentally Informed Parent (REDI-P) program which was designed to increase the sustained benefits of high-quality preschool programming by engaging parents and strengthening home learning support as children made the transition from Head Start into elementary school. We provide a brief overview of the developmental research that informed the REDI-P program design, identifying factors associated with early socioeconomic disadvantage that negatively affect the developing brain, along with intervention strategies that can boost families' capacities to buffer children and support early development and school readiness. We then review outcomes from a randomized-controlled trial demonstrating the efficacy of REDI-P in promoting neurodevelopment and school readiness and supporting gains in academic and social-behavioral school adjustment still evident at follow-up assessments conducted when children were in third grade, 4 years after intervention. We also present analyses that illustrate potential mechanisms of intervention action, with implications for future research and for intervention refinement and scaling.

3.1 Developmental Research Informing the REDI-P Intervention Design

The striking socioeconomic disparities in social, emotional, and cognitive domains of school readiness that are apparent at school entry appear multiply-determined, reflecting the negative developmental impact of adversities associated with growing up in poverty (Ryan et al., 2006). Limited financial resources often result in living conditions that are crowded and unsafe, with reduced access to high-quality child care and early education supports. Low levels of parent education, along with elevated rates of maternal depression, family instability, and single parenthood, all diminish parents' abilities to provide consistent, sensitive-responsive, and cognitively stimulating parenting support (Ryan et al., 2006). Exposure to these chronic stressors has an adverse impact on the development of key child skills that support adaptive functioning and learning, including the social-emotional skills that promote positive relationships with adults and peers, and the self-control skills that enhance impulse and attentional control (Blair & Raver, 2015). Concurrent delays in language and cognitive skill development often emerge as a function of reduced exposure to adult language use that includes complex oral vocabulary and syntax, and low levels of parent-child reading and book access (Senechal, 2006).

Integrating Interventions to Enrich Social-Emotional and Language Development Recognizing the multifaceted nature of the skill delays associated with early socioeconomic disadvantage, an initial REDI preschool enrichment program was designed with a dual focus on supporting social-emotional learning and language-emergent literacy skills. The REDI classroom program (REDI-C) provided Head Start teachers with manualized enrichment curricula and mentored professional development opportunities. To support the acquisition of social-emotional and self-control skills, REDI-C used the Preschool PATHS (Promoting Alternative Thinking Strategies) curriculum (Domitrovich et al., 2007) which provides classroom lessons and teaching support for social-emotional and self-regulatory skill development. To enhance language and emergent literacy skills, REDI-C also included an interactive reading program, using stories linked with PATHS themes to reinforce social-emotional understanding, along with a sound games program to build phonological awareness and alphabet center activities to strengthen print knowledge.

REDI-C's integrated focus on social-emotional learning and language-literacy support proved effective. A randomized-controlled trial demonstrated gains in both domains of child skills at the end of the prekindergarten year (Bierman et al., 2008). However, effects on language and literacy skills largely faded by the end of kindergarten, although social-emotional benefits were sustained (Bierman et al., 2014; Welsh et al., 2020). Subsequent analyses suggested that the REDI-related gains in social-emotional competencies and language-emergent literacy skills had synergistic benefits for children when they entered kindergarten (Nix et al., 2013), but that kindergarten instructional practices and teaching quality largely accounted for literacy skill growth after school entry (Bierman et al., 2014).

Logic Model for the REDI-P Intervention REDI-P was designed to reduce the fade-out associated with preschool classroom enrichment and provide ongoing support for child school adjustment by helping parents scaffold learning at home as children made the transition from preschool to elementary school. REDI-P extended the REDI-C emphasis from the classroom into the home to reinforce support for child social-emotional and language-literacy skill development. In designing strategies to support parents, REDI-P incorporated two distinct approaches for enhancing family-focused engagement that had proven effective in prior studies.

One of these approaches emphasized the use of parent-child learning activities designed specifically to support child skill acquisition. For example, prior research had demonstrated that teaching parents how to read interactively with their children (e.g., asking questions and using active listening to extend parent-child conversations about the pictures and stories) produced significant increases in receptive and expressive language skills (see reviews by Manz et al., 2010; Mol et al., 2008; Reese et al., 2010). Similarly, providing parents with games and activities that exposed children to letter and letter-sound identification (Evans & Shaw, 2008) and showing parents how to point out print while reading (Justice & Ezzell, 2000) boosted child emergent literacy skills and, in some cases, also enhanced their social-emotional skills (Ford et al., 2009).

A second intervention approach focused on enhancing the parent-child relationship and increasing parents' use of interaction strategies associated with positive child social-emotional development and behavioral adjustment (e.g., sensitive-responsive interaction, positive behavior management strategies, decreased directiveness, and punitive responding; see Webster-Stratton and Taylor (2001) for a review). Preschool interventions focused on promoting positive parenting have proven effective in improving child classroom behavior (Webster-Stratton et al., 2001) and in some cases have also promoted gains in child language and social skills (Landry et al., 2008; Lunkenheimer et al., 2008).

REDI-P Intervention Design REDI-P incorporated both of these approaches to parent engagement. During ten home visits scheduled in the spring of the prekindergarten year and six home visits scheduled during the fall of the kindergarten year, REDI-P provided parents with a prepared home learning curriculum and guidance regarding optimal teaching strategies. Monthly activity kits contained storybooks, guides, and props for parent-child dramatic play activities, conversation games, and literacy-focused games and activities. In alignment with the REDI-C program, REDI-P stories and games featured the characters introduced in the PATHS curriculum, emphasizing cooperation, caring, compliments, emotional understanding, and self-control (Domitrovich et al., 2007). Storybooks were written at a very basic literacy level, with embedded questions to help parents read interactively. Pretend play activities (supported with props and picture guides) featured letter and letter-sound identification practice; for example, playing restaurant included menus and alphabet placements, and playing post office involved drawing and writing notes to family members (for more details, see Bierman et al., 2015).

In addition to providing home learning materials, home visitors coached parents in strategies designed to support social-emotional learning (e.g., positive behavior management, emotion coaching, and the use of planned routines and social problem-solving dialogue) and strategies to enhance home language use and extend parent-child conversations (e.g., asking questions, using active listening, expanding on child statements). During their visits, home visitors used modeling videotapes, "parenting tips" handouts, discussion, and reflection activities to help parents become comfortable with these parenting strategies and customize their use to fit family preferences. In addition, at three time points during the intervention, parents were videotaped with their children using program materials and interaction strategies. These videotapes were reviewed by the parent and home visitor to highlight positive aspects of the parent-child relationship and reflect collaboratively on areas for troubleshooting and improvement. The logic model guiding the design of REDI-P and its hypothesized change processes is illustrated in Fig. 3.1.

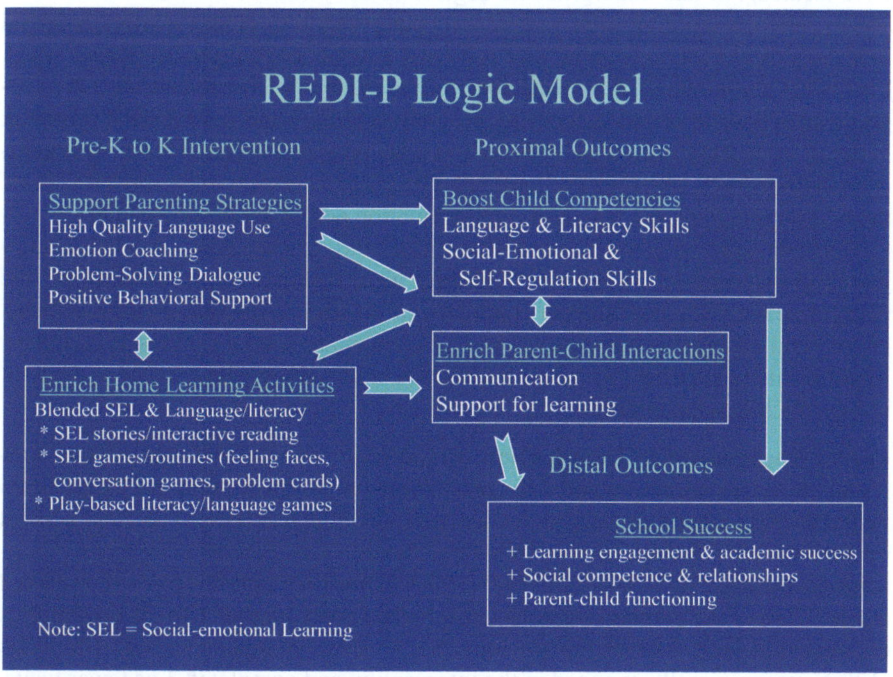

Fig. 3.1 REDI-P logic model

3.2 REDI-P Evaluation: Immediate and Longer-Term Outcomes

The impact of the REDI-P program was evaluated in a randomized-controlled efficacy trial. Participants included 200 4-year-old children recruited from Head Start classrooms using the REDI-C curriculum (55% European American, 26% African American, 19% Latinx, 56% male), age 4.45 years old at time of enrollment (*SD* = 0.29). Reflecting the Head Start population, families were generally low income (median annual family income = $18,000), with 54% of parents unemployed, and 39% single. Families were randomly assigned to receive REDI-P (intervention condition) or an alternative set of learning materials through the mail (control condition). All participating children were receiving the REDI-C program enrichments in the classroom; hence, this study examined the added value of extending the REDI curriculum into the home (REDI-P) beyond exposure to REDI-C alone.

Sixteen percent of the participating families spoke Spanish as their primary language; all of these families also spoke some English at home. These families were provided with a Spanish-speaking home visitor and were offered the home learning materials in Spanish. However, all families opted to use English materials when working with their child, no doubt influenced by the fact that their children would be entering schools where classroom instruction was provided only in English.

Home visitors were recruited from the communities where Head Start centers were located. All had undergraduate degrees in early education or human services and experience working with parents of young children. Home visitors received four days of workshop training and followed a manualized protocol during visits. Each week the home visitors participated in a group conference call with the program supervisor to review upcoming program activities and intervention protocol; in addition, weekly individual supervision calls provided home visitors with guidance in their work with specific families. The program supervisor attended 20% of the home visits to assure standard implementation across the home visitors.

Children were widely dispersed after Head Start, transitioning into 149 kindergarten classrooms in 74 schools. Children were followed longitudinally by the research team, with assessments conducted at the end of the intervention (kindergarten) and during the subsequent years of elementary school (grades 1, 2, and 3). Measures included direct assessments of child skills, along with teacher and parent ratings of child adjustment.

Parent Engagement in Intervention Home visitors completed regular logs, noting home visit completion and their perceptions of parent interest, use of program materials and parenting strategies, understanding of the parenting skills, and general openness to consultation. Out of 16 planned home visits, parents completed 12 sessions on average (SD = 5.48, range = 0–16). A majority of families (66%) completed at least 75% of the planned sessions (12–16 visits) and another 13% of the families completed at least 50% of the sessions (8–11 visits). A small number of families (13%) were minimally engaged in the intervention and completed 3 or fewer visits. These are high levels of attendance relative to the average rate of 50% attendance that characterizes many parent-focused intervention programs (Dumas et al., 2007; Webster-Stratton et al., 2001). We attribute the levels of attendance to several factors, including scheduling home visits at times selected by families (thereby reducing barriers to attendance), embedding REDI-P in the framework of the Head Start system which encourages and supports parent involvement, and providing the intervention at a time when parents were anticipating their child's transition into kindergarten and had both hopes and concerns that motivated interest in support strategies.

Ratings made by home visitors were scored to reflect two dimensions of intervention engagement (see Nix et al., 2018). Ratings of parent interest in and comfort with the intervention, openness to consultation, and understanding of the intervention strategies were averaged across all sessions to represent the quality of working alliance between the parent and home visitor. Overall, families showed relatively high levels of a positive working alliance, with a mean of 2.42 out of 3.00 ($SD = 0.59$), but there was variability in the sample, with a range from 0.67 to 3.00. Ratings of the parent's use of the home-based learning activities and teaching strategies were averaged across all sessions to reflect their use of program materials during the time between home visits. More variability emerged on this dimension of engagement with a mean of 1.72 out of 3.00 and a range of 0 to 3.00. Most parents (49%) used the home learning materials at a moderate level (e.g., some of the materials being used some of the time during the week), and another large portion of the sample (38%) used the materials frequently (e.g., most of the materials being used several times per week). The rest of the sample (13%) showed little to no use of the materials. Correlations among the dimensions of intervention engagement revealed that attendance was only mildly correlated with working alliance ($r = 0.30$) and use of program materials ($r = 0.23$), but working alliance and use of program materials were more highly correlated ($r = 0.71$).

Kindergarten Outcomes Cross-classified hierarchical linear models (nesting children within their Head Start classrooms and elementary school districts) were used to evaluate child and parent outcomes at the end of the intervention when children were in kindergarten, using demographics and pre-intervention baseline scores as covariates (Bierman et al., 2015). Relative to the control group who received only REDI-C, children who received REDI-P and REDI-C showed significantly higher scores on direct assessments of child emergent literacy skills ($d = 0.25$) and teacher-rated academic performance ($d = 0.28$) in kindergarten. They also showed higher levels of self-directed learning ($d = 0.29$) and social competence ($d = 0.28$) as rated by teachers. Parents who received the REDI-P intervention reported reading in a more interactive way with their children ($d = 0.28$) and having longer and more frequent conversations with their children ($d = 0.27$) than parents in the control condition. Interestingly, REDI-P also boosted parent's confidence in their children's ability to succeed in school, significantly increasing their expectations for their children's future grades and academic attainment ($d = 0.32$; Loughlin-Presnal & Bierman, 2017). On average, these effects for children and parents were moderate in size, roughly one-fourth of a standard deviation higher for families in the intervention versus control group. They demonstrate that adding a family engagement intervention (REDI-P) to cover the transition between a preschool classroom enrichment (REDI-C) and kindergarten entry significantly increased parent support for learning at home and significantly improved benefits to children in key areas of academic and social-emotional school adjustment.

Third-Grade Outcomes Study children were followed as they moved through the elementary school grades to determine whether REDI-P benefits were sustained in later grades. Hierarchical linear models with children nested within their Head Start classrooms were conducted on child assessments collected at the end of third grade revealed sustained effects. Relative to children in the control condition, children in the intervention condition continued to show significantly higher scores on direct assessments of child literacy skills ($d = 0.28$) and teacher-rated academic performance ($d = 0.29$) at the end of third grade (Bierman et al., 2018). Children in the REDI-P intervention condition also showed higher third-grade scores on observer ratings of task orientation ($d = 0.45$) and direct assessments of social understanding ($d = 0.31$) reflecting sustained effects in areas of adaptive approaches to learning and social competence, respectively. Although the specific measures included in the initial kindergarten and third-grade follow-up analyses differed, these findings illustrate sustained effects of a similar magnitude in both the academic and social-emotional domains through third grade (see Fig. 3.2).

In addition to these sustained child benefits, parent ratings at third grade revealed additional benefits at home. Parents who received REDI-P reported fewer child problems at home than parents in the control condition ($d = -0.28$) and they reported

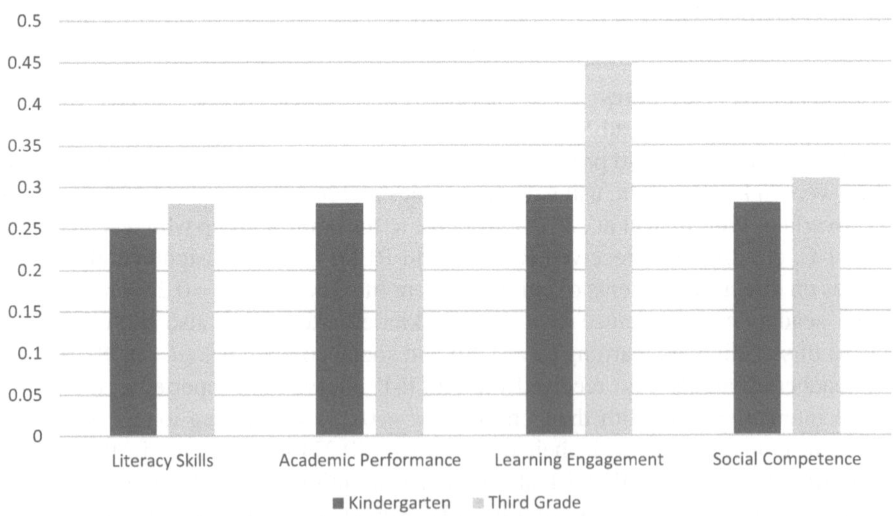

Fig. 3.2 REDI-P effects on child outcomes in kindergarten and third grade
Note: Effect sizes are in the small to moderate range and represent the average standard deviation difference between intervention and control groups. Different measures were used to in kindergarten and third grade to represent these outcome domains. Details are in Bierman et al. 2015 and Bierman et al. 2018

corresponding reductions in their experiences of parenting stress and hassles ($d = -0.27$). These are important findings regarding the degree to which boosting effective parent engagement at the critical developmental point of kindergarten transition can extend and augment preschool classroom enrichment. Not only did child school adjustment show sustained improvements in academic and social-emotional domains, but parent-child relationships also benefitted over time.

3.3 Exploring Potential Mechanisms of Action in the REDI-P Intervention

These findings are exciting, but it is important to keep in mind that REDI-P represents a fairly intensive parent engagement program. A careful cost analysis estimated the cost per family at $2491 for the 16-session home visiting program (Jones et al., 2019). The intensity and cost of the program represent potential barriers to wide-scale implementation, leading to questions about whether the program could be modified to simplify (and reduce) implementation costs without significantly reducing impact. To guide possible modifications of the intervention, analyses were undertaken to explore intervention mechanisms of action. The goal was to better understand whether certain components of REDI-P may have played a more central (or more peripheral) role in contributing to its positive impact. In the following sections, we describe these post hoc exploratory analyses and their implications for future intervention design refinement and research.

First, analyses were conducted within the intervention group to understand variation in parent engagement in and response to REDI-P, including baseline family characteristics that predicted intervention engagement, and associations between intervention engagement and child outcomes (Nix et al., 2018). A second set of analyses was then conducted to explore links between initial intervention response and later child and family benefits, illuminating possible mechanisms of action supporting sustained effects for REDI-P (Bierman et al., 2019).

Predictors of Intervention Engagement As noted above, families living in poverty often experience multiple adversities that impede their ability to provide consistent, positive, and stimulating educational support for their young children. We wondered whether these adversities might also reduce parent engagement in REDI-P. Within the intervention group, we tested the degree to which three baseline family factors associated with adversity (parent education levels, unemployment, and parent depressive symptoms) predicted intervention engagement. We also looked at three factors that might make parent-child interaction more difficult or less rewarding – the degree of warmth observed in the parent-child relationship, child attention problems, and child behavior problems.

Correlations were computed to determine how each of these baseline family characteristics predicted the three dimensions of intervention engagement. None of the family characteristics studied predicted rates of intervention attendance, although families who were white and lived primarily in rural counties attended more sessions on average ($M = 13.72$) than families of color who lived primarily in urban areas ($M = 10.79$). The lack of association between other family characteristics and home visit attendance may be due to the efforts of home visitors to reschedule visits as needed, resulting in a majority of families (79%) receiving at least 50% or more of the intervention.

Somewhat surprisingly, none of the baseline parent characteristics studied (e.g., parent education, employment status, or depressive symptoms) predicted the quality of the working alliance in REDI-P nor did parent race/ethnicity. However, the working alliance was significantly promoted by the three baseline factors reflecting parent-child functioning: the warmth of the parent-child relationship ($r = 0.37$), child attention skills ($r = 0.21$), and low levels of child behavior problems ($r = 0.23$). Prior studies have identified low parent education, being a parent of color, maternal depression, and severity of child behavior problems as predictors of lower levels of working alliance and quality of participation in parent group interventions (Baydar et al., 2003; Nix et al., 2009). Because REDI-P was delivered individually and not in group sessions, home visitors had more latitude to adjust their support to better align with the needs and preferences of parents who varied in education level, cultural beliefs, and family context, thereby reducing the extent to which these factors attenuated parent connection with the home visitor or interest in the intervention. Even so, parent enthusiasm and uptake of the REDI-P intervention appears reduced by child characteristics and parent-child relationship difficulties that made home learning activities and intervention strategies more challenging and less rewarding to implement.

A very similar set of baseline characteristics predicted the degree to which families used REDI-P home learning books and activities in between home visits, which were promoted by fewer parent depressive symptoms ($r = -0.23$), higher warmth in the parent-child relationship ($r = 0.30$), better child attention skills ($r = 0.34$), and fewer child behavior problems ($r = 0.35$). On the one hand, these findings suggest that REDI-P was successful at mitigating many of the barriers to parent engagement that occur in the face of the adversities associated with poverty. On the other hand, these findings suggest that parents were most enthusiastic about REDI-P parenting strategies and active in using REDI-P home learning materials when they had a warmer relationship with their child at the start of the program and when their child was more easily engaged.

Predictive Associations Between Intervention Engagement and Child Outcomes The next set of analyses explored the degree to which the three dimensions of parent engagement predicted subsequent child acquisition of the targeted academic and social-emotional skills.

Hierarchical multiple regression equations were estimated to isolate the unique effect of each dimension of intervention engagement (e.g., attendance, working alliance, use of home learning materials) on each child outcome. In these analyses, baseline family characteristics and child skills (e.g., emergent literacy skills, attention skills, behavior problems) were entered first to control for preexisting differences that might affect both intervention engagement and child outcomes. Two sets of child outcomes were examined: (1) those reflecting the immediate post-intervention school functioning of children in kindergarten and (2) those reflecting later school functioning of children at the second-grade follow-up assessments (for more details, see Nix et al., 2018).

The regression equations predicting kindergarten outcomes revealed one significant effect for intervention attendance, as it uniquely predicted improvements in children's behavior at home. Somewhat surprisingly, the working alliance did not uniquely predict any of the child outcomes in kindergarten. In contrast, use of the program materials at home significantly predicted multiple kindergarten outcomes – improved child literacy skills and attention skills at school and reduced behavior problems at home. Thus, parent use of the home learning materials emerged as the most important unique feature of program engagement contributing to immediate child outcomes assessed at the end of kindergarten.

However, a somewhat different picture emerged when the measures of parent intervention engagement were used to predict sustained child outcomes at the second-grade follow-up assessments. In these regression equations, neither intervention attendance nor use of program materials was a significant unique predictor of outcomes. Instead, the quality of the working alliance emerged as the significant unique predictor of second-grade language arts skills (e.g., reading and writing), attention skills, and social competence.

This switch in the engagement dimensions that uniquely predicted outcomes may be best understood by taking a developmental perspective. The home learning activities used during the intervention period were selected to support the acquisition of the literacy-language and social-emotional skills children would need at kindergarten entry. In this way, these learning activities were limited in their developmental scope. In contrast, the REDI-P parenting strategies had more developmental generalizability, including strategies useful for enriching parent-child conversation, improving parent-child interaction quality, and increasing cognitive stimulation. A good working alliance between parents and home visitors likely contributed to parents' deeper understanding and acceptance of the REDI-P approach to learning support. In turn, that deeper understanding and acceptance may have allowed parents to generalize REDI-P strategies to new challenges their children faced after the end of the intervention period. Hence, children made early gains as long as parents used the learning materials REDI-P provided; however, sustained benefits required greater reliance on broader parenting strategies related to learning support.

Given the high correlation between use of home learning materials and the home visitor-parent working alliance ($r = 0.71$), it is likely that these facets of intervention engagement were intertwined and interdependent. Having concrete activities to use at home may have provided important scaffolds for initial parent behavior and attitude change (and boosted immediate child skill acquisition). More frequent parent use of the materials likely increased parent reflections on and conversations with the home visitors about the parenting strategies that seemed effective with their children and likely enriched problem solving discussions and tailoring of parenting strategies to fit the child's needs and parent preferences. These reflections and discussions about the parent-child interaction strategies may have increased parent feelings of efficacy in their general use, thereby fostering longer-term use and adaptation, contributing to sustained gains in child functioning. Together these analyses suggest that both facets of intervention engagement played important and unique roles in supporting positive child outcomes. Beyond promoting sufficient intervention attendance, working alliance and use of program materials are both important to optimize initial and longer-term child outcomes.

Associations Between Initial REDI-P Response and Sustained Benefits Another way to explore the relative utility of the dual-pronged REDI-P program focus on building child skills and coaching parenting strategies was to examine the relative contributions of initial gains in child and parenting skills to the later intervention outcomes that were sustained in third grade. These additional analyses were conducted using both the intervention and control groups.

Conceptually, the dual focus of REDI-P might contribute to sustained benefits for children by strengthening either child skills or enhancing parenting strategies (or both). For example, by promoting child skills, REDI-P might enhance child success at school entry, increasing opportunities for positive socialization and learning at school (or reducing socialization and learning risks), thereby setting children on more positive developmental trajectories (Bailey et al., 2017; Sandler et al., 2011). Alternatively or in addition, REDI-P might enhance parenting skills that generalize over time, extending parent capacity to support positive child development and home support for learning in subsequent years and thereby producing sustained benefits (Reid et al., 2004; Webster-Stratton & Taylor, 2001). Researchers have also suggested that parent-focused interventions might improve parental self-efficacy, thereby fueling more positive and engaged parenting efforts in subsequent years (Sandler et al., 2011).

A set of multilevel path analyses using structural equation models tested three areas of REDI-P post-intervention gains as potential mediators of third-grade sustained effects: (1) child emergent literacy skills, (2) child social-emotional skills (e.g., social competence, self-directed learning), and (3) parenting strategies (e.g., parent-child conversations, reading quality) and efficacy (parent academic expectations). Separate mediation models were run for third-grade outcomes in the four areas of child academic performance, social-emotional functioning, child problems at home, and reduced parenting stress. These models included multiple covariates to control for possible confounders, including demographics and baseline measures of child skill (Bierman et al., 2019).

The first model revealed that sustained intervention effects on child academic performance were significantly mediated by initial intervention gains in child emergent literacy skills and parent academic expectations, which together accounted for 34% of the total third-grade intervention effect. A second model revealed that sustained intervention effects on child social-emotional competence were significantly mediated by initial intervention gains in child social-emotional competence, which accounted for 50% of the third-grade intervention effect. The third model revealed that sustained intervention effects on child problems at home were significantly mediated by initial intervention gains in child social-emotional skills, parent-child conversations, and parent academic expectations, which accounted for 60% of the third-grade intervention effect. Finally, the fourth model revealed that sustained intervention effects on parenting stress were significantly mediated by initial intervention gains in child social-emotional skills and parent-child conversations, which accounted for 37% of the third-grade intervention effect.

These analyses validate the multifaceted approach of REDI-P, suggesting that the dual focus on building child skills and enhancing parenting strategies, along with the dual emphasis on social-emotional learning and language-literacy skills produced sustained benefits through multiple pathways. Of particular importance to later outcomes were the initial intervention effects on child social-emotional skills, including social competence and adaptive approaches to learning. Initial gains in this domain were sustained within domain, and they also made unique contributions to later reductions in child behavior problems and parenting stress. Home learning curricula have traditionally focused primarily on academic skills (e.g., Manz et al., 2010; Mol et al., 2008; Reese et al., 2010). The current findings validate this emphasis, as initial intervention gains in the area of emergent literacy skills uniquely contributed to sustained gains in the same domain. However, the findings also suggest that an integrated intervention emphasis on stories, games, and activities that have social-emotional content and support parent-child conversations about feelings and problem solving may be uniquely valuable for children growing up under conditions of adversity.

It is notable that the initial gains in high-quality parent-child conversations and parent academic expectations played a critical role in supporting longer-term improvements. Several prior studies have documented that improving positive parenting and behavior management skills lead to reductions in child conduct problems (Brotman et al., 2009; Reid et al., 2004). REDI-P showed something similar, but only for parents with low levels of warmth at baseline (Mathis & Bierman, 2015). In general, about 25–30% of children attending Head Start have problems with impulsive, oppositional, and aggressive behaviors (Reid et al., 2004). Families who struggled with those child behavior problems sometimes found REDI-P difficult to implement. They may have benefitted more from a parent management training prior to a learning support program like REDI-P. For the larger majority of Head Start families who were not struggling with elevated child behavior problems and were able to implement and enjoy the REDI-P reading and learning activities with their children, this home learning enrichment promoted sustained gains in social-emotional, self-regulation, and language competencies, fueled by enhanced parent-child communication skills and parent feelings of hope and efficacy regarding their child's academic potential.

3.4 Implications of REDI-P Findings for Future Intervention Design and Research

Despite strong evidence of its efficacy in reducing socioeconomic gaps in child school readiness and school success, REDI-P has several features that are likely to limit its broad diffusion. In particular, the intensity and cost of the intervention services are likely to reduce program use. One of the goals of examining how (and for whom) REDI-P worked was to inform future intervention design and research. A better understanding of intervention mechanisms of action could guide future design efforts by suggesting critical intervention features that should be maintained in future adaptations as well as identifying aspects of the intervention that might be streamlined. In the following section of this chapter, we consider the implications of the research completed to "unpack" the active mechanisms driving REDI-P effects for future program adjustments. We also consider additional research that is needed on REDI-P and similar family engagement programs.

Critical Intervention Features Accounting for Beneficial Effects In large part, REDI-P's positive effects were attained by engaging parents effectively in home learning activities that were easy and fun for parents to use and designed to support the child's acquisition of key social-emotional and emergent literacy skills. Analyses suggest that the use of these home learning activities functioned as a critical lever promoting child skill acquisition and provided parents with concrete guides for how to interact with their children in ways that promoted parent-child communication and child learning. Analyses further suggest that coaching by the home visitors in parenting strategies designed to support social-emotional learning (positive behavior management, emotion coaching, and the use of planned routines and social problem-solving dialogue) and strategies to enhance home language use and extend parent-child conversations (questions, active listening, expansions) contributed to the sustainability of child gains. The integrated approach of REDI-P with its focus on boosting child social-emotional and language-literacy skills also appears validated in the REDI-P analyses. Hence, these three elements (e.g., use of scaffolded home learning materials, coaching support in parenting strategies, and integrated focus on child social-emotional and language-literacy skills) likely represent the central features of REDI-P that account for its benefits and should be maintained in any future program adaptation.

At the same time, there are several other aspects of REDI-P design that might possibly be modified without reducing the benefits. Next, we consider these aspects of intervention design and the future research needed to explore them.

Delivery System and Dose The most expensive element of REDI-P is the provision of 16 home visits to each family. Interestingly, the number of home visits that parents received was not significantly associated with their use of the home learning materials or their working alliance nor with child outcomes (with the exception of reduced behavior problems at home). These findings suggest that it might be possible to attain similar results with fewer home visits, particularly for parents who were not struggling with child behavior problems at home and who found the learning materials and teaching strategies easy to use. At the same time, most families received at least 12 home visits, so determining the number of visits needed to produce beneficial effects is a topic that requires future research. It would also be less expensive to deliver REDI-P coaching in an alternative format, such as a parent group workshop or via online demonstrations rather than in-person home visits. These alternative formats would reduce the amount of personalized coaching that could be done but might still be effective in generating parent self-reflection and strategy understanding. Future research is needed to determine the potential benefits of delivering REDI-P with a less costly delivery system than individual home visits.

Use of a Tailored or Adaptive Intervention Design In a tailored or adaptive intervention design, the content, length, or nature of the intervention is altered based upon the characteristics or response of individual families (Collins et al., 2004). The implementation research presented here suggests that families with strained parent-child relationships and difficulties managing child behaviors at home struggled to use the home learning materials and REDI-P parenting strategies effectively with their children. Additional research documents that these parents showed progress, becoming warmer and more effective during the course of the REDI-P intervention (Mathis & Bierman, 2015). However, they were not as effective as other parents at building child skills. These findings raise questions about whether this subgroup of parents would have been better served with a parenting program that focused more exclusively on positive management strategies prior to introducing home learning materials. At the other end of the spectrum, it is possible that some parents were well-prepared to take on the REDI-P home learning curriculum with their children and would have made similar progress with a less intensive intervention that involved fewer home visits. Additional research is needed to better understand the family characteristics that moderated response to REDI-P. A good sense of those moderators would provide an empirical basis for tailored approaches that might involve variations in the parenting strategies that were a focus of the intervention or that might involve different levels of intervention intensity and delivery. Additional research is also needed to determine whether parent engagement interventions like REDI-P could be equally effective and more cost-effective if they used an adaptive or tailored design, in which the focus and timing of intervention support was determined by initial screening assessments or by family response during intervention.

Timing and Administrative Home REDI-P was designed to cover the time period before and after children transitioned into kindergarten. We believed that timing the intervention over this critically important developmental transition point was a feature crucial to intervention impact. Certainly, parent interest and motivation to participate in the intervention seemed heightened at this major transition point for their child. However, covering this transition period with intervention services is challenging due to the lack of alignment between early education programs and public school programs. Only the research funding and staffing available for REDI-P made it possible to track children and follow their families as they widely dispersed across the transition from Head Start to kindergarten. With the exception of the subset of public schools that house their own prekindergarten programs, it is very difficult for preschool programs to follow their students forward into elementary school and conversely very difficult for elementary schools to "reach back" and identify and connect with parents of rising kindergarten students prior to school entry.

This disconnect between early childhood education programs and public schools raises questions about the best administrative home to sustain a program like REDI-P that covers the chasm between the two systems. Future research might determine whether REDI-P could work equally well if it did not extend across the prekindergarten and kindergarten years and whether it could be more effectively implemented and sustained as a prekindergarten program or as a kindergarten program.

Coordinating and Aligning Home and School Curricula A related issue that requires additional research is the degree to which the impact of REDI-P or a program like it depends upon coordination with the preschool or kindergarten curriculum. REDI-P was designed to align with REDI-C. In the evaluation trial, all children in both the intervention and control groups received the enriched REDI-C program in Head Start. Although the effects of the classroom program were thereby controlled in the evaluation of REDI-P, it remains unclear whether the alignment with REDI-C played an important role in "priming" children for the home-based intervention materials. REDI-P was not coordinated in any specific way with the kindergarten programming that children experienced. It remains unknown whether home-school curriculum alignment in kindergarten may have strengthened impact.

Ongoing Implementation Research As research on REDI-P and other family engagement programs moves forward, additional research evaluating the mediation and moderation of short-term and long-term outcomes is a priority. Most efficacy trials are set up to determine whether a program is successful in producing targeted outcomes. Although this is important, mediation studies are also critical to help build a better understanding of how different intervention approaches achieve their goals. Studies such as those described in this chapter that explore the dynamics of parent engagement in intervention and that test the mediators identified in intervention logic models can contribute to a better understanding of the pathways by which preschool parent interventions produce downstream benefits and thereby inform the design and refinement of future interventions and guide future research. In addition, moderation studies are important to illuminate which parents and children benefit most from different intervention approaches. Parents seemed to engage more effectively in REDI-P when they had a warm relationship with their child and less effectively when their child had significant preexisting attention deficits and behavior problems. Additional research is needed to determine whether an adaptive version of REDI-P or an alternative approach to family engagement support might improve benefits for this subgroup of families.

3.5 Summary

Parents provide critical ongoing support for children's well-being and education. Family engagement programs that empower parents to promote their children's learning and development at the transition into formal schooling may be particularly strategic because of the potential for downstream benefits associated with improved trajectories of school success. For these reasons, federal and state policies mandate parent engagement efforts, especially for children with vulnerabilities that may mitigate school achievement. However in response to these policy mandates, typical family engagement strategies remain limited to orientation sessions, parent-teacher conferences, and volunteer opportunities.

Research on REDI-P and the other programs presented in this volume highlight the potential power of more intensive and strategic family engagement programming to promote child success, reduce the fade-out of benefits associated with center-based preschool interventions, and reduce the school achievement gap associated with socioeconomic disadvantage. Children change teachers each year, but they remain with their parents, giving parents potential opportunities to support child development and school adjustment across the entire span of the child's education. Ongoing research holds promise for identifying the best ways to optimize preschool and kindergarten parent engagement programs, to the benefit of the children, families, and schools involved.

Acknowledgments This project was supported by National Institute of Child Health and Human Development Grant HD046064. We greatly appreciate the cooperation of our partners in this project: the parents, students, teachers, and program personnel of the Head Start programs of Huntingdon, Blair, and York counties in Pennsylvania and of the school districts that participated in the follow-up study. In addition, this work reflects the particular efforts and talents of Gloria Rhule and Julia Gest, who contributed to the home visiting program development and served as program supervisors.

References

Bailey, D., Duncan, G. J., Odgers, C. L., & Yu, W. (2017). Persistence and fadeout in the impacts of child and adolescent interventions. *Journal of Research on Educational Effectiveness, 10*, 7–39.

Baydar, N., Reid, M. J., & Webster-Stratton, C. (2003). The role of mental health factors and program engagement in the effectiveness of a preventative parenting program for head start mothers. *Child Development, 74*, 1433–1453.

Bierman, K. L., Domitrovich, C. E., Nix, R. L., Gest, S. D., Welsh, J. A., Greenberg, M. T., Blair, C., Nelson, K., & Gill, S. (2008). Promoting academic and social-emotional school readiness: The head start REDI program. *Child Development, 79*, 1802–1817.

Bierman, K. L., Nix, R. L., Heinrichs, B. S., Domitrovich, C. E., Gest, S. D., Welsh, J. A., & Gill, S. (2014). Effects of head start REDI on children's outcomes one year later in different kindergarten contexts. *Child Development, 85*, 140–159.

Bierman, K. L., Welsh, J., Heinrichs, B. S., Nix, R. L., & Mathis, E. T. (2015). Helping head start parents promote their children's kindergarten adjustment: The REDI parent program. *Child Development, 86*, 1877–1891.

Bierman, K.L., Welsh, J.A., Heinrichs, B.S., & Nix, R.L. (2018). Preschool home visiting boosts school readiness and reduces need for services in elementary school: A randomized program evaluation. *JAMA Pediatrics,*172(8): e181029.

Bierman, K.L., McDoniel, M. & Loughlin-Presnal, J.E. (2019). How a preschool parent intervention produced later benefits: A longitudinal mediation analysis. *Journal of Applied Developmental Psychology, 64*,101058.

Blair, C., & Raver, C. C. (2015). School readiness and self-regulation: A developmental psychobiological approach. *Annual Review of Psychology, 66*, 711–731.

Brotman, L. M., O'Neal, C. R., Huang, K., Gouley, K. K., Rosenfelt, A., & Shrout, P. E. (2009). An experimental test of parenting practices as mediator of early childhood physical aggression. *Journal of Child Psychology and Psychiatry, 50*, 235–245.

Collins, L. M., Murphy, S. A., Bierman, K. L., & the Conduct Problems Prevention Research Group. (2004). A conceptual framework for adaptive preventive interventions. *Prevention Science, 5*, 185–196.

Committee on Integrating the Science of Early Childhood Development. (2000). *From neurons to neighborhoods: The science of early childhood development*. Washington, D.C.: National Academy Press.

Domitrovich, C. E., Cortes, R., & Greenberg, M. T. (2007). Improving young children's social and emotional competence: A randomized trial of the preschool PATHS curriculum. *Journal of Primary Prevention, 28*, 67–91.

Dumas, J. E., Nissley-Tsiopinis, J., & Moreland, A. D. (2007). From intent to enrollment, attendance, and participation in preventive parenting groups. *Journal of Child and Family Studies, 16*, 1–26.

Evans, M. A., & Shaw, D. (2008). Home grown for reading: Parental contributions to young children's emergent literacy and word recognition. *Canadian Psychology, 49*, 89–95.

Ford, R. M., McDougall, S. J. P., & Evans, D. (2009). Parent-delivered compensatory education for children at risk of educational failure: Improving the academic and self-regulatory skills of a sure start preschool sample. *British Journal of Psychology, 100*, 773–797.

Isaacs, J.B. (2012) *Starting school at a disadvantage: The school readiness of poor children*. Brookings Institution. Retrieved July 7, 2019 from https://www.brookings.edu/wp-content/uploads/2016/06/0319_school_disadvantage_isaacs.pdf

Jones, D.E., Bierman, K.L., Crowley, D.M., Welsh, J.A., & Gest, J. (2019). *Important issues in estimating costs of early childhood educational interventions: An example from the REDI program*. Unpublished manuscript.

Justice, L. M., & Ezzell, H. K. (2000). Enhancing children's print and word awareness through home-based parent intervention. *American Journal of Speech-Language Pathology, 9*, 257–269.

Landry, S. H., Smith, K. E., Swank, P. R., & Guttentag, C. (2008). A responsive parenting intervention: The optimal timing across early childhood for impacting maternal behaviors and child outcomes. *Developmental Psychology, 44*, 1335–1353.

Loughlin-Presnal, J. E., & Bierman, K. L. (2017). Promoting parent academic expectations predicts improved school outcomes for low-income children entering kindergarten. *Journal of School Psychology, 62*, 67–80.

Lunkenheimer, E. S., Dishion, T. J., Shaw, D. S., Connell, A. M., Gardner, F., Wilson, M. N., & Skuban, E. M. (2008). Collateral benefits of the family check-up on early childhood school readiness: Indirect effects of parents' positive behavior support. *Developmental Psychology, 44*, 1737–1752.

Manz, P. H., Hughes, C., Barnabas, E., Bracaliello, C., & Ginsburg-Block, M. (2010). A descriptive review and meta-analysis of family-based emergent literacy interventions: To what extent is the research applicable to low-income, ethnic-minority or linguistically-diverse young children? *Early Childhood Research Quarterly, 25*, 409–431.

Mathis, E. T., & Bierman, K. L. (2015). Effects of parent and child pre-intervention characteristics on child skill acquisition during a school readiness intervention. *Early Childhood Research Quarterly, 33*, 87–97.

Mol, S. E., Bus, A. G., de Jong, M. T., & Smeets, D. J. H. (2008). Added value of dialogic parent-child book readings: A meta-analysis. *Early Education and Development, 19*, 7–26.

Nix, R. L., Bierman, K. L., McMahon, R. J., & Conduct Problems Prevention Research Group. (2009). How attendance and quality of participation affect treatment response to parent management training. *Journal of Consulting and Clinical Psychology, 77*, 429–438.

Nix, R. L., Bierman, K. L., Domitrovich, C. E., & Gill, S. (2013). Promoting preschool social-emotional skills with the head start REDI program enhances academic and behavioral outcomes in kindergarten. *Early Education and Development, 24*, 1000–1019.

Nix, R. L., Bierman, K. L., Motamedi, M., Heinrichs, B. S., & Gill, S. (2018). Parent engagement in an enriched head start home visiting program: Predictors and associations with child outcomes. *Early Childhood Research Quarterly, 45*, 106–114.

Reardon, S. F. (2011). The widening socioeconomic status achievement gap: New evidence and possible explanations. In R. J. Murnane & G. J. Duncan (Eds.), *Whither opportunity?Rising inequality, schools, and children's life chances* (pp. 91–115). New York: Russell Sage.

Reese, E., Sparks, A., & Leyva, D. (2010). A review of parent interventions for preschool children's language and emergent literacy. *Journal of Early Childhood Literacy, 10*, 97–117.

Reid, M. J., Webster-Stratton, C., & Baydar, N. (2004). Halting the development of conduct problems in head start children: The effects of parent training. *Journal of Clinical Child and Adolescent Psychology, 33*, 279–291.

Ryan, R. M., Fauth, R. C., & Brooks-Gunn, J. (2006). Childhood poverty: Implications for school readiness and early childhood education. In B. Spodek & O. N. Saracho (Eds.), *Handbook of research on the education of children* (2nd ed., pp. 323–346). Mahwah: Erlbaum Associates.

Sandler, I., Schoenfelder, E., Wolchik, S., & MacKinnon, D. (2011). Long-term impact of prevention programs to promote effective parenting: Lasting effects but uncertain processes. *Annual Review of Psychology, 62*, 299–329.

Senechal, M. (2006). Testing the home literacy model: Parent involvement in kindergarten is differentially related to grade 4 reading comprehension, fluency, spelling, and reading for pleasure. *Scientific Studies on Reading, 10*, 59–87.

Webster-Stratton, C., & Taylor, T. K. (2001). Nipping early risk factors in the bud: Preventing substance abuse, delinquency, and violence in adolescence through interventions targeted at young children (0-8 years). *Prevention Science, 2*, 165–192.

Webster-Stratton, C., Reid, M. J., & Hammond, M. (2001). Preventing conduct problems, promoting social competence: A parent and teacher training partnership in head start. *Journal of Clinical Child Psychology, 30*, 283–302.

Welsh, J.A., Bierman, K.L., Nix, R.L., Heinrichs, B., & Gest, S.D. (2020). Sustained effects of a school readiness intervention: Fifth grade outcomes of the Head Start REDI program. *Early Childhood Research Quarterly, 53*, 151–160.

Yoshikawa, H., Weiland, C., Brooks-Gunn, J., Burchinal, M. R., Espinosa, L. M., Gormley, W. T., … Phillips, M. D. (2013). *Investing in our future: The evidence base on preschool education* (Vol. 9). Ann Arbor: Society for Research in Child Development.

Chapter 4
Understanding ParentCorps' Essential Elements for Building Adult Capacity to Support Young Children's Health and Development

Spring Dawson-McClure, Dana Rhule, Kai-ama Hamer, Esther Calzada, Bukky Kolawole, Michelle Mondesir, Katherine Rosenblatt, and Laurie Brotman

Abstract ParentCorps is an enhancement to pre-Kindergarten designed to reduce racial and socioeconomic disparities in children's educational and health outcomes. It includes multiple components to bolster parent and teacher capacity to support children's development in the face of early childhood adversity, including poverty, racism, discrimination, and immigration-related stress. Two trials with primarily Black and Latinx children in schools in historically disinvested neighborhoods document positive impacts of ParentCorps for children's achievement, mental health, and physical health. The theory of action specifies the following as essential processes through which ParentCorps professional development and parenting program strengthen adult capacity: building authentic relationships, honoring culture, understanding race and racism, translating the science of early childhood development, and practicing self-reflection. The third component, Friends School, directly promotes children's social-emotional learning. Together, these three ParentCorps components support early childhood self-regulation. This chapter identifies priorities for future research to understand core pathways that account for positive

---

S. Dawson-McClure (✉) · D. Rhule · K.-a. Hamer · M. Mondesir · K. Rosenblatt
L. Brotman
NYU Grossman School of Medicine, New York University, New York, NY, USA
e-mail: Spring.Dawson-McClure@nyulangone.org; Dana.Rhule@nyulangone.org; Kai-ama.Hamer@nyulangone.org; Michelle.Mondesir@nyulangone.org; Katherine.Rosenblatt@nyulangone.org; Laurie.Brotman@nyulangone.org

E. Calzada
Steve Hicks School of Social Work, University of Texas at Austin, Austin, TX, USA
e-mail: Esther.Calzada@austin.utexas.edu

B. Kolawole
Relationship HQ, New York, NY, USA
e-mail: drbukky@myrelationshiphq.com

© Springer Nature Switzerland AG 2022

K. L. Bierman, S. M. Sheridan (eds.), *Family-School Partnerships During the Early School Years*, Research on Family-School Partnerships,
https://doi.org/10.1007/978-3-030-74617-9_4

outcomes and to optimize impact at scale to realize the promise of early childhood family-centered programs.

Keywords Early childhood · Parenting program · Professional development · Relationships · Self-reflection · Race · Culture · Disparity

ParentCorps was developed to reduce racial and socioeconomic disparities in educational and health outcomes. The program was designed to be accessible, engaging, and effective for culturally diverse families, with professional development to directly support family-school partnerships. From the outset, ParentCorps was designed to be embedded in early education settings and facilitated by teachers and school staff with the aim of creating a sustainable program to reach the majority of children early in life. Two randomized controlled trials documented short- and longer-term impact on children's health and development and offered the promise of achieving positive outcomes for children at a large scale. This chapter describes the ParentCorps theory of action, the evidence of impact, and critical future directions for research to realize the promise of early childhood family-centered programs. In conducting studies to understand core pathways and optimize impact at scale, we are driven by the importance of developing social-emotional learning (SEL) in early childhood, supporting the adults in young children's lives, and transforming the pre-K experiences of families of color to create equitable education systems. We partner with district and school leaders to deliver and evaluate ParentCorps as an enhancement to pre-Kindergarten (pre-K) programs in historically disinvested neighborhoods. We use the term *historically disinvested neighborhoods* to recognize that systemic racism has contributed to high concentrations of families of color living in poverty, with deep implications for educational opportunities.

4.1 ParentCorps Theory of Action

ParentCorps is a multicomponent program that aims to strengthen relationships between parents and teachers and to support both teachers and parents in creating safe, nurturing, and predictable environments that scaffold children's SEL and self-regulation. The components are (1) professional development (PD), including group-based experiential training and one-on-one coaching for pre-K teachers, mental health professionals, and family support staff; (2) a 14-week group-based parenting program for all parents as part of the pre-K experience; and (3) Friends School, a 14-week social-emotional learning program for pre-K children. ParentCorps coaches provide PD to teachers and staff, who in turn facilitate the programs for children and parents.

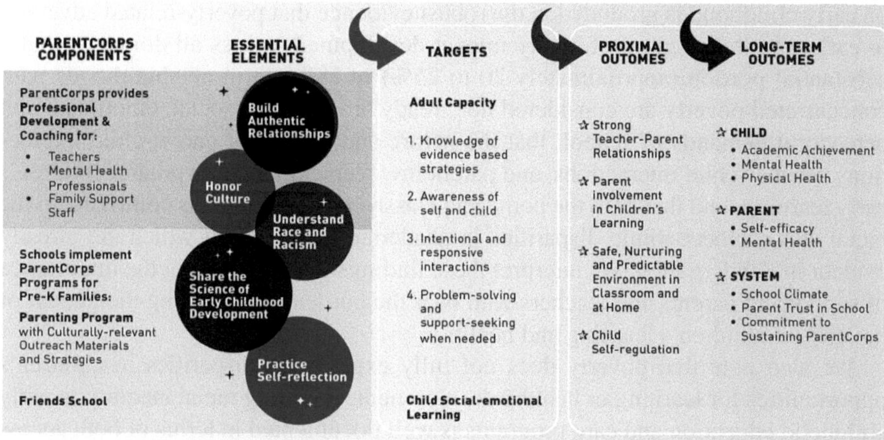

Fig. 4.1 ParentCorps theory of action

The theory of action specifies five elements through which ParentCorps strengthens adult capacity: building authentic relationships, honoring culture, understanding race and racism, translating the science of early childhood development, and practicing self-reflection (see Fig. 4.1). As discussed in the section on future research to understand core pathways, these essential elements explain the extent to which the targets change. Specifically, we hypothesize that high quality, high fidelity facilitation supports parents and teachers in developing increased capacity as defined by (1) knowledge of evidence-based strategies (strategies detailed below in the section on program components); (2) awareness of self and child; (3) intentional and responsive interactions; and (4) problem-solving and support-seeking as needed. In parallel, child social-emotional learning is targeted directly by Friends School. Over time, increased adult capacity is expected to lead to proximal outcomes: strong teacher-parent relationships, parent involvement in children's learning, and safe, nurturing, and predictable classroom and home environments. These proximal changes are expected to synergistically support self-regulation in early childhood and contribute to longer-term outcomes in childhood and adolescence: academic achievement and mental and physical health. We also hypothesize that there are cascading benefits for parent well-being, including self-efficacy and mental health, and for the system, including improved school climate and parent trust in teachers and school leaders, as well as increased commitment of school leaders to sustain ParentCorps programs.

The theory of action draws on several models, including Mindful Parenting (Duncan et al., 2009), Prosocial Classroom (Jennings & Greenberg, 2009), Five Awarenesses of Teaching (Rodriguez et al., 2020); Cascading Resilience (Doty et al., 2017), Transformative Learning Theory (Taylor, 2008), Critical Race Theory (Ladson-Billings & Tate, 1995), and the Critical Consciousness paradigm (Marchand et al., 2019). It is based on the strong evidence that parenting programs support healthy developmental trajectories (see review by Sandler et al., 2011). Our focus on early childhood is grounded in the robust evidence that poverty-related adversity in early childhood can profoundly impact development across all domains; that a substantial portion (approximately 20 to 25%) of children in neighborhoods with concentrated poverty are considered not "ready" to meet the social, emotional, and behavioral demands of school; that the nature and quality of parent-child interactions, teacher-child interactions, and parent involvement uniquely predict children's early learning; and that both the home and classroom environments contribute to the racial and socioeconomic disparities in academic achievement which are already evident in Kindergarten. We interpret these findings as documenting the importance of supporting parents and teachers who bear the burden of mitigating the impact of poverty on children's learning and health.

We also note that poverty does not fully explain the disparities in children's opportunities for learning or healthy development. Enduring racial inequity in early childhood education and care programs is well documented in terms of both access and quality (including the use of exclusionary discipline), as well as access to health care and other structural determinants of health and development (e.g., Bailey et al., 2017). Critical Race Theory in education highlights the fundamental role of racism in creating and maintaining inequitable student outcomes (Dixson & Rousseau Anderson, 2018; Ladson-Billings & Tate, 1995). Scholars articulate the educational policies and practices that regulate and denigrate the cultural expressions of Black and brown students, and perpetuate the normativeness and superiority of white students and white culture (e.g., Hilliard, 2003; Ogbu 1992). Indeed, the term "achievement gap" locates the problem in Black and brown children, and in their parents and teachers (Wise Whitehead, 2017). Ladson-Billings (2006) proposes "educational debt" as a more accurate term to explicitly recognize the problem as systemic and structural. Thus, we believe scaling of evidence-based programs is essential to bolster adult capacity to support children's health and development, as parents and teachers continue to navigate interpersonally mediated and structural racism. Further, we join others in advocating for racial equity training for all involved in scaling (e.g., program developers, coaches, facilitators, evaluators) to deepen understanding of race and racism and develop capacity to address inequities in children's school experiences.

4.2 Program Components

The content and structure of the ParentCorps components are aligned. Both professional development and the parenting program begin with an explicit focus on building relationships, honoring culture, understanding race, and practicing self-reflection. Both preserve these elements throughout as facilitators shift their focus to encourage parents' and teachers' use of strategies that promote children's social-emotional learning (SEL) and prevent behavior problems. Together, this array of strategies creates safe, nurturing, and predictable environments in which children can thrive (e.g., Biglan, 2015; National Academies of Sciences, Engineering, and

Medicine, 2016). For both teachers and parents, the strategies include establishing routines, providing positive attention during adult-child play, using positive reinforcement, ignoring mild misbehavior, delivering proactive strategies, disciplining effectively, managing emotions, and problem solving. For teachers, this also includes strategies to build strong relationships with families (i.e., active listening, perspective taking, navigating difficult conversations). Table 4.1 includes key messages to both parents and teachers, and examples of program activities alternating between the parenting program and professional development, to illustrate the parallel process through which facilitators and coaches engage. The essential elements are described in more detail in the section "Priorities for Research to Understand Core Pathways to Impact."

Friends School is designed to promote SEL skills that are considered foundational for self-regulation and early learning (Raver et al., 2007) and are common to many programs for young children (e.g., sharing, paying attention, identifying feelings, asking for help, solving problems, calming body). Additional lessons support emerging identity and healthy living skills related to food and activity. Exposure to strategies taught to their parents (e.g., routine chart, sticker chart) is intended to increase children's familiarity with and acceptance of these practices when parents try them at home.

Professional Development ParentCorps coaches provide four days of experiential training (ParentCorps FUNdamentals) on evidence-based strategies to engage families and create safe, nurturing, and predictable classrooms. This initial training also provides the rationale and evidence base for the ParentCorps programs for families. Building on this foundation, there is additional experiential training and one-on-one coaching for (1) school- and district-based mental health professionals to facilitate the parenting program, (2) pre-K teachers to implement Friends School in the classroom and in parallel to the parenting program when offered after school hours, and (3) family support staff to invite parents to the parenting program using culturally relevant, affirming materials.

Our approach to behavior change and the combination of training with ongoing in vivo and distant coaching are based on iterative learning from educators who have participated in ParentCorps over the past two decades. Research on professional development strategies that support sustained change in behavior (Lundahl et al., 2010; Sheridan et al., 2009; Snyder et al., 2012) and theoretical and empirical support for reflective practice (Sellars, 2012; Taylor, 2008) provides further foundations for our work. Facilitators of professional development and the parenting program are trained in motivational interviewing (MI), a counseling approach with strong evidentiary foundations to support behavior change through the exploration and resolution of ambivalence, with a spirit of partnership, acceptance, compassion, and evocation (Miller & Rollnick, 2013). Facilitators practice listening to participants and reflecting responses to draw out beliefs, feelings, and meaning. Based in MI principles, there is an emphasis on exploration of beliefs rather than on sharing information and creating a context for learning in which shifts in beliefs, and subsequently behavior, are possible. Experiential activities aim to increase teachers'

Table 4.1 Essential elements, core messages to parents and teachers, and example program activities

Essential elements	Core messages to parents and teachers	Example program activities
Build authentic relationships	*We believe we must interrupt patterns where parents are told how to parent by people and systems outside of their homes, and teachers are told how to teach by those outside their classrooms. Instead we believe that families are the experts of their children, and teachers are the experts of their classrooms We aim to join with all the adults in young children's lives to build a community that can learn from and support each other.*	In professional development, coaches begin to build authentic relationships by deeply affirming teachers' tremendous impact on children's lives, offering freedom in how teachers engage, and establishing group norms or "traditions" that explicitly invite teachers to share candidly when they disagree with us or a colleague ("tell us when you have an "itch") and to express their negative and often unspoken emotions ("permission to feel!"). This allows professional development to quickly become a space for authentic dialogue about the real struggles teachers are experiencing. With this foundation, coaches can then tailor and connect the science and evidence-based strategies to teachers' real lived experiences.
Honor culture	*We believe that we cannot talk about parenting or teaching without an explicit focus on race and culture (ethnicity, nationality, religion, gender, sexual orientation). Each of us brings our own perspective to the table, based on where we come from and what we have experienced. We are committed to honoring everyone's culture and understanding how it connects to parenting and teaching for every individual.*	In parenting program, facilitators begin by exploring what we mean by culture and then inviting parents to share with the group the parts of their culture that they are most proud of. This session dedicated to culture sets a foundation early in the formation of the group that who parents are and where they come from matters deeply in the program.
Understand race and racism	*We believe that supporting social-emotional learning requires understanding intimately the challenges families face related to immigration, income, and particularly race. We strive to always center the perspectives of people of color and ask ourselves how we can interrupt oppression.*	In professional development, coaches introduce tools to interrupt our society's pattern of avoiding conversations about race and racism. One such tool ("gardener video") offers teachers a framework to understand different forms of racism impacting students. Teachers are asked to reflect and explore what role they play. This centering of race continues throughout the series as family engagement and classroom strategies are explored. Coaches model using new knowledge and tools to enter difficult conversations.

(continued)

Table 4.1 (continued)

Essential elements	Core messages to parents and teachers	Example program activities
Translate science	*We believe that everyone should have access to the latest science about children's development. We present evidence-based strategies and trust you to make the best decision for your children/your classroom.*	In parenting program, facilitators share candidly about both the power of science ("we know from the evidence that just a few minutes a day playing with your child in this way can have a really positive impact") and its limitations ("we need more studies with families from different cultures to really understand how spanking affects children's behavior. We believe that you, as a parent, are the one who can best decide what works for you and your child. Let's talk about the reasons that parents may choose to spank and not to spank.")
Practice self-reflection	*We believe that who you are is how you parent/how you teach. We believe an understanding of self is critical for all the adults in children's lives. We believe that self-reflection is an ongoing practice, not a single action. We believe that it is important to have space as parents and teachers to engage in this practice. We believe that it is in a practice of self-reflection that we can consider relationships, culture, race, and science to make the best decisions for the children in our lives.*	In professional development, coaches support self-reflection through both the content covered and in their facilitation choices. Teachers are guided through self-reflection activities that call them back to their best and worst memories of teachers they had in childhood. They are asked to think about the impact those early experiences had on them as people and teachers, and how they show up with some of those positive or negative attributes in different moments with students. Utilizing motivational interviewing techniques, facilitators consistently reflect back what teachers are bringing in the room and cultivate a sense of curiosity about what might be impacting the thoughts, feelings, behaviors, and actions of teachers each day.

empathy for challenges parents face and to practice self-reflection, while group norms or "traditions" aim to establish an unusual level of honesty that disrupts dominant norms (see Table 4.1 for examples).

Parenting Program and Outreach The parenting program includes 14 weekly 2-hour group-based sessions, held at school, and facilitated by a mental health professional. School leaders are encouraged to schedule the program flexibly based on parents' availability and preferences and school capacity, offering both daytime and evening options, in the languages spoken by the majority of pre-K parents. Manuals and materials are currently available in English, Spanish, and Chinese. All pre-K families are invited to participate as part of the pre-K experience (see Dawson-McClure et al. (2017) for more details on our approach to outreach).

Designated family support staff lead parent outreach, ideally with involvement of school leaders and pre-K teachers. ParentCorps materials and strategies are used flexibly to fit with their school context. Outreach is designed to support relationship-building from the start of the year in hopes of reducing the stigma parents may feel when invited to a parenting program. For example, print materials portray images representing racially diverse families in community together and use the tagline "Together We: Parent. Share. Learn. Grow." Welcome events and personalized communication are also used to engage with parents. Parents are always welcome to join the parenting program regardless of the parameters (e.g., arriving late from work, being unable to attend every session), and the invitation extends to all adults who are important in the child's life (e.g., grandparent, aunt). As with many evidence-based parenting programs, ParentCorps provides meals, small incentives (i.e., raffle tickets for gift cards), and childcare when the program is offered in the evenings (i.e., Friends School for pre-K children, arts program for older siblings, led by teachers and staff who choose after-hours work).

Friends School Throughout the 14-week program, teachers use a consistent structure (e.g., lesson with puppets, play, activity) and evidence-based strategies to scaffold children in learning new SEL skills. In addition to delivering Friends School in the evening for families who attend an evening parenting program, the current delivery model includes teachers and teaching assistants facilitating Friends School in pre-K classrooms, integrated flexibly into the school day (e.g., 1.5- to 2-hour block per week; lesson and activities spread across several days). The evening program includes two additional activities that are optional during the school day: (1) teachers provide positive feedback to parents about children's progress toward individualized goals, grounded in observations of the child's strengths and challenges, and (2) four sessions conclude with parent-child activities to enjoy fun time together and to practice new skills with support from facilitators.

4.3 Evidence of Impact

Two randomized controlled trials (RCTs) in schools with pre-K programs in historically disinvested neighborhoods document positive impacts of ParentCorps for children's health and development. Both RCTs were conducted in New York City (NYC) in partnership with NYC Department of Education pre-K leaders to evaluate impact in schools with large numbers of children living in poverty. Schools were randomly assigned to pre-K as usual (control condition) or to deliver ParentCorps as an enhancement to pre-K. University-based mental health professionals provided professional development and co-facilitated the parenting program with school-based mental health professionals and Friends School with teachers and teaching assistants.

The first RCT was conducted in 8 schools with a racially and ethnically diverse sample (N = 171 families; 39% Black, 24% Latinx, 13% White, 12% Asian, and 12% multiracial; >50% immigrant parents). Schools were selected because they represented all of the schools in one community school district with at least one pre-K class designated to serve lower-income children (relative to the general community, through a federally subsidized program). This RCT demonstrated feasibility and impact on parenting and child behavior at school at the end of pre-K (Brotman et al., 2008, 2011).

The second RCT was conducted in 10 schools with a primarily Black sample (N = 1050 families; 86% Black, 10% Latinx, 4% other races; >50% immigrant parents). Schools from two community districts were selected if they had more than 70% students eligible for free lunch and were 80% Black. Race was included as a school selection criterion to maximize the proportion of families who would meet the only eligibility criterion that a parent could provide informed consent in English (7% of families were ineligible). Notably, nearly 90% of the pre-K population enrolled in the study. Similar to other large urban school systems in the USA, these two community districts served segregated neighborhoods, in which the vast majority of students were children of color, a majority of families were immigrants, and about one-third of residents were living in poverty. Consistent with the evidence that schools in segregated neighborhoods with concentrated poverty are under-resourced and therefore may offer fewer opportunities for learning (e.g., Logan et al., 2012), the high school graduation rate in these two districts was approximately 50% and nearly half of elementary school students scored below grade level in reading and math. Evidence from the second RCT is summarized below.

Parent Participation The majority (58%) of pre-K families attended at least one parenting program session; the proportion of families attending ranged across schools (44–75%) and tended to increase from the first to fourth year of program implementation (50–65%). Among families who ever attended, the average attendance was half the sessions. For heuristic purposes, we set a threshold for "meaningful dose" at five or more sessions; this subgroup (40% of families) came to an average of 10 sessions. Participation was not predicted by ethnicity, neighborhood poverty, or baseline parenting or child behavior (Dawson-McClure et al., 2014a, 2014b), indicating that a wide spectrum of families was engaged.

Meaningful and Sustained Impacts on Academic Achievement, Mental Health, and Physical Health ParentCorps resulted in improved academic achievement by the end of kindergarten, particularly for reading, and improved teacher ratings of academic performance through the end of second grade (Brotman et al., 2013, 2016). Test scores at the end of kindergarten showed a 24% lower risk of reading below grade level for children in ParentCorps schools (Kaufman Test of Educational Achievement, Second Edition) (Kaufman, 2005). To place the magnitude of impact into context, it is useful to consider the size of disparities as measured by standardized tests in kindergarten; the mean difference between Black and White students is 0.50 standard deviation units (SD) and the mean difference between students from low- and high-income families is 1.0 SD units. The estimate of ParentCorps impact for reading achievement (mean difference between ParentCorps and control conditions) was 0.34 SD, based on intent-to-treat analyses. There was a stepwise increase in impact with each of year of implementation in ParentCorps schools up to 0.49 SD in the fourth and final year studied (and 0.88 SD for the "meaningful dose" subgroup; Brotman et al., 2013), consistent with the pattern observed for other school-based programs (Borman et al., 2003). These findings suggest the potential to reduce disparities by bolstering adult capacity to support children's achievement.

ParentCorps prevented the development of mental health problems, including both emotional and behavioral problems at school, through second grade (Brotman et al., 2016). For children enrolled in pre-K in control schools, both emotional and behavioral problems at school (as reported by teachers) increased substantially during the early years. This pattern is consistent with the well-described impact of adversity on early childhood development (National Scientific Council on the Developing Child, 2012). In sharp contrast, children in pre-K programs enhanced with ParentCorps showed no increase in mental health problems over time. These different trajectories resulted in clinically meaningful differences by second grade, such that children in ParentCorps schools were 50% less likely to score in the clinical range on a norm-referenced teacher rating scale (Behavior Assessment System for Children, Second Edition; Reynolds & Kamphaus, 2004).

Finally, ParentCorps prevented the development of obesity and unhealthful behaviors (e.g., low physical activity, high sedentary activity) for a high risk subgroup. Children without strong behavior regulation skills are at high risk for a range of problems including obesity (e.g., Mamun et al., 2009). Within this subgroup (about one-quarter of the RCT sample), 54% of children in the control condition were obese (Body Mass Index >95th percentile) by second grade, relative to 24% of children in ParentCorps schools (Brotman et al., 2012).

Impacts on Proximal Outcomes at Home and School Parents showed increases in knowledge of evidence-based practices and greater use of practices (such as positive reinforcement and proactive strategies) in the ParentCorps condition relative to controls (Dawson-McClure et al., 2014a, 2014b). Among families of children who entered pre-K without strong behavior regulation skills, ParentCorps also reduced inconsistent behavior management. ParentCorps also supported parent involvement in children's learning as perceived by both parents and teachers in pre-K and kindergarten (Dawson-McClure et al., 2014a, 2014b). Parallel changes were observed in pre-K classrooms in ParentCorps schools, including more nurturing teacher-student interactions and effective behavior management relative to control schools, as assessed on the Classroom Assessment Scoring System – Emotional Support domain (Pianta et al., 2008), with effect sizes >0.60 SD (Dawson-McClure et al., *unpublished manuscript*).

In sum, there were sustained benefits of ParentCorps across three critical domains of children's development (i.e., academic achievement, mental health, and physical health). Notably, because ParentCorps was delivered as an enhancement to pre-K, these impacts are over and above the benefits of pre-K. A mathematical simulation study demonstrated that the prevention of these cross-domain problems in elementary school significantly increases each individual's quality adjusted life expectancy and saves over $4000 per child over the life course (Hajizadeh et al., 2017), resulting in approximately 4:1 return on investment.

4.4 Priorities for Research to Understand Core Pathways to Impact

Several decades of prevention trials have demonstrated the efficacy of parenting programs and established that specific parenting strategies often mediate program impacts on child outcomes (e.g., Sandler et al., 2011). Critical next steps are to articulate the full theory of action that specifies precisely how different programs work and to test the strength of pathways from program elements to targets to proximal outcomes (Berkel et al., 2018a; Center on the Developing Child at Harvard University, 2019). This level of specificity can illuminate how the program is actually working at scale, for whom and in which settings it is most effective and why, and what has gone awry when the program falls short. A precise theory of action allows for measurement of adaptations (e.g., added or modified content or processes) and characterization of the counterfactual (e.g., other services being provided that may activate the same pathways). Building on this knowledge, researchers and practitioners can advance the field by developing and testing new innovations or implementation supports to overcome contextual and systemic barriers and bolster elements that are shown to be essential. We highlight some steps our team is taking in this direction.

Articulate a Precise Theory of Action We have refined the ParentCorps theory of action to include essential elements and targets (see Fig. 4.1), drawing on insights from parents, teachers, facilitators, and coaches about how the program supports changes in the proximal outcomes. These are hypothesized mechanisms that we have not yet tested. We describe the elements with respect to interactions between facilitators and parents in the parenting program; coaches engage with teachers and staff in professional development in a parallel process (see Table 4.1 for examples). Building authentic relationships is fundamental to our model of embedding an evidence-based parenting program in school settings, consistent with this recent definition of family engagement as a "process of relationship building" that must include treating "families as essential partners while providing services that encourage children's learning and development" (US Department of Health and Human Services, 2016). Our approach includes facilitators embodying empathy and using specific strategies to build relationships with and a sense of community among parents (an enduring "corps" of support), explicitly affirming parents' inherent value and capacity to succeed, and actively supporting their autonomy to make decisions about what is best for their children – in stark contrast to the commonly held stereotypes that parents living in poverty and Black and brown parents are uncaring, unable to be involved, or ill-equipped to raise successful children (Cooper, 2009; Marchand et al., 2019).

From its inception, ParentCorps was designed to honor culture by inviting parents to share about their cultures and explicitly respecting cultural values, beliefs, and practices as important and adaptive (Garcia Coll et al., 1996) and embracing a broad definition of culture that includes race, ethnicity, religion, and sexuality to encourage each parent to share about the aspects of identity that are salient for them. More recently, we have articulated the importance of facilitators' understanding of race and racism; this includes recognizing that race affects all aspects of daily experiences, learning about and believing others' lived experiences of racism, both interpersonally mediated and structural, and interrupting one's own biases in daily interactions. We applied a racial equity lens to reexamine program content and materials. The parenting program now includes more explicit reflection on racial identity and more intentional conversations about race and daily lived experiences of racism, discrimination, and immigration-related stress. Professional development now scaffolds examination of implicit racial and gender bias and supports teachers and staff in beginning to consider how to interrupt bias in their daily interactions with children and parents.

In this context of participants being seen, heard, and cared for, facilitators translate the science of early childhood development by sharing information about evidence-based strategies, encouraging consideration of the fit and relevance of strategies, and creating space for parents to share ideas with each other and continually reflect on their values and beliefs in reaction to strategies introduced by the facilitator, in a mutual transfer of expertise that respects each person's culture and lived experience. In this way, facilitators model and provide opportunities for parents to practice self-reflection on their values and beliefs about parenting and child development and increasing their moment-to-moment awareness of thoughts, feelings, beliefs, and behaviors. These in-session experiences are expected to strengthen parents' capacity to engage in responsive interactions with their child, in alignment with their values and beliefs, based on the science of early childhood development and other trusted sources of information.

Thoroughly Measure and Test the Theory of Action In order to test our hypothesis that the five elements shown in Fig. 4.1 are indeed essential to building adult capacity and achieving positive outcomes for children, our measures of implementation must include assessment of these elements, ideally considering the multiple perspectives of participants, facilitators, and coaches. Durlak and DuPre's (2008) review of implementation dimensions emphasizes the value of measuring quality (how well facilitators deliver the material, facilitator engagement and support) in addition to fidelity (the quantity of the content delivered as in the manual), both of which are distinct from adaptation (additions or modifications to process or content). We highlight a series of studies by Berkel and colleagues, testing the theory of action for an evidence-based program for divorcing families delivered at scale in the court system, as an exemplar in this critical area of research. With multi-method measurement of implementation, based on a precise theory of action, a series of tests revealed unique relations for fidelity and two of the three aspects of quality that they hypothesized were essential (facilitators' positive engagement predicted parent attendance, skillful presentation predicted parents' efficacy and competence in trying new strategies at home). Consistent with their expectation that home practice is the core pathway to outcomes, they found that it mediated program impacts on parenting and child mental health (Berkel et al., 2018a, 2018b). Building on these findings, they propose a staged approach to implementation monitoring and continuous improvement: (1) consistently track attendance and home practice through relatively low-cost, low-burden online data entry by facilitators and, (2) when those indicators fall below the threshold determined sufficient for positive outcomes, supplement with more costly and burdensome observations of fidelity and quality (Berkel et al., 2019).

In this vein, we have been iteratively refining our tools for measuring the quality of facilitation to fully tap into our coaches' conceptualization of the essential elements and the in-session experiences of parents and teachers. We hypothesize that quality will complement measures of fidelity in explaining the extent to which the program targets change. Of course, testing the theory of action also requires careful measurement of program targets, the specific aspects of adult capacity that we expect ParentCorps to strengthen, at logical times during and/or after the program, with methods that are sensitive to change. We are measuring aspects of adult capacity with new measures of mindfulness developed specifically for teachers and parents (Frank et al., 2016; McCaffrey et al., 2017) that tap into both awareness of self and child (e.g., for parents, "how often did you notice when your child's behavior was making you upset"; for teachers, "when you're upset with your students, how often do you notice how you are feeling before you take action?") and intentional and responsive interactions (e.g., "how often did you try to slow down your reactions in order to accomplish your goals," "how often did you believe that the way you were parenting/teaching was consistent with best practices"). We have stopped using tests of knowledge based on consistent negative feedback from teachers and parents about being tested. We are also utilizing some new measures for the proximal outcomes that were developed with early childhood educators and Black and Latinx families to improve their relevance and breadth (parent involvement in children's learning and parenting (McWayne et al., 2013), teacher-parent relationships (Porter et al., 2015). In particular, this supports expanded consideration of safe, nurturing, and predictable environments to include parents' use of culturally relevant strategies (e.g., storytelling, teaching about own and others' culture, setting expectations for the importance of education) in addition to the use of evidence-based strategies (e.g., routines, proactive strategies, positive reinforcement, book sharing).

As researchers and practitioners, we are eager to understand the variability in quality and fidelity as the program is implemented at greater scale, to begin to establish empirical thresholds for sufficient quality and fidelity, and learn about adaptations that may be problematic or brilliant responses to improve the fit of the program into context (Lyons & Bruns, 2019). We are formulating a series of research questions to test our beliefs about how the program works. For example, we hypothesize that when facilitators are strong in the essential elements based on observations and parent/teacher report of in-session experiences (e.g., "cares about me," "explains strategies so I understand how to use them," "consistently listens, reflects, and seeks our perspectives"), participants are more likely to attend subsequent sessions, engage actively, and try new strategies. Further, we expect that the more that they perceive strategies as helpful in reaching their goals, the more likely it is that trying new strategies through intentional and responsive interactions will consolidate into their consistent use to create safe, nurturing, and predictable environments. Additionally, we hypothesize that when facilitators are strong in the essential elements, participants will continue to practice self-reflection outside of sessions, increasing their capacity to slow down and notice their thoughts and feelings and the children in front of them; this increased awareness in turn supports the consistent use of new strategies. We expect that teacher awareness as a pathway to changing interactions with both children and parents is particularly salient when teachers have a different cultural identity and lived racial experience than their students, which is very often the case for children of color given that fewer than 20% of teachers in the USA are people of color.

In sum, specifying, measuring, and testing precise theories of action are necessary steps to advance the field and hold great potential to rapidly increase knowledge that will support continuous improvement and the development of innovative supports for evidence-based programs.

4.5 Priorities for Research to Support Impact at Scale

Many early childhood interventions developed by researchers that show great potential in early testing phases fail to scale effectively (Dodge, 2019). Likewise, school districts and other public systems may introduce evidence-based interventions (EBIs) to improve program quality and promote child and family outcomes, but without adequate implementation and improvement supports, interventions often remain underutilized or fail to achieve intended outcomes (Fagan et al., 2019). Dodge (2019) argued that the traditional Institute of Medicine model of moving from efficacy trials to effectiveness trials to scaling up has not worked, in part due to failure to consider key aspects of the system (policies and practices) in which the early childhood intervention is being scaled. The Society for Prevention Research's Mapping Advances in Prevention Science (MAPS) IV Translational Research Task Force noted that although there is evidence that it is possible to implement EBIs at scale and improve population level outcomes, achieving scaled impact "remains one of the most vexing challenges facing prevention science" (Fagan et al., 2019; pg. 1148).

Numerous recent reviews about EBIs in public education systems conclude that practitioners, scientists, policy makers, and community stakeholders need to work together in new ways. There is increasing interest in the potential of Research Practice Partnerships (RPP) to support EBI implementation at scale and to produce sustainable improvements at scale across systems (Cohen-Vogel et al., 2015; Dodge, 2019; Fagan et al., 2019; World Health Organization, 2010). We have been in a long-standing and continuously evolving RPP between the Center for Early Childhood Health and Development (CEHD) at the NYU Grossman School of Medicine and the Division of Early Childhood Education of the New York City Department of Education (NYCDOE). The goals and activities of this RPP have included both efforts to (1) implement ParentCorps at scale as an enhancement to public Pre-K programs and (2) improve the early childhood educational system at scale by integrating new tools and practices within public Pre-K programs and building collective knowledge about how practices lead to improved outcomes for children and families (Brotman et al., 2021). This partnership work blends the worlds of research, policy, and practice and attempts to advance evidence-based practice and practice-based evidence.

The SPR Task Force identified a common set of factors that interfered with implementation at scale across public systems, with the most important factor being the degree to which these systems enacted public policies (i.e., statutes, regulations, and guidance) requiring or recommending EBIs, and provided public funds for EBIs. They identified additional facilitators of scale up, including creating EBIs that are ready for scale up, leadership support for EBIs, a skilled workforce capable of delivering EBIs, and data monitoring and evaluation capacity.

Our learnings about scaling are grounded in experiences in New York City, where investment in universal, high-quality pre-K (Pre-K for All established in 2014) brought recognition of the importance of EBIs and a city-wide mental health initiative drastically increased public funding and advanced policies to facilitate the integration of EBIs across public systems (ThriveNYC established in 2016). In this context, NYCDOE contracted with CEHD to provide evidence-based services and resources to promote family engagement and SEL, which accelerated and broadened the scope of our plans for scaling ParentCorps. For example, because Pre-K for All provided about 60% of pre-K programs in community-based organizations (CBOs), the public system was invested in scaling ParentCorps in both elementary school and CBO contexts. Since ParentCorps was developed as an enhancement to pre-K in elementary schools and the prior trials were conducted in that context, the decision to implement in CBOs raised questions about whether impacts would be sustained once children transition to other buildings for kindergarten. We have interpreted the prior finding of sustained impact as being due in part to families remaining in the same buildings, such that the "corps" of parents that formed in pre-K may continue to be a source of support and strong relationships with pre-K teachers may increase parents' trust and sense of belonging in the building. The decision to implement in CBOs also required adjustments to fit this new context (with different financial, staffing, and logistical considerations).

A second example involves the public system's need to provide professional development for its early childhood workforce at scale (across more than 1800 pre-K programs serving approximately 70,000 children annually). The ParentCorps team worked in partnership with NYCDOE partners to adapt the existing ParentCorps PD series to fit into the system-wide model (e.g., 4 days across the school year) to be provided to teachers and leaders from approximately 125–250 pre-K programs annually. This decision to implement one component of ParentCorps at scale presented the opportunity to rigorously test the added value of the parenting program and Friends School over and above PD alone. It also allowed for a comparison of ParentCorps PD to PD as usual.

We have prioritized a series of policy and practice relevant questions to learn about facilitators and barriers to implementing ParentCorps at scale within a large, complex public education system serving racially and culturally diverse children and families. In partnership with key stakeholders across the public school system, we designed three hybrid implementation-effectiveness trials including approximately 180 pre-K sites. These studies will answer a range of pressing questions including the following: (1) will ParentCorps impact be replicated with independent facilitation by teachers and district/school-based mental health professionals (a shift from co-facilitation with university-based staff in the prior trials); (2) will impact be replicated in CBOs; and (3) what are the impacts of ParentCorps professional development alone and the added impacts of the full program? These studies go beyond testing replication of meaningful impact on child outcomes. They also examine child-, family-, and classroom-level moderators, consider contextual influences on fidelity and quality, and characterize the population reached and examine the extent to which the parenting program is engaging parents across the racial, linguistic, and cultural diversity within a given setting. Finally, these studies evaluate impact on parent and system outcomes, based on the cascading resilience model which specifies mechanisms through which parenting programs may activate positive cascades in other domains of parents' lives (Doty et al., 2017) and based on Brown et al.' (2019) hypothesis that system-level outcomes may result from early childhood programs that alter multiple drivers of health disparities.

In addition to these three trials in NYC, we are conducting a fourth hybrid implementation-effectiveness trial of ParentCorps implementation in a small school district in Texas and a series of rapid cycle tests in NYC, Michigan, and Texas. We also engage with parents through focus groups and interviews to understand deeply the perspectives of the families whom we seek to support (e.g., the kinds of programs parents want to see in their schools, the advice they would give policy makers, and pre-K leaders on how to invest time and resources). Our hope is also to learn from parents about ways in which they would find value in advising or partnering with our team in making decisions about scaling, identifying high priority research questions, and interpreting findings. For a family-centered program seeking to reach parents experiencing adversity related to poverty, racism, discrimination, and immigration-related stress, across settings and geographies, the centering of parent voice is foundational for success by any typical measure and to begin to address structural inequity.

4.6 Conclusion

This volume offers a unique opportunity to reflect on what we know, what we believe to be essential, and our top priorities for research to realize the promise of early childhood family-centered programs. New approaches to cross-sector partnerships and the proliferation of tools from implementation science and improvement science boost confidence and urgency to accelerate the pace of learnings. Building on the decades of prevention research that established the evidence base, it is within reach for researchers and practitioners to take these programs to scale – promoting SEL in early childhood, supporting the adults in young children's lives, and transforming the pre-K experiences of families of color to create more equitable education systems.

References

Bailey, Z. D., Krieger, N., Agénor, M., Graves, J., Linos, N., & Bassett, M. T. (2017). Structural racism and health inequities in the USA: Evidence and interventions. *The Lancet, 389*(10077), 1453–1463. https://doi.org/10.1016/S0140-6736(17)30569-X.

Berkel, C., Gallo, C. G., Sandler, I. N., Mauricio, A. M., Smith, J. D., & Brown, C. H. (2019). Redesigning implementation measurement for monitoring and quality improvement in community delivery settings. *The Journal of Primary Prevention, 40*(1), 111–127. https://doi.org/10.1007/s10935-018-00534-z.

Berkel, C., Mauricio, A. M., Sandler, I. N., Wolchik, S. A., Gallo, C. G., & Brown, C. H. (2018a). The cascading effects of multiple dimensions of implementation on program outcomes: A test of a theoretical model. *Prevention Science, 19*(6), 782–794. https://doi.org/10.1007/s11121-017-0855-4.

Berkel, C., Sandler, I. N., Wolchik, S. A., Brown, C. H., Gallo, C. G., Chiapa, A., Mauricio, A. M., & Jones, S. (2018b). "Home practice is the program": Parents' practice of program skills as predictors of outcomes in the new beginnings program effectiveness trial. *Prevention Science, 19*(5), 663–673. https://doi.org/10.1007/s11121-016-0738-0.

Biglan, A. (2015). *The nurture effect: How the science of human behavior can improve our lives and our world*. New Harbinger Publications.

Borman, G. D., Hewes, G. M., Overman, L. T., & Brown, S. (2003). Comprehensive school reform and achievement: A meta-analysis. *Review of Educational Research, 73*(2), 125–230. https://doi.org/10.3102/00346543073002125.

Brotman, L., Calzada, E., Huang, K., Kingston, S., Dawson-McClure, S., Kamboukos, D., Rosenfelt, A., Schwab, A., & Petkova, E. (2011). Promoting effective parenting practices and preventing child behavior problems in school among ethnically diverse families from underserved, urban communities. *Child Development, 82*(1), 258–276. https://doi.org/10.1111/j.1467-8624.2010.01554.x.

Brotman, L., Dawson-McClure, S., Calzada, E., Huang, K., Kamboukos, D., Palamar, J., & Petkova, E. (2013). Cluster (school) RCT of ParentCorps: Impact on Kindergarten academic achievement. *Pediatrics, 131*(5), e1521–e1529. https://doi.org/10.1542/peds.2012-2632.

Brotman, L., Dawson-McClure, S., Huang, K., Theise, R., Kamboukos, D., Wang, J., Petkova, E., & Ogedegbe, G. (2012). Early childhood family intervention and long-term obesity prevention among high-risk minority youth. *Pediatrics, 129*(3), e621–e628. https://doi.org/10.1542/peds.2011-1568.

Brotman, L., Dawson-McClure, S. R., Kamboukos, D., Huang, K. Y., Calzada, E. J., Palamar, J., & Petkova, E. (2016). Effects of family-centered intervention in public school pre-kindergarten programs: Follow-up of a randomized trial through second grade. *JAMA Pediatrics, 2016, 170*(12), 1–7. https://doi.org/10.1001/jamapediatrics.2016.1891.

Brotman, L., Dawson-McClure, S., Rhule, D., Rosenblatt, K., Hamer, K., Kamboukos, D., Boyd, M., Mondesir, M., Chau, I., Lashua-Shriftman, E., Rodriguez, V., Barajas-Gonzalez, R.G & Huang, K. Y. (2021). Scaling early childhood evidence-based interventions through RPPs. *The Future of Children, 31*(1), 57–74. https://futureofchildren.princeton.edu/sites/futureofchildren/files/foc_combined_5.3.21.pdf

Brotman, L., Kingston, S., Bat-Chava, Y., Caldwell, M. B., & Calzada, E. J. (2008). Training school personnel to facilitate a family intervention to prevent conduct problems. *Early Education and Development, 19*(4), 622–642. https://doi.org/10.1080/15374410802231057.

Brown, A. F., Ma, G. X., Miranda, J., Eng, E., Castille, D., Brockie, T., Jones, P., Airhihenbuwa, C. O., Farhat, T., Zhu, L., & Trinh-Shevrin, C. (2019). Structural interventions to reduce and eliminate health disparities. *American Journal of Public Health, 109*(S1), S72–S78.

Center on the Developing Child at Harvard University. (2019). *Frontiers of Innovation: The IDEAS. Impact Framework.* https://developingchild.harvard.edu/innovation-application/innovation-approach/

Cohen-Vogel, L., Tichnor-Wagner, A., Allen, D., Harrison, C., Kainz, K., Socol, A. R., & Wang, Q. (2015). Implementing educational innovations at scale: Transforming researchers into continuous improvement scientists. *Educational Policy, 29*(1), 257–277.

Cooper, C. W. (2009). Parent involvement, African American mothers, and the politics of educational care. *Equity & Excellence in Education, 42*(4), 379–394. https://doi.org/10.1080/10665680903228389.

Dawson-McClure, S., Calzada, E. J., & Brotman, L. M. (2017). Engaging parents in preventive interventions for young children: Working with cultural diversity within low-income, urban neighborhoods. *Prevention Science, 18*(6), 660–670. https://doi.org/10.1007/s11121-017-0763-7.

Dawson-McClure, S. R., Calzada, E. J., Huang, K. Y., Kamboukos, D., Kolawole, B., Rhule, D., Acra, F. A., & Brotman, L. (2014a). *Promoting high quality early childhood classroom environments and family engagement through culturally-informed professional development* [Unpublished manuscript]. Department of Population Health, New York University School of Medicine, New York, NY.

Dawson-McClure, S. R., Calzada, E. J., Huang, K. Y., Kamboukos, D., Rhule, D., Kolawole, B., Petkova, E., & Brotman, L. (2014b). A population-level approach to promoting healthy child development and school success in low-income urban neighborhoods: Impact on parenting and child conduct problems. *Prevention Science, 16*, 279–290.

Dixson, A. D., & Rousseau Anderson, C. (2018). Where are we? Critical race theory in education 20 years later. *Peabody Journal of Education, 93*(1), 121–131. https://doi.org/10.1080/0161956X.2017.1403194.

Dodge, K. A. (2019). Redefining the science and policy of early childhood intervention programs. *Pediatrics, 144*(6), 1–3. https://doi.org/10.1542/peds.2019-2606.

Doty, J. L., Davis, L., & Arditti, J. A. (2017). Cascading resilience: Leverage points in promoting parent and child well-being. *Journal of Family Theory & Review, 9*, 111–126. https://doi.org/10.1111/jftr.12175.

Duncan, L. G., Coatsworth, J. D., & Greenberg, M. T. (2009). A model of mindful parenting: Implications for parent–child relationships and prevention research. *Clinical Child and Family Psychology Review, 12*(3), 255–270. https://doi.org/10.1007/s10567-009-0046-3.

Durlak, J., & DuPre, E. (2008). Implementation matters: A review of research on the influence of implementation on program outcomes and the factors affecting implementation. *American Journal of Community Psychology, 41*, 327–350. https://doi.org/10.1007/s10464-008-9165-0.

Fagan, A. A., Bumbarger, B. K., Barth, R. P., Bradshaw, C. P., Cooper, B. R., Supplee, L. H., & Walker, D. K. (2019). Scaling up evidence-based interventions in US public systems to prevent behavioral health problems: Challenges and opportunities. *Prevention Science, 20*(8), 1147–1168. https://doi.org/10.1007/s11121-019-01048-8.

Frank, J. L., Jennings, P. A., & Greenberg, M. T. (2016). Validation of the mindfulness in teaching scale. *Mindfulness, 7*(1), 155–163. https://doi.org/10.1007/s12671-015-0461-0.

Garcia Coll, C., Crnic, K., Lamberty, G., Wasik, B. H., Jenkins, R., Garcia, H. V., & McAdoo, H. P. (1996). An integrative model for the study of developmental competencies in minority children. *Child Development, 67*(5), 1891–1914. https://doi.org/10.1111/j.1467-8624.1996.tb01834.x.

Hajizadeh, N., Stevens, E. R., Applegate, M., Huang, K. Y., Kamboukos, D., Braithwaite, R. S., & Brotman, L. M. (2017). Potential return on investment of a family-centered early childhood intervention: A cost-effectiveness analysis. *BMC Public Health, 17*(1), 796. https://doi.org/10.1186/s12889-017-4805-7.

Hilliard, A. (2003). No mystery: Closing the achievement gap between Africans and excellence. In T. Perry, C. Steele, & A. G. Hilliard III (Eds.), *Young, gifted, and Black: Promoting high achievement among African-American Students* (pp. 131–165). Beacon Press.

Jennings, P. A., & Greenberg, M. T. (2009). The prosocial classroom: Teacher social and emotional competence in relation to student and classroom outcomes. *Review of Educational Research, 79*(1), 491–525. https://doi.org/10.3102/0034654308325693.

Kaufman, A. S. (2005). *Kaufman test of educational achievement second edition, brief form manual*. AGS Publishing.

Ladson-Billings, G., & Tate, W. F. (1995). Toward a critical race theory of education. *Teacher's College Record, 97*, 47–68.

Ladson-Billings, G. (2006). From the achievement gap to the education debt: Understanding achievement in US schools. *Educational Researcher, 35*(7), 3–12. https://doi.org/10.3102/0013189X035007003.

Logan, J. R., Minca, E., & Adar, S. (2012). The geography of inequality: Why separate means unequal in American public schools. *Sociology of Education, 85*(3), 287–301. https://doi.org/10.1177/0038040711431588.

Lundahl, B. W., Kunz, C., Brownell, C., Tollefson, D., & Burke, B. L. (2010). A meta-analysis of motivational interviewing: Twenty-five years of empirical studies. *Research on Social Work Practice, 20*(2), 137–160. https://doi.org/10.1177/1049731509347850.

Lyon, A. R., & Bruns, E. J. (2019). From evidence to impact: Joining our best school mental health practices with our best implementation strategies. *School Mental Health, 11*(1), 106–114. https://doi.org/10.1007/s12310-018-09306-w.

Mamun, A. A., O'Callaghan, M. J., Cramb, S. M., Najman, J. M., Williams, G. M., & Bor, W. (2009). Childhood behavioral problems predict young adults' BMI and obesity: Evidence from a birth cohort stud. *Obesity, 17*(4), 761–766. https://doi.org/10.1038/oby.2008.594.

Marchand, A. D., Vassar, R. R., Diemer, M. A., & Rowley, S. J. (2019). Integrating race, racism, and critical consciousness in Black parents' engagement with schools. *Journal of Family Theory & Review, 11*(3), 367–384. https://doi.org/10.1111/jftr.12344.

McCaffrey, S., Reitman, D., & Black, R. (2017). Mindfulness in parenting questionnaire (MIPQ): Development and validation of a measure of mindful parenting. *Mindfulness, 8*(1), 232–246. https://doi.org/10.1007/s12671-016-0596-7.

McWayne, C. M., Melzi, G., Schick, A. R., Kennedy, J. L., & Mundt, K. (2013). Defining family engagement among Latino head start parents: A mixed-methods measurement development study. *Early Childhood Research Quarterly, 28*(3), 593–607. https://doi.org/10.1016/j.ecresq.2013.03.008.

Miller, W. R., & Rollnick, S. (2013). Applications of motivational interviewing. *Motivational interviewing: Helping people change* (3rd edition). Guilford Press.

National Academies of Sciences, Engineering, and Medicine. (2016). *Parenting matters: Supporting parents of children ages 0–8*. National Academies Press. https://doi.org/10.17226/21868.

National Scientific Council on the Developing Child. (2012). *Establishing a level Foundation for Life: Mental health begins in early childhood.* Harvard University, Center on the Developing Child. https://developingchild.harvard.edu/resources/establishing-a-level-foundation-for-life-mental-health-begins-in-early-childhood/

Ogbu, J.U. (1992). Understanding Cultural Diversity and Learning. *Educational Researcher, 21*(8), 5–14. https://doi.org/10.3102/0013189X021008005

Pianta, R. C., La Paro, K. M., & Hamre, B. K. (2008). *Classroom assessment scoring system™: Manual K-3*. Paul H Brookes Publishing.

Porter, T., Bromer, J., & Forry, N. (2015). *Assessing Quality in Family and Provider/Teacher Relationships: Using the Family and Provider/Teacher Relationship Quality (FPTRQ) Measures in Conjunction with Strengthening Families and the Head Start Parent, Family and*

Community Engagement Frameworks and Self-Assessments Tools. OPRE Report 2015–56. Office of Planning, Research and Evaluation, Administration for Children and Families, U.S. Department of Health and Human Services. https://www.acf.hhs.gov/sites/default/files/opre/assessing_quality_in_family_provider_teacher_relationships_a.pdf

Raver, C. C., Garner, P., & Smith-Donald, R. (2007). The roles of emotion regulation and emotion knowledge for children's academic readiness: Are the links causal? In B. Pianta, K. Snow, & M. Cox (Eds.), *Kindergarten transition and early school success* (pp. 121–148). Brookes Publishing.

Reynolds, C. R., & Kamphaus, R. W. (2004). *BASC-2 behavior assessment for children manual.* American Guidance Service.

Rodriguez, V., Solis, S. L., Mascio, B., Kiely Gouley, K., Jennings, P. A., & Brotman, L. M. (2020). With awareness comes competency: The five Awarenesses of teaching as a framework for understanding teacher social emotional competency and Well-being. Early Education and Development, Special Issue: *Early Care and Education Professionals' Social and Emotional Well-Being.* Advance online publication. https://doi.org/10.1080/10409289.2020.1794496.

Sandler, I. N., Schoenfelder, E. N., Wolchik, S. A., & MacKinnon, D. P. (2011). Long-term impact of prevention programs to promote effective parenting: Lasting effects but uncertain processes. *Annual Review of Psychology, 62*, 299–329.

Sellars, M. (2012). Teachers and change: The role of reflective practice. *Procedia-Social and Behavioral Sciences, 55*, 461–469. https://doi.org/10.1016/j.sbspro.2012.09.525.

Sheridan, S. M., Edwards, C. P., Marvin, C. A., & Knoche, L. L. (2009). Professional development in early childhood programs: Process issues and research needs. *Early Education and Development, 20*(3), 377–401. https://doi.org/10.1080/10409280802582795.

Snyder, P., Hemmeter, M. L., Meeker, K. A., Kinder, K., Pasia, C., & McLaughlin, T. (2012). Characterizing key features of the early childhood professional development literature. *Infants & Young Children, 25*(3), 188–212.

Taylor, E. W. (2008). Transformative learning theory. In S. B. Merriam (Ed.), *Third update of adult learning. New directions for adult and continuing education, Book 119* (pp. 5–15). Jossey-Bass.

U.S. Department of Health and Human Services. (2016). *The Family Engagement Inventory (FEI): A brief cross-disciplinary synthesis.* U.S. Department of Health and Human Services, Children's Bureau. https://www.childwelfare.gov/pubPDFs/synthesis.pdf

Wise Whitehead, K. (2017, June 1). *Achievement gap is our fault, not the kids'*. Baltimore Sun. https://www.baltimoresun.com/opinion/op-ed/bs-ed-education-liberation-20170601-story.html

World Health Organization. (2010). *Nine steps for developing a scaling-up strategy.* World Health Organization. https://www.who.int/immunization/hpv/deliver/nine_steps_for_developing_a_scalingup_strategy_who_2010.pdf

Chapter 5
Research on the Family Check-Up to Support Social and Behavioral Adjustment in Early Elementary School

Elizabeth A. Stormshak, Alyssa L. Kennedy, Robyn E. Metcalfe, and Jordan M. Matulis

Abstract Developmental transitions are critical time points for intervention and prevention. The successful transition to elementary school is associated with several key skills, including sustained attention, self-regulation, social skills, and early literacy skills. Research suggests that family-centered interventions can promote these competencies associated with a successful school transition during early childhood. One such intervention is the Family Check-Up (FCU). In this chapter, we review research on the FCU and discuss the intervention as an effective approach for promoting school success during early elementary school. The FCU is a brief, family-centered intervention that is comprised of three components: an initial interview, an assessment, and a feedback and motivation session followed by tailored and adaptive intervention modules geared to family needs. The model is intended to prevent emotional, behavioral, and academic problems in children by improving family functioning and parenting skills. In early childhood, the FCU has been shown to reduce problem behaviors and increase school readiness. As researchers continue to explore strategies for the successful implementation and scale-up of the FCU, the fundamental mechanisms of change remain consistent across adaptations to unique populations and settings. Next steps involve understanding dosage and key ingredients of the FCU that predict positive adjustment.

Keywords School entry · Family-centered prevention · Parenting skills · School-based prevention

E. A. Stormshak (✉) · A. L. Kennedy · R. E. Metcalfe · J. M. Matulis
Prevention Science Institute, University of Oregon, Eugene, OR, USA
e-mail: bstorm@uoregon.edu; akenned8@uoregon.edu; robynm@uoregon.edu; jmatulis@uoregon.edu

© Springer Nature Switzerland AG 2022

K. L. Bierman, S. M. Sheridan (eds.), *Family-School Partnerships During the Early School Years*, Research on Family-School Partnerships,
https://doi.org/10.1007/978-3-030-74617-9_5

The transition into school is one of the most important developmental transitions in a child's life. A successful school transition that facilitates the development of reading and math skills predicts achievement through the high school years (Hooper et al., 2010). As they enter formal schooling, students encounter a wide variety of academic and social experiences that pose new emotional and behavioral challenges (Hughes, 2015). Students are better positioned to manage these challenges and experience a successful school transition when they have age-appropriate self-regulation, sustained attention, and early literacy skills (Cadima et al., 2015; Garbacz et al., 2018). Research has demonstrated that these skills also foster later academic achievement (Fink et al., 2019). In contrast, children who exhibit emotional and behavioral problems in early elementary school are at risk for problems at school entry that may persist into adolescence and young adulthood, including mental health problems and high-risk behaviors (Dishion et al., 2008). These problems, if not ameliorated in early childhood, can lead to adjustment difficulties that last a lifetime.

One of the most influential contexts affecting development in early childhood is the family environment. Decades of research have now demonstrated the significance of the family environment and parent-child interactions for predicting children's adjustment over time. The consistent use of positive family management techniques supports the development of children's school readiness skills predictive of school success (Hughes, 2015), whereas deficits in parenting skills during early childhood predict child problem behaviors and later risk. Given the significant impact of parenting practices on child skill development, family-centered interventions delivered during this developmental period can promote school readiness and help prevent school and home-based problem behaviors that have an impact on academic performance (Brotman et al., 2013). Research has demonstrated that family-centered interventions in the early years can help to disrupt the long-term effects of problem behaviors, increase self-regulation, and decrease problem behaviors (Chang et al., 2014; Shelleby et al., 2018). The early years are particularly suited to prevention because parents are typically more invested in their child's educational progress at this time in development than in the later years and, therefore, may be more inclined to participate in interventions and associated services to improve child functioning (Powell et al., 2012).

5.1 The Family Check-Up Model

Overview The Family Check-Up (FCU) is a brief, family-centered, school-based intervention designed to prevent emotional, behavioral, and academic problems. The FCU uses motivational interviewing to engage families in a change process focused on enhancing family management skills including supporting positive behavior, strengthening family relationships, using proactive parenting strategies, and setting healthy limits (Dishion & Stormshak, 2007). Across multiple randomized, controlled trials, the FCU has been demonstrated to be effective at reducing

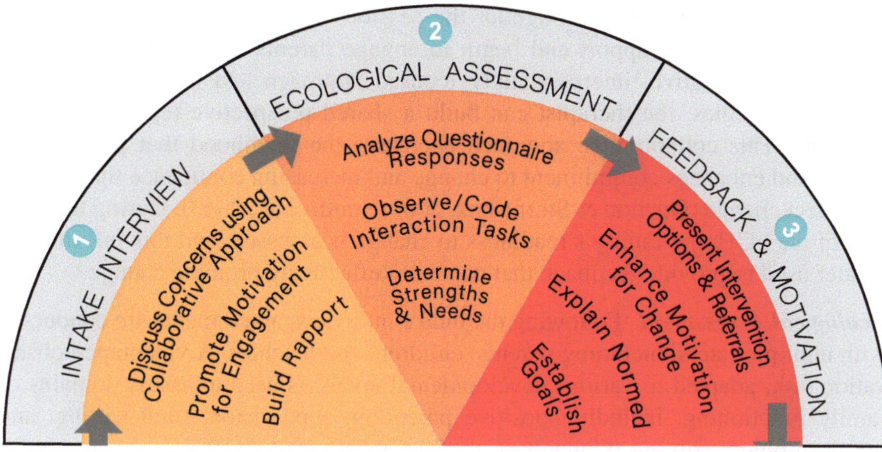

Fig. 5.1 The Family Check-up model components

problem behaviors and emotional distress as well as improving academic skills from early childhood to late adolescence, ages 2 to 17 (Garbacz et al., 2018; Mauricio et al., 2019). The goals of the FCU are to increase parent motivation to maintain effective parenting practices, decrease interactions that are detrimental to parent-child relationships or child behavior, and promote parenting behaviors that support positive youth adjustment (Dishion et al., 2008; Stormshak et al., 2018). Specifically, the intervention targets parenting practices, including parental knowledge of and involvement in children's activities, positive reinforcement and support of desired behaviors, and proactive planning and structuring to anticipate and avoid child problems (Smith et al., 2013). The ecologically based approach of the FCU has facilitated its use with populations characterized by diverse demographics and a range of severity in problem behaviors and has allowed for implementation in a variety of settings, including schools, outpatient and residential treatment settings, and community mental health centers (Smith et al., 2015a; Spirito et al., 2017).

FCU Components The traditional FCU model is comprised of three components: (1) an initial intake interview, (2) an ecological assessment, and (3) a feedback and motivation session, as demonstrated in Fig. 5.1 (Dishion & Stormshak, 2007). These components are typically completed during two to three visits, which may be conducted through home visits or appointments at a clinic or school, with variability dependent upon family needs, service delivery context, and other considerations such as constraints imposed by managed care. Visits can be accomplished in 50-minute sessions, with the option of completing both the intake interview and ecological assessment during one 75- to 90-minute session.

Intake Interview The intake interview is the first component of the FCU model. The therapist and parent(s) discuss the family's presenting concerns and goals for the intervention. The therapist aims to integrate a focus on family management and the active role of parents throughout the session. This first contact provides an opportunity to build rapport and begin to engage parents in the change process. Using a collaborative, interpersonally focused approach and motivational interviewing strategies, the therapist can build a shared perspective regarding family concerns. This collaborative approach decreases the likelihood that parents feel judged and enhances commitment to change and increasing confidence that parents can affect change (Dishion & Stormshak, 2007; Smith et al., 2013). During this portion of the FCU, the family's readiness to change is assessed, and this information is later used to provide feedback that can more effectively promote change.

Ecological Assessment Following the intake interview, assessments are conducted with multiple raters, including parents, children, and teachers. A videotaped observation task, adapted to various developmental levels, is used to assess domains of family functioning, including positive parenting, supervision, limit setting, and family problem solving (Connell et al., 2007). The ecological assessment is also intended to assess various levels and contexts of influence that can impact child outcomes, including individual- and family-level factors, peer environment, and additional considerations that influence family management practices (e.g., parent mental health and financial stress; Dishion & Stormshak, 2007). The videotaped observation comprises three to five semi-structured interaction tasks, dependent upon the age and developmental level of the youth. These interaction tasks are coded for various observed family management practices and compared to clinical and nonclinical norms. Prior research has documented the validity of these tasks as predictors of later child problem behaviors as well as sensitive indicators of responsiveness to the FCU intervention, and parents who engage in the FCU show improved interactions over time (Dishion et al., 2017).

Feedback and Motivation During the final FCU session, the therapist provides the results of the ecological family assessment and elicits input from parents regarding the results, focusing throughout on the essential role of parenting practices for child well-being (Connell et al., 2007; Dishion & Stormshak, 2007). Specifically, norm-based data are used to prompt a discussion of the family's areas of strength and areas that could benefit from further support. These results are represented on a feedback form with continuums ranging from "area of strength" to "needs attention" for each domain assessed. The therapist builds upon the rapport established during the initial session to motivate change and connect the family to appropriate services and resources. These goals are accomplished through the use of motivational interviewing techniques to reframe parents' appraisals of their child and their concerns, target parents' ambivalence or resistance, and promote parents' feelings of efficacy. The therapist uses a collaborative approach to determine treatment goals and provides a menu of individually tailored intervention options and available resources with which the family can engage to work toward the established goals (Stormshak & Dishion, 2009).

5.2 Empirical Support

Historical Research The FCU was initially developed as a school-based intervention based upon evidence emerging from randomized trials targeting problem behaviors and substance use in adolescents that highlighted the critical role of parent monitoring in successful intervention (Dishion et al., 2008; Dishion & Stormshak, 2007). Specifically, early implementation of the FCU was intended as a brief approach for motivating parents to monitor and manage adolescents at high risk for substance use. Intervention effects were found for youth substance use during seventh through ninth grades and were mediated by parental monitoring (Dishion et al., 2003). The FCU was designed to be an ecologically based intervention implemented within preexisting service systems (e.g., schools) with the goal of effectively engaging families and schools in change (Stormshak et al., 2005). Since that time, research has demonstrated intervention effects of the FCU at promoting improvements in grade point average, attendance, school engagement, and self-regulation as well as reducing problem behavior, depression, substance use, high-risk sexual behavior, and weight gain and obesity (Connell et al., 2007; Smith et al., 2015b; Stormshak et al., 2019a).

Early Childhood Research The Early Steps Multisite Study conducted by Dishion et al. (2008) was the first evaluation of the adaptation of the FCU for use in early childhood contexts. The authors examined the efficacy of the FCU among a sample of 731 at-risk and ethnically diverse families from three geographically disparate sites across the United States. Families with children ages 2–5 were recruited from the Special Supplemental Nutrition Program for Women, Infants, and Children (WIC) and were randomly assigned to the treatment condition (FCU) or control condition, where they received services as usual. All families received a standardized in-home assessment that targeted parenting strategies (i.e., positive behavior support) and child problem behavior starting at age two. Guided by a developmental, ecological model, the Early Steps Multisite Study targeted parenting skills as the primary mechanism associated with change in problem behavior, with a specific focus on positive parenting.

The results of the Early Steps Multisite Study suggest that the FCU is effective as an early childhood prevention program with benefits in areas of problem behavior, self-regulation, and school-related skills, which were measured as both proximal and distal outcomes. Random assignment to the treatment condition significantly predicted improvements on parent reports of child behavior problems at 2, 3, and 4 years of age, as well as the direct observation of parent positive behavior support from ages two to three. Increases in parent positive behavior support inhibited the growth of child problem behavior during early childhood experienced by families in the control condition (Dishion et al., 2008; Sitnick et al., 2015). These results were consistent across ethnic groups and gender. In addition, the FCU also promoted aspects of school readiness, including inhibitory control, improved language development in early childhood, and fostered a healthier trajectory of BMI in later childhood and young adulthood relative to the control group (Dishion et al., 2014; Lunkenheimer et al., 2008; Smith et al., 2015a).

Moreover, assignment to the FCU condition in the Early Steps Multisite Study has been associated with positive academic outcomes over time. Findings indicate that, when compared to control families, inclusion in the treatment condition predicted higher levels of academic achievement years later at ages 5 and 7, mediated by the increased use of positive behavior supports by parents and higher parental reports of child inhibitory control. The results also suggested indirect effects via parenting and self-regulation on ratings of oppositional behavior at age 7.5 by teachers (Brennan et al., 2013; Chang et al., 2014).

5.3 Adaptations for School Entry: The Family Check-Up for Kindergarteners

The outcomes associated with the Early Steps Multisite Study predicted positive adjustment through school entry; however, Early Steps was not a school-based intervention trial. Until recently, the FCU has not been applied or rigorously evaluated as a school-based intervention delivered at school entry. In the FCU-Kindergarten study, we adapted the model for school entry and tested the effects of the FCU in a randomized trial with kindergarten, first-grade, and second-grade children (Garbacz et al., 2018). Kindergarten families were randomly assigned to the FCU or school-as-usual at school entry (N = 365). The FCU was adapted for this population in several ways. First, assessments that focused on key skills needed for a successful transition to kindergarten were collected from parents and teachers. For children, this included measures of self-regulation, sustained attention, and school readiness skills. For parents, the assessment was tailored to measure parenting skills associated with adjustment during early childhood, such as positive parenting, family routines, school involvement, and consistent parenting. Families were observed in a videotaped interaction engaging in a variety of developmentally appropriate tasks designed to elicit parenting skills during the transition to school, including a teaching task where children built a Lego tower, a homework task where parents assisted children with math worksheets, and a reading task where parents read to their child. The recordings from these interactions were then coded by therapists, and the results were used to provide feedback to parents on homework and reading skills with their children in a process consistent with the overall FCU model. Other adaptations included the provision of books at the developmental level of the child to support reading at home, and parents in the FCU condition received support to engage with their child in reading and homework using effective parenting skills, such as positive support, creating a reading routine, and choosing books at the child's reading level. Parenting skills training was derived from two general content areas described below.

Positive Behavior Support (PBS) for Daily Routines PBS for daily routines was based on our *Everyday Parenting* curriculum (Dishion et al., 2011), an empirically supported intervention for parents that emphasizes daily family management practices that promote child adaptation. Our intervention for Kindergarten parents supported parents' efforts to promote child self-regulatory behaviors related to homework, chores, and bedtime routines. Consistent and effective parenting skills are crucial processes for promoting self-regulation (Fosco et al., 2013; Purdie et al., 2004). Three sets of parenting skills are enacted in PBS: (a) identifying realistic goals for the child, (b) identifying salient incentives, and (c) practicing and role-playing praise and encouragement and avoiding critical statements or unclear globally positive statements.

Early Literacy and Home-to-School Behavior Support Kindergarten is an important transition year for the socialization of children and their parents. Children learn the rules and structure of the public school environment, and parents are socialized in the expectations for involvement in their child's learning. Kindergarten teachers and school staff play a key role in this process by creating expectations for parent involvement. One key expectation for involvement in kindergarten is parent-teacher coordination for students' early literacy skills. Parent involvement is associated with enhanced student literacy (Dearing et al., 2006). Our Kindergarten intervention materials built on the important relationship between caretakers and the school during this transition. Trained therapists served as home–school links who build parent capacity for sustained advocacy for their child by facilitating partnership-centered interactions with school personnel. We developed a range of materials to support the home–school linkages during this transition, which included support for parents to structure reading tasks with their child in the home. We also worked directly with families to create predictable environments across home and school to support student success and building on partnership-centered strategies (Garbacz et al., 2008). Parents received this support as part of the tailored menu of options after their feedback session, and the level of support was titrated based on parent need and assessment results. Most of the families invited to participate in the intervention completed the FCU process (75%), and about two-thirds (66%) received additional support in the form of tailored sessions after the feedback.

Results of the FCU-Kindergarten model were promising. Guided by a developmental, ecological model consistent with prior FCU research, the FCU model is based on the expectation that parenting skills and child self-regulation skills serve as key mediators that promote positive child outcomes over time. Teachers completed ratings of child behavior each year during kindergarten, first grade, and second grade. Initial results indicated that children in the FCU treatment condition, relative to the "usual practice" control group, performed better on teacher report measures of emotional and behavioral problems during the first and second grade (Garbacz et al., 2018). Furthermore, children with higher initial levels of emotional and behavioral problems at the initial assessments experienced greater benefit from treatment (Garbacz et al., 2018). These outcomes were consistent regardless of special services received by the children in school and are consistent with prior FCU research suggesting greater effects for children and families at higher risk (Pelham et al., 2017).

5.4 Mechanisms of Change

Self-regulation is a key construct that mediates outcomes associated with family-centered prevention and intervention. In the context of warm, consistent, and supportive parenting relationships, children learn behavior regulation, emotional control, and coping skills. Results from various studies examining mediational pathways suggest that the FCU may function through a two-step process in which the intervention improves parenting skills that, in turn, promote child self-regulation. Through more skilled parenting, children may develop more capacity for and be more apt to implement self-regulation strategies, thus improving their behavioral and academic outcomes.

Ample research now supports the link between self-regulation and positive outcomes for youth, as well as a focus on self-regulation skills as key targets of interventions that lead to improvements in behavior over time. Across multiple studies, changes in self-regulation as a function of parenting support predict positive youth outcomes, including problem behavior and peer acceptance during early childhood and depression and school engagement during middle and high school (Chang et al., 2014; Chang et al., 2017; Stormshak et al., 2010; see Fig. 5.2). Children who participated in the FCU showed levels of growth in inhibitory control between ages two to seven that were higher than children in the control condition, which mediated intervention effects on teacher reports of child self-control and oppositional defiant behavior (Chang et al., 2014). Similar effects have been found when the FCU has been implemented during the middle school years. We demonstrated that the FCU implemented during the sixth grade had a positive effect on youth self-regulation,

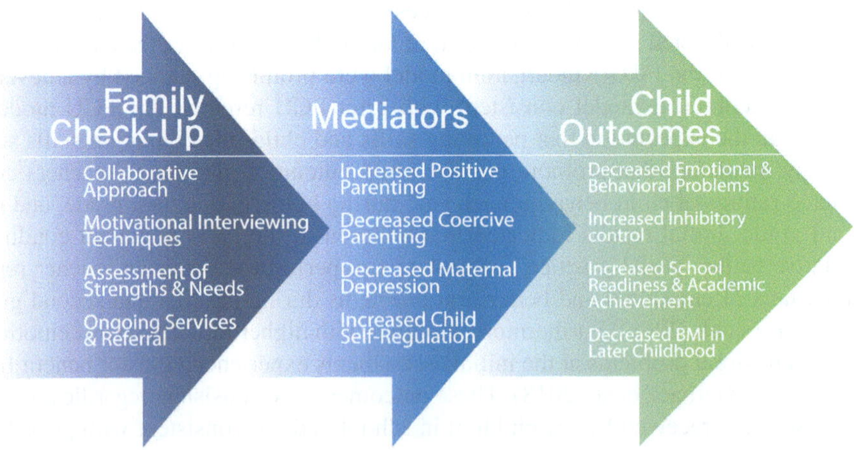

Fig. 5.2 Empirically-supported critical elements of the family check-up during early childhood

leading to decreases in youth depressive symptoms and higher levels of school engagement during the transition to high school (Stormshak et al., 2010).

When examining the effect of the FCU at school entry on parenting skills, results demonstrated that random assignment was related to improved parenting skills, especially for families at high risk based on initial assessments. Contextual stress moderated outcomes for kindergarten families, with higher levels of stress associated with improvements including reductions in negative parenting and increases in monitoring/family routines (Stormshak et al., 2019b). Improvements in parenting skills during first grade predicted reductions in child behavior problems through second grade (Stormshak et al., in press). In sum, these results suggest that the FCU is an efficacious intervention for school entry when delivered by staff selected and trained by the program developers. However, additional research is needed to determine if schools can be successful at implementing this intervention at scale. Furthermore, further examination of child self-regulation in addition to parenting skills during kindergarten will help to clarify mediational processes of the FCU during school entry.

5.5 Implementation of the FCU at School Entry in Real-World Settings

Translating evidence-based practices such as the FCU from research settings to typical care settings is challenging, with multiple barriers documented (Smith et al., 2018; Smolkowski et al., 2017). Dissemination and implementation often require broad changes at the levels of both the systemic and organizational contexts (Aarons et al., 2018). Most mental health and social service interventions occur within organizations, making it particularly important to consider organizational processes such as organizational culture, implementation climate, leadership, and organizational readiness to change when designing sustainable interventions (Aarons et al., 2018). A focus on specific implementation strategies as well as targeting populations that can benefit most from interventions may be effective at enhancing implementation broadly. In the next sections, we consider a set of issues that require attention and additional research to support the broader diffusion of the FCU Kindergarten intervention model.

Adaptation One strategy for expanding the scalability of an intervention approach involves tailoring aspects of the intervention to better fit the organization that will administer it or the population being served while maintaining the core critical elements of the intervention responsible for positive effects (Smith et al., 2018). When core components of the intervention are sustained with adequate fidelity, adapted interventions should yield effect sizes comparable to the original studies with results across time reflecting the effective tailoring of the intervention to the population or setting (Chambers et al., 2013). Thus, the FCU can be "scaled out" to address new target behaviors, delivery systems, or populations, while retaining the three steps encompassing the FCU, including the intake interview, ecological assessment, and motivation/feedback (Aarons et al., 2017). This ensures that the evidence-based components of the FCU that are essential for its mechanism of change are protected, even when adaptations are made. The FCU was developed as a school-based intervention to reduce adolescent risk behavior; it has been adapted for various contexts and populations. These adaptations have included early childhood modifications, out-of-school settings such as mental health clinics and home visitation, and Internet-based delivery (Danaher et al., 2018; Smith et al., 2018). In each setting, although the context and population have varied, the fundamental mechanism of change – increased self-regulation by the improvement of family functioning – has stayed constant. Most recently, based on data suggesting that the FCU can help effectively reduce obesity risks in children, a new adaptation called the Family Check-Up 4 Health (FCU4H) has specifically targeted health-promoting behaviors such as nutrition, physical activity, and sleep (Smith et al., 2018). Maintaining key components of the FCU along with context-appropriate adaptations can help target a variety of clinical goals for underserved children and families, such as expansion into kindergarten settings. Our adaptations to the FCU for kindergarten, such as parenting support for reading at home, should be key ingredients in the model as it is disseminated to real-world settings.

Applicability to Diverse Populations In addition to these adaptations, services should be specifically adapted to ethnically diverse groups. Children from diverse backgrounds continue to face systematic barriers to mental health service access (Pumariega et al., 2005). Evidence-based treatments appear to be equally effective for diverse populations when appropriate access is offered, even before accounting for culturally specific adaptations (Smith et al., 2014). Indeed, the FCU's adaptive and flexible framework was developed using a culturally diverse sample of families to be applicable to the individual family unit (Dishion & Kavanagh, 2003). The collaborative stance and ecological focus enable a multiculturally competent therapist to tailor feedback to the specific cultural context of the family.

However, culturally specific adaptations may still help improve the relevance of the FCU for specific populations (Smith et al., 2014). For example, the first culturally specific adaptation of the FCU was aimed at Native American adolescents, incorporating cultural traditions such as the public acknowledgment of youth and access to traditional supports such as healers and spiritual advisors (Boyd-Ball & Dishion, 2006). In this project, the FCU was delivered community-wide without randomization, using a quasi-experimental evaluation design that supported community leaders during uptake of the model. A variety of barriers reduced the sustainability of the model, including the lack of trained staff to implement the model after the project ended and high levels of trauma and health-related issues among the population. These barriers, coupled with lack of funding, impeded the sustained impact of the FCU in these communities. Community-based participatory research strategies may help identify culturally specific strategies to sustain the intervention over time in these highly underserved communities.

Dosage Broadly, the concept of dosage refers to the amount of intervention that is delivered to families. Intended dosage is operationalized in various ways in the clinical literature, but is most often characterized by amount, frequency, and duration, as well as the interactions between these variables (Voils et al., 2012). Because the evaluation process of the FCU is concrete, the short, adapted sessions may be particularly effective in assessment and skill-building (Halle et al., 2010). However, not all families fully engage in interventions. Thus, it may be valuable to explore effective dosage, or the mean intervention dosage in which a family must engage, to show "measurable functional progress" (Bagnato et al., 2011). This is measured by the intended dosage, as well as parent engagement and involvement. For many early childhood interventions, parent participation rate is a particularly potent predictor of clinical outcomes (e.g., Stormshak et al., 2003). The evaluation of effective dosage in early childhood interventions is still developing, with traditional views assuming that, typically, higher dosage will improve outcomes (Neuman & Dwyer, 2009). Consistent with predictions, outcomes typically improve over time as families receive a larger "dose" of the FCU (Stormshak et al., 2018). Dosage also varies across ages and intervention trials, based on both the context of the delivery and developmental issues.

Consider the FCU delivered at both middle school and early elementary school. Table 5.1 shows the dosage and engagement rates associated with several FCU studies across development, from early childhood to the young adult years. Engagement rates varied based on the context of delivery and age of the children. In the first Project Alliance trial (PAL 1), which was delivered in middle school, 23% of families received the FCU, but only those with high-risk behaviors were targeted for treatment. In the second Project Alliance trial (PAL 2), all families of middle school youth assigned to intervention were offered the FCU. Interestingly, when the treatment was targeted to a high-risk population, rates of follow-up sessions appeared to increase, with 100% of PAL 1 families receiving follow-up services versus 80% of PAL 2 families. Using similar methods for recruitment across projects can provide comparable data on engagement rates. PAL 2 and the FCU Kindergarten study used the same methods for recruitment and engagement, delivering the FCU as a school-based model to the whole population. After the consent process was complete, intervention families were invited to participate in the intervention or could opt out of the

Table 5.1 Dosage and engagement rates across randomized trials of the Family Check-UP (FCU)

Project	Families completing FCU (%)	Families receiving follow-up (%)	Minutes of treatment (average)	Age range of child (years)
Project Alliance trial (PAL 1; MS)	23%	100%	688	12–14
Project Alliance trial (PAL 2; MS)	42%	80%	337	12–16
Project Alliance trial (PAL 2; YA)	35%	33%	117	20
Early steps	88%	86%	713	2–5
FCU kindergarten study	75%	66%	214	5–7

Note. MS middle school, *YA* young adult

intervention at this juncture. In middle school, 42% of families randomly assigned to intervention received the FCU, whereas at kindergarten entry, 75% of families received the intervention (Garbacz et al., 2018; Stormshak et al., 2010), suggesting that families are more likely to engage in family-centered support during elementary school than middle school. However, when we examined rates of engagement in parenting skills training after completion of the FCU, the opposite was true. Kindergarten families engaged in follow-up sessions 66% of the time, whereas 80% of middle school families engaged at this level. Perhaps the issues with which middle school students struggle require additional and persistent support, whereas during kindergarten many of the parents' concerns were addressed in the context of the FCU feedback session. More research is needed on dosage as it relates to outcomes associated with the FCU Kindergarten, especially given the wide range of dosage differences both between and within research studies.

Cost-Effectiveness Economic analyses have become increasingly important in the evaluation of prevention-based research and help guide decisions for community agencies about feasibility of evidence-based programs (Kuklinski et al., 2012). When public policymakers and other decision-makers are not given information about implementation cost, they often are unable to make choices about effective interventions, widening the research-practice gap. Several cost analyses of the FCU have been conducted to support the uptake of the FCU by communities and inform providers. A recent rigorous cost analysis of the FCU for early childhood was conducted by Kuklinski and colleagues. The study found that the FCU could be delivered at an average annual cost of $1066 per family (*SD* = $400), and additional families could be served at roughly half the cost once FCU infrastructure was established (Kuklinski et al., in press). Costs increased for higher-risk families, but investment was associated with stronger impacts among these families. Similar cost analyses of the FCU4H have also been conducted and suggest that implementation preparation would cost between $15,000 and $18,000 per site (Jordan et al., 2019). The primary costs associated with implementation are training costs, and when these are accounted for, the cost of implementing and sustaining the program decreases. However, schools are faced with high staff turnover and personnel costs, which limits the ability of schools to sustain this type of programming. Further cost analysis should examine the specific implementation costs for the FCU Kindergarten within the context of existing elementary school infrastructure and staff.

Assessing Fidelity Inadequate treatment fidelity compromises the therapist's adherence (or use of treatment-specific interventions) and competence (or therapist skill level) during the intervention (Waltz et al., 1993). Implementation fidelity is plausibly linked to overall treatment outcomes, with particular consistency in the literature for family-based interventions (Smith et al., 2013). Using the Fidelity of Implementation Rating System as a conceptual base, Smith et al. (2013) proposed a fidelity monitoring system called COACH, an acronym that refers to "Conceptual accuracy and adherence," "Observant and relevant to client needs," "Actively structures sessions," "Careful and appropriate teaching," and "Hope and motivation generated." They found that implementation fidelity predicted parent engagement and that engagement predicted positive behavior support one year later. Both engagement and positive behavior support directly predicted reductions in child problem behavior two years after the intervention. This suggests that FCU implementation fidelity is particularly important in predicting beneficial outcomes, highlighting the need for fidelity monitoring for this type of parenting intervention.

5.6 Future Research Directions

Research on the FCU from early childhood through elementary school has shown promising results. Real-world implementation of the FCU is just beginning, however, and research focusing on ways to implement this intervention in schools that are sustainable and realistic is needed. It is not realistic for schools to train their staff in the traditional FCU model because it requires significant staff time and effort. Schools are faced with many barriers to implementing family-centered programs, and they need tools that are practical, brief, and accessible for their staff.

Without doubt, identifying effective strategies to deliver the FCU through more accessible modalities is a critical component of future research. We have recently developed an electronic health version of the FCU (FCU Online), which has been tested in a school-based, randomized controlled trial (RCT) targeting middle school children (Danaher et al., 2018; Stormshak et al., 2019c). Families who participated were randomly assigned to either an online-only delivery of the intervention, an online plus coach delivery, or a waitlist control group. The coaching was delivered through a telehealth model, making it more cost-effective and accessible than prior versions of the FCU. Coaching was targeted during the feedback and as follow-up when parents were working on skill development. We found that the online intervention that included coaching improved both parent self-efficacy and confidence as well as child emotional problems and that families with initial risk showed greater improvements than those with no risk. This innovative delivery of the intervention will potentially address many of the barriers of traditional school-based implementation, especially in under-resourced areas and rural areas. Our next priority is to continue research on the FCU Online to evaluate its efficacy in other age groups, including children in the early childhood and school entry years.

Last, understanding the key ingredients of the FCU related to changes in child and parent behavior will be important for future research. Embry and Biglan (2008) discuss evidence-based kernels, defined as fundamental units of behavioral influence, and the need for our work to identify these kernels and apply them to real-world, community prevention. Identifying the aspects of the FCU that lead to behavioral change is an important piece of understanding the translation of efficacy to effectiveness. Through the identification of essential elements, we can ensure their retention within intervention techniques as we continue scale-up efforts. One example of a possible kernel is the use of videotaping and feedback to families in the FCU. In the majority of FCU clinical trials, videotaped observations of families are collected and used to provide feedback to parents (as well as to code for later analyses of parenting skills as an outcome variable). Motivational interviewing is used to guide parents' self-discovery, support their strengths, and highlight areas of growth related to interactions with their child. In general, few studies have been published using the observational data as a key outcome, primarily because observation data rarely correlates with parent self-report, and the findings using the observational data as a key outcome across projects have been limited. Nonetheless, observational data, in particular using these data to provide feedback to families, is a core process component of the FCU. However, when we adapt the FCU for school and clinical settings, collecting observations of parent-child interactions is less feasible. In all of our effectiveness trials of the FCU, we have dropped the observational task from the intervention. There is no video-feedback component in the FCU Online or the Positive Family Support project, which included 41 schools across the state of Oregon (Smolkowski et al., 2017). Although many factors predict limited effectiveness, it is possible that the video-observation and tailored feedback to parents using observations may be a key ingredient of the FCU's efficacy. This speculation remains unproven. Future research should examine the FCU with and without video-observed feedback to evaluate the impact of this step in the FCU process on outcomes. Understanding the key ingredients, dosage, and mechanisms of change associated with the FCU will help refine the intervention over time for large-scale dissemination in schools and community settings.

5.7 Conclusion

Research has demonstrated the critical importance of successful transition into school and the significant role the family environment plays in fostering healthy development. In this chapter, we discussed how family-centered interventions can promote school readiness and prevent later problem behaviors that impact school success. One such intervention is the FCU, an ecologically based approach targeting parenting practices to support positive youth adjustment. While the FCU was initially developed as a school-based intervention for adolescent populations at high risk, it has been adapted for use in early childhood and kindergarten populations. Furthermore, research for these adaptations has shown promising results on measures of self-regulation through second grade.

This chapter considered factors related to the implementation of the FCU and raised a set of issues that will be important in future research focused on translating the intervention to broader use in real-world settings. These issues include adapting the FCU to better fit different delivery contexts and address the needs of diverse populations in varied settings while retaining the core intervention components that produce positive change. In addition, FCU researchers are designing and evaluating variations in program delivery that might help address the many barriers associated with scaling up the intervention for sustainable and high-fidelity school-based implementation. Some key areas of future research to support this focus include evaluating efficacy of the FCU Online and understanding the key ingredients related to positive impact.

References

Aarons, G. A., Sklar, M., Mustanski, B., Benbow, N., & Brown, C. H. (2017). "Scaling-out" evidence-based interventions to new populations or new health care delivery systems. *Implementation Science, 12*(1), 1–11. https://doi.org/10.1186/s13012-017-0640-6.

Aarons, G. A., Moullin, J. C., & Ehrhart, M. G. (2018). The role of organizational processes in dissemination and implementation research. In R. C. Brownson, G. A. Colditz, & E. K. Proctor (Eds.), *Dissemination and implementation research in health: Translating science to practice* (pp. 122–142). Oxford University Press.

Bagnato, S. J., Suen, H. K., & Fevola, A. V. (2011). "Dosage" effects on developmental progress during early childhood intervention: Accessible metrics for real-life research and advocacy. *Infants & Young Children, 24*(2), 117–132. https://doi.org/10.1097/IYC.0b013e3182104896.

Boyd-Ball, A. J., & Dishion, T. J. (2006). Family-centered treatment for American Indian adolescent substance abuse: Toward a culturally and historically informed strategy. In *Adolescent Substance Abuse: Research and Clinical Advances* (pp. 421–448). Cambridge University Press. https://doi.org/10.1017/CBO9780511543968.022.

Brennan, L. M., Shelleby, E. C., Shaw, D. S., Gardner, F., Dishion, T. J., & Wilson, M. (2013). Indirect effects of the family check-up on school-age academic achievement through improvements in parenting in early childhood. *Journal of Educational Psychology, 105*(3), 762. https://doi.org/10.1037/a0032096.

Brotman, L. M., Dawson-McClure, S., Calzada, E. J., Huang, K.-Y., Kamboukos, D., Palamar, J. J., & Petkova, E. (2013). Cluster (school) RCT of ParentCorps: Impact on kindergarten academic achievement. *Pediatrics, 131*(5), e1521–e1529. https://doi.org/10.1542/peds.2012-2632.

Cadima, J., Doumen, S., Verschueren, K., & Buyse, E. (2015). Child engagement in the transition to school: Contributions of self-regulation, teacher–child relationships and classroom climate. *Early Childhood Research Quarterly, 32*, 1–12. https://doi.org/10.1016/j.ecresq.2015.01.008.

Chambers, D. A., Glasgow, R. E., & Stange, K. C. (2013). The dynamic sustainability framework: Addressing the paradox of sustainment amid ongoing change. *Implementation Science, 8*(1), 1–11. https://doi.org/10.1186/1748-5908-8-117.

Chang, H., Shaw, D. S., Dishion, T. J., Gardner, F., & Wilson, M. N. (2014). Direct and indirect effects of the family check-up on self-regulation from toddlerhood to early school-age. *Journal of Abnormal Child Psychology, 42*(7), 1117–1128. https://doi.org/10.1007/s10802-014-9859-8.

Chang, H., Shaw, D. S., Shelleby, E. C., Dishion, T. J., & Wilson, M. N. (2017). The long-term effectiveness of the family check-up on peer preference: Parent-child interaction and child effortful control as sequential mediators. *Journal of Abnormal Child Psychology, 45*(4), 705–717. https://doi.org/10.1007/s10802-016-0198-9.

Connell, A. M., Dishion, T. J., Yasui, M., & Kavanagh, K. (2007). An adaptive approach to family intervention: Linking engagement in family-centered intervention to reductions in adolescent problem behavior. *Journal of Consulting and Clinical Psychology, 75*(4), 568–579. https://doi.org/10.1037/0022-006x.75.4.568.

Danaher, B. G., Seeley, J. R., Stormshak, E. A., Tyler, M. S., Caruthers, A. S., Moore, K. J., & Cardenas, L. (2018). The family check-up online program for parents of middle school students: Protocol for a randomized controlled trial. *JMIR research protocols, 7*(7), e11106. https://doi.org/10.2196/11106.

Dearing, E., Kreider, H., Simpkins, S., & Weiss, H. B. (2006). Family involvement in school and low-income children's literacy: Longitudinal associations between and within families. *Journal of Educational Psychology, 98*(4), 653–664. https://doi.org/10.1037/0022-0663.98.4.653.

Dishion, T. J., & Kavanagh, K. (2003). *Intervening in adolescent problem behavior: A family-centered approach*. New York: Guilford Press.

Dishion, T. J., & Stormshak, E. A. (2007). *Intervening in children's lives: An ecological, family-centered approach to mental health care*. Washington, DC: American Psychological Association.

Dishion, T. J., Nelson, S. E., & Kavanagh, K. (2003). The family check-up with high-risk young adolescents: Preventing early-onset substance use by parent monitoring. *Behavior Therapy, 34*(4), 553–571. https://doi.org/10.1016/s0005-7894(03)80035-7.

Dishion, T. J., Shaw, D., Connell, A., Gardner, F., Weaver, C., & Wilson, M. (2008). The family check-up with high-risk indigent families: Preventing problem behavior by increasing parents' positive behavior support in early childhood. *Child Development, 79*(5), 1395–1414. https://doi.org/10.1111/j.1467-8624.2008.01195.x.

Dishion, T. J., Stormshak, E. A., & Kavanagh, K. (2011). *Everyday parenting: A professional's guide to building family management practices*. Research Press.

Dishion, T. J., Brennan, L. M., Shaw, D. S., McEachern, A. D., Wilson, M. N., & Jo, B. (2014). Prevention of problem behavior through annual family check-ups in early childhood: Intervention effects from home to early elementary school. *Journal of Abnormal Child Psychology, 42*(3), 343–354. https://doi.org/10.1007/s10802-013-9768-2.

Dishion, T. J., Mun, C. J., Tein, J. Y., Kim, H., Shaw, D. S., Gardner, F., Wilson, M. N., & Peterson, J. (2017). The validation of macro and micro observations of parent–child dynamics using the relationship affect coding system in early childhood. *Prevention Science, 18*(3), 268–280. https://doi.org/10.1007/s11121-016-0697-5.

Embry, D. D., & Biglan, A. (2008). Evidence-based kernels: Fundamental units of behavioral influence. *Clinical Child and Family Psychology Review, 11*(3), 75–113. https://doi.org/10.1007/s10567-008-0036-x.

Fink, E., Browne, W. V., Hughes, C., & Gibson, J. (2019). Using a "child's-eye view" of social success to understand the importance of school readiness at the transition to formal schooling. *Social Development, 28*(1), 186–199. https://doi.org/10.1111/sode.12323.

Fosco, G. M., Frank, J. L., Stormshak, E. A., & Dishion, T. J. (2013). Opening the "black box": Family check-up intervention effects on self-regulation that prevents growth in problem behavior and substance use. *Journal of School Psychology, 51*(4), 455–468. https://doi.org/10.1016/j.jsp/2013.02.001.

Garbacz, S. A., Woods, K. E., Swanger-Gagné, M. S., Taylor, A. M., Black, K. A., & Sheridan, S. M. (2008). The effectiveness of a partnership-centered approach in conjoint behavioral consultation. *School Psychology Quarterly, 23*(3), 313–326. https://doi.org/10.1037/1045-3830.23.3.313.

Garbacz, S. A., McIntyre, L. L., Stormshak, E. A., & Kosty, D. B. (2018). The efficacy of the family check-up on children's emotional and behavior problems in early elementary school. *Journal of Emotional and Behavioral Disorders*, 1–13. https://doi.org/10.1177/1063426618806258.

Halle, T., Zaslow, M., Tout, K., Starr, R., Wessel, J., & McSwiggan, M. (2010). Beyond how much: What we are learning about structuring effective early childhood professional development preparing teachers for the early childhood classroom. In S. B. Neuman & M. Kamil (Eds.), *Preparing teachers for the early childhood classroom: Proven models and key principles* (pp. 175–188). Brookes Publishing.

Hooper, S. R., Roberts, J., Sideris, J., Burchinal, M., & Zeisel, S. (2010). Longitudinal predictors of reading and math trajectories through middle school for African American versus Caucasian students across two samples. *Developmental Psychology, 46*(5), 1018–1029. https://doi.org/10.1037/a0018877.

Hughes, C. (2015). The transition to school. *The Psychologist, 28*(9), 714–717.

Jordan, N., Graham, A. K., Berkel, C., & Smith, J. D. (2019). Costs of preparing to implement a family-based intervention to prevent pediatric obesity in primary care: A budget impact analysis. *Prevention Science, 20*(5), 655–66409. https://doi.org/10.1007/s11121-018-70-x.

Kuklinski, M. R., Briney, J. S., Hawkins, J. D., & Catalano, R. F. (2012). Cost-benefit analysis of communities that care outcomes at eighth grade. *Prevention Science, 13*(2), 150–161. https://doi.org/10.1007/s11121-011-0259-9.

Kuklinski, M. R., Crowley, D. M., Dishion, T. J., Shaw, D. S., Wilson, M. N., & Pelham, W. E., III. (in press). Supporting strategic Investment in Social Programs: A high-utility cost analysis of the family check-up. *Prevention Science*.

Lunkenheimer, E. S., Dishion, T. J., Shaw, D. S., Connell, A. M., Gardner, F., Wilson, M. N., & Skuban, E. M. (2008). Collateral benefits of the family check-up on early childhood school readiness: Indirect effects of parents' positive behavior support. *Developmental Psychology, 44*(6), 1737–1752. https://doi.org/10.1037/a0013858.

Mauricio, A. M., Rudo-Stern, J., Dishion, T. J., Letham, K., & Lopez, M. (2019). Provider readiness and adaptations of competency drivers during scale-up of the family check-up. *The Journal of Primary Prevention, 40*(1), 51–68. https://doi.org/10.1007/s10935-018-00533-0.

Neuman, S. B., & Dwyer, J. (2009). Missing in action: Vocabulary instruction in pre-K. *The Reading Teacher, 62*(5), 384–392. https://doi.org/10.1598/rt.62.5.2.

Pelham, W. E., Dishion, T. J., Tein, J. Y., Shaw, D. S., & Wilson, M. N. (2017). What doesn't work for whom? Exploring heterogeneity in responsiveness to the family check-up in early childhood using a mixture model approach. *Prevention Science, 18*(8), 911–922. https://doi.org/10.1007/s11121-017-0805-1.

Powell, D. R., Son, S. H., File, N., & Froiland, J. M. (2012). Changes in parent involvement across the transition from public school prekindergarten to first grade and children's academic outcomes. *The Elementary School Journal, 113*(2), 276–300. https://doi.org/10.1086/667726.

Pumariega, A. J., Rogers, K., & Rothe, E. (2005). Culturally competent systems of care for children's mental health: Advances and challenges. *Community Mental Health Journal, 41*(5), 539–555. https://doi.org/10.1007/s10597-005-6360-4.

Purdie, N., Carroll, A., & Roche, L. (2004). Parenting and adolescent self-regulation. *Journal of Adolescence, 27*(6), 663–676. https://doi.org/10.1016/j.adolescence.2004.01.002.

Shelleby, E. C., Shaw, D. S., Dishion, T. J., Wilson, M. N., & Gardner, F. (2018). Effects of the family check-up on reducing growth in conduct problems from toddlerhood through school age: An analysis of moderated mediation. *Journal of Consulting and Clinical Psychology, 86*(10), 856–867. https://doi.org/10.1037/ccp0000337.

Sitnick, S. L., Shaw, D. S., Gill, A., Dishion, T. J., Winter, C., Waller, R., Gardner, F., & Wilson, M. (2015). Parenting and the family check-up: Changes in observed parent-child interaction following early childhood intervention. *Journal of Clinical Child & Adolescent Psychology, 44*(6), 970–984. https://doi.org/10.1080/15374416.2014.940623.

Smith, J. D., Dishion, T. J., Shaw, D. S., & Wilson, M. N. (2013). Indirect effects of fidelity to the family check-up on changes in parenting and early childhood problem behaviors. *Journal of Consulting and Clinical Psychology, 81*(6), 962–974. https://doi.org/10.1037/a0033950.

Smith, J. D., Knoble, N. B., Zerr, A. A., Dishion, T. J., & Stormshak, E. A. (2014). Family check-up effects across diverse ethnic groups: Reducing early-adolescence antisocial behavior by reducing family conflict. *Journal of Clinical Child Adolescent Psychology, 43*(3), 400–414. https://doi.org/10.1080/15374416.2014.888670.

Smith, J. D., Montaño, Z., Dishion, T. J., Shaw, D. S., & Wilson, M. N. (2015a). Preventing weight gain and obesity: Indirect effects of the family check-up in early childhood. *Prevention Science, 16*(3), 408–419. https://doi.org/10.1007/s11121-014-0505-z.

Smith, J. D., Stormshak, E. A., & Kavanagh, K. (2015b). Results of a pragmatic effectiveness–implementation hybrid trial of the family check-up in community mental health agencies. *Administration and Policy in Mental Health and Mental Health Services Research, 42*(3), 265–278. https://doi.org/10.1007/s10488-014-0566-0.

Smith, J. D., Berkel, C., Hails, K. A., Dishion, T. J., Shaw, D. S., & Wilson, M. N. (2018). Predictors of participation in the family check-up program: A randomized trial of yearly services from age 2 to 10 years. *Prevention Science, 19*(5), 652–662. https://doi.org/10.1007/s11121-016-0679-7.

Smolkowski, K., Seeley, J. R., Gau, J. M., Dishion, T. J., Stormshak, E. A., Moore, K. J., Falkenstein, C. A., Fosco, G. M., & Garbacz, S. A. (2017). Effectiveness evaluation of the positive family support intervention: A three-tiered public health delivery model for middle schools. *Journal of School Psychology, 62*, 103–125. https://doi.org/10.1016/j.jsp.2017.03.004.

Spirito, A., Hernandez, L., Marceau, K., Cancilliere, M. K., Barnett, N. P., Graves, H. R., Rodriguez, A. M., & Knopik, V. S. (2017). Effects of a brief, parent-focused intervention for substance using adolescents and their sibling. *Journal of Substance Abuse Treatment, 77*, 156–165. https://doi.org/10.1016/j.jsat.2017.02.002.

Stormshak, E. A., & Dishion, T. J. (2009). A school-based, family-centered intervention to prevent substance use: The family check-up. *American Journal of Drug and Alcohol Abuse, 35*(4), 227–232. https://doi.org/10.1080/00952990903005908.

Stormshak, E. A., Kaminski, R. A., & Goodman, M. R. (2003). Enhancing the parenting skills of head start families during the transition to kindergarten. *Prevention Science, 3*(3), 223–234. https://doi.org/10.1023/A:1019998601210.

Stormshak, E. A., Dishion, T. J., Light, J., & Yasui, M. (2005). Implementing family-centered interventions within the public middle school: Linking service delivery to change in student problem behavior. *Journal of Abnormal Child Psychology, 33*(6), 723–733. https://doi.org/10.1007/s10802-005-7650-6.

Stormshak, E. A., Fosco, G. M., & Dishion, T. J. (2010). Implementing interventions with families in schools to increase youth school engagement: The family check-up model. *School Mental Health, 2*(2), 82–92. https://doi.org/10.1007/s12310-009-9025-6.

Stormshak, E. A., DeGarmo, D. D., Chronister, K. M., & Caruthers, A. (2018). The impact of family-centered prevention on self-regulation and subsequent long-term risk in emerging adults. *Prevention Science, 19*(4), 549–558. https://doi.org/10.1007/s11121-017-0852-7.

Stormshak, E. A., Caruthers, A., Chronister, K. M., DeGarmo, D. D., Stapleton, J., Falkenstein, C., DeVargas, E., & Nash, W. (2019a). Reducing risk behavior with family-centered prevention during the young adult years. *Prevention Science, 2*(3), 321–330. NIHMS991171. https://doi.org/10.1007/s11121-018-0917-2.

Stormshak, E. A., McIntyre, L. L., Garbacz, S. A., & Kosty, D. B. (2019b). Family-centered prevention to enhance parenting skills during the transition to elementary school: A randomized trial. *Journal of Family Psychology, 34*(1), 122–127. https://doi.org/10.1037/fam0000570.

Stormshak, E. A., Seeley, J. R., Caruthers, A. S., Cardenas, L., Moore, K. J., Tyler, M. S., Fleming, C. M., Gau, J., & Danaher, B. (2019c). Evaluating the efficacy of the family check-up online: A school-based, ehealth model for the prevention of problem behavior during the middle school years. *Development and Psychopathology, 31*(5), 1873–1886. https://doi.org/10.1017/S0954579419000907.

Stormshak, E. A., DeGarmo, D. D., Garbacz, S. A., McIntyre, L. L., & Caruthers, A. (in press). Using motivational interviewing to improve parenting skills and prevent problem behavior during the transition to kindergarten. *Prevention Science*. https://doi.org/10.1007/s11121-020-01102-w.

Voils, C. I., Chang, Y., Crandell, J., Leeman, J., Sandelowski, M., & Maciejewski, M. L. (2012). Informing the dosing of interventions in randomized trials. *Contemporary Clinical Trials, 33*(6), 1225–1230. https://doi.org/10.1016/j.cct.2012.07.011.

Waltz, J., Addis, M. E., Koerner, K., & Jacobson, N. S. (1993). Testing the integrity of a psychotherapy protocol: Assessment of adherence and competence. *Journal of Consulting and Clinical Psychology, 61*(4), 620–630. https://doi.org/10.1037//0022-006x.61.4.620.

Chapter 6
Parental Involvement and Engagement in Early Education Contribute to Children's Success and Well-Being

Arthur J. Reynolds, Sangyoo Lee, Lauren Eales, Nishank Varshney, and Nicole Smerillo

Abstract Parent involvement has long been considered a key component of early childhood programs. Yet efforts to engage parents have waned in recent years when policy and research support have focused on promoting children's school readiness skills with few resources devoted to family support services. This chapter illustrates the central role that parental involvement and engagement plays in promoting the lasting benefits of high-quality early education. We describe the Child-Parent Center (CPC) program and its emphasis on facilitating productive family engagement across the early childhood years (ages 3–9). In addition to prescribing specific strategies designed to involve parents in their children's education as well as for their own personal and career development, CPC creates school infrastructure supports (e.g., small class, resource centers) to sustain family engagement and align home-based and school-based learning. We describe the positive impact of the CPC program on parent involvement in their child's school, parent support for their child's learning at home, and parent expectations for child academic success. Parental involvement in children's learning is not only a key element of effective early education, but, as many studies have shown, it is a primary mechanism through which long-term benefits are achieved. We also review longitudinal research that documents the long-term child benefits of parental involvement and family engagement in the CPC model, including educational attainment, economic well-being, and health and well-being more generally.

Keywords Parent involvement · Family engagement · Child-Parent Center Program · Early childhood education · Longitudinal benefits

---

A. J. Reynolds (✉)
Institute of Child Development, University of Minnesota, Minneapolis, MN, USA
e-mail: ajr@umn.edu

S. Lee · L. Eales · N. Varshney · N. Smerillo
Human Capital Research Collaborative, University of Minnesota, Minneapolis, MN, USA
e-mail: leex5172@umn.edu; eales009@umn.edu; varsh011@umn.edu; nsmerill@umn.edu

© Springer Nature Switzerland AG 2022

K. L. Bierman, S. M. Sheridan (eds.), *Family-School Partnerships During the Early School Years*, Research on Family-School Partnerships,
https://doi.org/10.1007/978-3-030-74617-9_6

6.1 Introduction

Parental involvement has been a fundamental component of early childhood programs for decades.[1] The founding of the Head Start preschool program in the 1960s brought widespread attention to the importance of developing and implementing comprehensive family services that benefit parents personally and professionally and that foster children's well-being. Engaging parents in meaningful relationships with their child's schools also provides the context for ensuring that learning gains are sustained. As noted by Urie Bronfenbrenner (1974), a member of Head Start's planning committee, "the involvement of the child's family as an active participant is critical to the success of any intervention program [without which gains] erode fairly rapidly" (p. 17).

Since the early years of preschool expansion across the nation, however, the curricular and educational components of early education have become predominant, such that most state- and school-district-funded programs today provide few if any direct resources for parental involvement. Although cost is a factor, as the goal of public programs is to scale up to the entire population (O'Connell et al., 2009), this trend is inconsistent with evidence that the most effective programs include strong family components and demonstrate high economic returns into adulthood (Consortium for Longitudinal Studies, 1983; Schweinhart et al., 2005; Reynolds & Temple, 2019; Reynolds et al., 2017).

6.2 Parental Involvement in Early Education: The Child-Parent Center Model

This chapter describes the Child-Parent Center (CPC) program model that includes a sustainable school infrastructure to support productive family engagement across the early childhood years (ages 3–9). Longitudinal research evaluating the CPC illustrates how parent engagement in early childhood contributes to a variety of life course outcomes, including academic success and better adult health, reflected in data from two major studies: the Chicago Longitudinal Study (CLS) and Midwest Longitudinal Study (MLS) (Reynolds, 1999; Chicago Longitudinal Study, 2005; Reynolds et al., 2014; Reynolds et al., 2016a).

[1] In this chapter the terms parent involvement and parent engagement are used interchangeably.

6.2.1 The Child-Parent Center (CPC) Program

The Child-Parent Center (CPC) program is a center-based early intervention that began in 1967 to provide high-quality educational and family-support services to young children. CPC centers primarily serve children from preschool through third grade in Chicago public schools with high concentrations of economically disadvantaged students. In 2012, the Chicago CPC model was expanded to four school districts in mid-western cities of the United States: Chicago, Evanston, and Normal, Illinois, and St. Paul, Minnesota. The expansion program was targeted towards more than 2500 children from preschool through third grade across 26 schools in these four school districts.

The CPC model begins with comprehensive early intervention including health and social services, with program continuity that links and aligns the preschool and early school-age years. CPC places a strong focus on six core elements: collaborative leadership teams, effective learning experiences, aligned curriculum and practices, parent involvement, professional development, and continuity and stability (Reynolds et al., 2016a; Reynolds et al., 2019b). Rather than only prescribing a specific set of intervention strategies like other programs featured in this volume, the CPC model involves structural changes in school design and staffing to support dynamic and community-informed activities that strengthen family engagement and align home and school learning supports. The program also requires the implementation of an array of child- and teacher-directed instructional activities as well family support behaviors in school, at home, and in the community (Reynolds et al., 2016a).

As shown in Fig. 6.1, the centers provide comprehensive services under the direction of a head teacher and in collaboration with the elementary school principal.

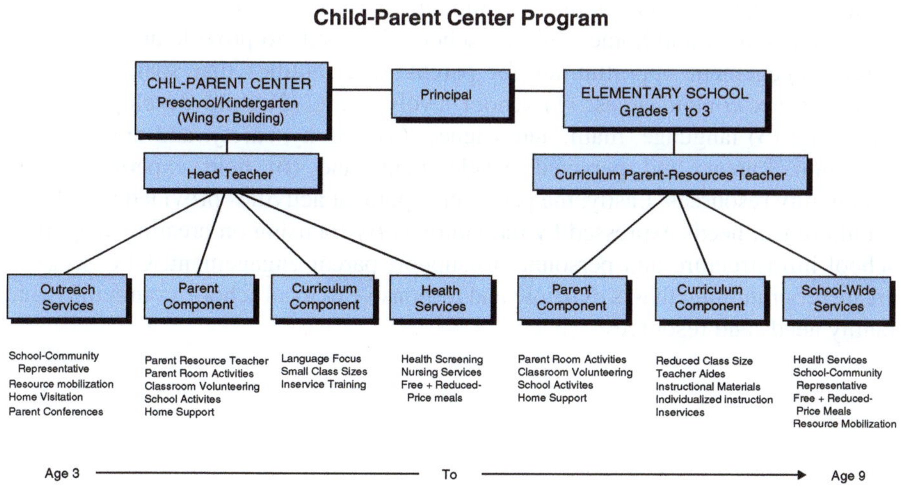

Fig. 6.1 Chicago Child-Parent Center program

Each center also includes on their staff a parent resource teacher, a school-community representative, classroom teachers and aides, nurses, speech therapists, and school psychologists. The major rationale of the program is that the foundation for school success is facilitated (a) by the presence of a stable and enriched learning environment during the entire early childhood period (ages 3–9) and (b) when parents are active participants in their children's education. Service continuity from preschool into kindergarten and the primary grades is emphasized to increase and sustain learning gains (Fig. 6.1).

6.2.2 CPC Parent Engagement Component

The CPC model emphasizes the role of family members in supporting a child's learning, achievement, and readiness for school (Hayakawa & Reynolds, 2016). Parent involvement and engagement (terms used interchangeably in this chapter) is one of the six key CPC program elements. Therefore, the program makes substantial efforts to involve parents in the education of their children, with guidelines encouraging at least 2.5 hours per week of parental activities in support of the child's learning (Reynolds, Hayakawa et al., 2016). There are four central features of the parent engagement element in the CPC model as described below.

First, a school site must have a parent resource room, which is a specific room solely dedicated for activities that support parent engagement. These activities include parent interactions, meetings with program staff, and hosting parent classes on topics ranging from nutritional education to learning financial skills, among others. Second, a school site should have specific, dedicated personnel to support parent engagement, including a parent resource teacher and a school-community representative. These staff members are employed by the school site to plan parent engagement activities and facilitate community outreach efforts to assist in engaging families at school and home. Third, a school site needs to provide ample, diverse parent engagement opportunities for parents and families that span across the following six content areas: (1) school involvement; (2) child development and parenting; (3) language, math, and science; (4) healthy, safety, and nutrition; (5) education, career, and personal development; and (6) field experiences and community resources. Lastly, the parent engagement activities provided by schools should reflect needs expressed by the families. By focusing on creating supportive school infrastructure and personnel to support parent engagement, CPC seeks to create programming that is dynamic and responsive to local school, community, and family needs and resources.

6.2.3 Evidence Documenting the Positive Impact of the CPC Model on Child Outcomes

Evidence documenting the positive long-term benefits of the CPC comes from two longitudinal studies. The Chicago Longitudinal Study (CLS) is an ongoing longitudinal study with 1539 participants born in 1979 to 1980 (93% African American). The study included children who participated in the CPC program in 1983–1984 and a matched comparison group that was not part of CPC. The study has had multiple collection waves since that time point, with the most recent large data collection effort completed in 2017. The Midwest Longitudinal Study (MLS) began once the CPC program was extended into the Midwest through the Midwest Child-Parent Center (MCPC) Expansion Project, including more cities in Illinois and Minnesota (see below). The MLS includes more than 3000 participants who enrolled in CPC programs in 2012. The goals of both the CLS and MLS are to examine the effectiveness of the CPC centers, examine early predictors of life course outcomes, and examine the extent to which long-term effects of the CPC program map onto two different cohorts.

The role of parent engagement in promoting the efficacy of early education programs has been well documented through the CLS (Reynolds & Shlafer, 2010). Children who participated in the CPC preschool program have shown better educational performance and social behaviors compared to children who attended an existing preschool program available in the neighborhood (Reynolds et al., 2001; Reynolds et al., 2018). Table 6.1 shows the common types of parental involvement and engagement activities in the CPC program and example indicators. Involvement in school and learning (e.g., help with homework, communication with school and teachers) is a prominent focus in the CPC program.

Table 6.2 summarizes program impacts on life-course outcomes from the CLS, most of which have cost savings to families and society. Compared to the usual early childhood experiences available in the participating cities, CPC program graduates have greater school readiness skills in kindergarten, lower rates of later child maltreatment and need for school remediation, lower rates of juvenile and adult arrest (court records), higher levels of educational attainment, and higher income in adulthood. These impacts are of practical significance. For example, rates of child maltreatment, grade repetition, and special education for program graduates by age 18 were lower by 51%, 40%, and 41%, respectively (Reynolds & Ou, 2011; Reynolds et al., 2001).

Data from these studies also document the fidelity of implementation of the parent engagement components of the CPC model across sites and the corresponding positive impact of the model on rates of parent engagement. In both Chicago and St. Paul public school districts (MCPC expansion project districts), CPC classrooms were more likely to include more of the site and staffing configurations designed to enhance parent engagement compared to non-CPC classrooms (e.g., parent resource room, parent resource teacher, school-community representative, and parent engagement opportunities in six content areas). In the Chicago school district, CPC

Table 6.1 Common types of parent involvement in CPC and relevant indicators

Common types of parent involvement	Indicators
Parent participation at school	
	Parent participation in school activities
	Parent helps in child's classroom
Parent involvement at home	
	Parent reads to child
	Parent cooks with child
	Parent goes on outings with child
	Parent and child take trips to other cities
	Parent takes trips to the zoo
Parent involvement in school and learning	
	Parent helps child with homework
	Parent makes sure child does homework
	Parent provides learning experiences for the child
	Parent communicates with the school regularly
	Parent talks to child's teacher
	Parent communicates with the school
	Parent discusses school progress with child
	Parent and child discuss school at home
	Parent picks up child's report cards
Parent participation in community activities	
	Parent attends local school council meetings
	Parent votes in school elections
	Parent is a member of a community organization
	Parent is a member of PTA or other school group

classrooms met, on average, 3.5 out of 4 recommended indicators of implementation fidelity, whereas non-CPC classrooms met 0.2 out of 4. In the St. Paul school district, CPC classrooms met, on average, 2.1 out of 4 recommended implementation fidelity indicators compared to non-CPC classrooms which met 0.0 out of 4. Parents were significantly more likely to attend parent engagement events in schools that implemented 3 or more of recommended implementation fidelity indicators (Reynolds et al., 2019c). In addition, students who had more involved parents were more likely to meet the national norms of school readiness assessment than students with less engaged parents (Reynolds et al., 2019c). Similarly, program evaluation studies done in the Chicago and St. Paul districts showed that CPC program participants recorded higher levels of parent involvement on both teachers' ratings of parent participation and parents' rating of their own involvement in the school when compared to the comparison group (Varshney et al., 2020; Reynolds et al., 2016b). The next sections consider the mechanisms of action in CPC and how the enhancement of parent engagement may have its long-term benefits for children.

Table 6.2 Proportion of the Chicago CPC preschool and comparison group participants achieving school and social competence

Outcome	Age	Program group	Comparison group	Difference	Change (%)
Child and youth development	5	46.7	25.1	21.6	86
At/above national norm on scholastic readiness					
Child maltreatment	4–17	5.0	10.3	−5.3	−51
Socio-emotional adjustment	6–8	19.6	18.3	1.3	7
Repeated a grade	6–15	23.0	38.4	−15.4	−40
Special education	6–18	14.4	24.6	−10.2	−41
Juvenile arrest	10–18	16.9	25.1	−8.2	−33
Arrest for violent offense	10–18	9.0	15.3	−6.3	−41
Acting out	12–13	12.1	12.9	−0.8	-6
At/above grade level on reading achievement	13–14	34.2	25.2	9.0	36
Completed high school	18–24	63.1	53.3	9.8	18
Adulthood development					
Adult felony arrest	18–24	15.3	21.6	−6.3	−29
Adult incarceration	18–24	18.4	24.9	−6.5	−26
Adult depression	18–24	13.7	18.5	−4.8	−26
Average income equal to or higher than nat'l average	22–24	37.7	33.5	4.2	13
College attendance or stable employment	22–24	49.5	42.4	7.1	17
Attended a 4-year college	22–24	13.2	7.9	5.3	67

6.3 Parental Engagement as a Mechanism Promoting Long-Term Benefits

Parent engagement in school has a strong association with academic success, even after controlling for background variables like socioeconomic status (Barger et al., 2019; Hill & Tyson, 2009; Reynolds & Gill, 1994; Reynolds et al., 2016b; Reynolds et al., 2019a, b; Seefeldt et al., 1998; Sheridan et al., 2019). Various early childhood intervention programs with a parent engagement component have been evaluated through meta-analyses. A meta-analysis of 448 independent studies regarding the influence of parent engagement on children's development showed a positive association between parent involvement and multiple dimensions of child academic and socio-emotional adjustment (Barger et al., 2019). Moreover, these positive associations were persistent over time regardless of child's developmental period. Another meta-analysis that reviewed early childhood education evaluation studies from 1960 to 2007 similarly concluded that parent-targeted programs further enhance children's outcomes beyond center-based programs alone (Joo et al., 2019).

6.3.1 Contributions of the CPC Family Support Component to Children's Well-Being

What is the contribution of the family support component of the CPC program to children's well-being? Although it is difficult to separate the effects of parent engagement from other child and family services, one approach is to investigate the extent to which the main effects of program participation are explained by parent engagement and other family support behaviors. In models testing parent engagement as a mechanism of program participation effects, the focus is on identifying the intervening or indirect influences on children's well-being. That is, the models test parent engagement as a mediator of the association between program participation and child outcomes. Because indirect effects are more subtle than direct effects, they are underrepresented in the education and prevention literature. Few studies have investigated parent engagement as a mechanism accounting for the long-term effects of early childhood programs (Reynolds & Ou, 2011; Reynolds et al., 2017). In recognition of the complex array of factors during and after program participation that account for long-term effects, research has increasingly emphasized examination of explanatory processes. Research evaluating parent engagement as a mechanism contributing to CPC program effects has been based on the Five-Hypothesis Model of Intervention Effects (5HM; Reynolds, 2000). Derived from the accumulated research over five decades, 5HM posits, as shown in Fig. 6.2, that the effects of CPC (and other similar early childhood programs) can be explained by indicators of five general paths of influence described in more detail below: family support behavior, cognitive-scholastic advantage, school quality and support, motivational advantage, and socio-emotional adjustment. Because the major purpose of early childhood programs is to promote enduring effects into adulthood, the extent to which this pattern is observed will depend on the magnitude of effects on one or more of the processes.

As shown in Fig. 6.2, the family support hypothesis suggests that longer-term effects will occur to the extent that CPC participation enhances parenting skills, attitudes and expectations, and the parent behaviors that support children's education (Ou & Reynolds, 2010; Reynolds et al., 2004). To test this hypothesis, we use measures of parent involvement in school (i.e., participation in activities and instruction), parent expectations for child achievement, and parent support for learning at home. Conceptually, these parenting attitudes and behaviors should lead to improved child achievement and school attainment by increasing children's learning time directly (e.g., reading with parents, higher school attendance) or

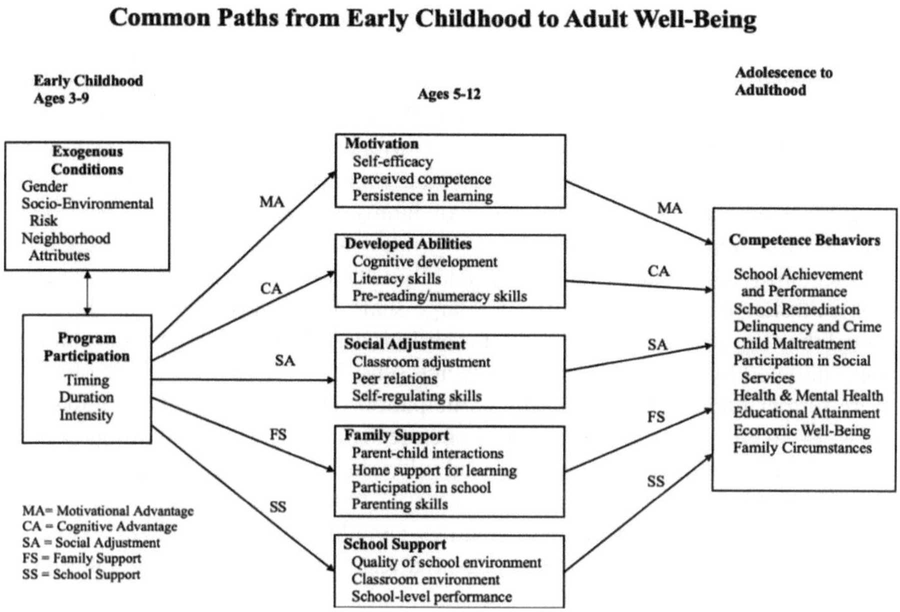

Fig. 6.2 Five hypothesis model for the Chicago longitudinal study

indirectly (e.g., parental monitoring), enhancing children's motivation and school commitment, and increasing children's own expectations for their educational attainment and success. These parenting attitudes and behaviors may also reflect improvements in parenting skills and social support, which would reduce social isolation and the risk of child maltreatment. Supporting this mechanism of action in general, meta-analyses of family interventions and parenting behaviors (Farrington & Welsh, 2007; Jeynes, 2007) show that involvement and monitoring link to higher achievement and crime prevention.

Research on the CPC suggests that promoting increases in family support plays a critical role in the program's positive impact promoting children's academic success and long-term well-being. Using longitudinal data, Hayakawa and colleagues (Hayakawa et al., 2013) reported that the increases in kindergarten parent engagement associated with CPC participation influenced later child achievement via two major pathways. First, increased parent engagement in kindergarten was sustained over time, leading to later and ongoing parent engagement and support for child learning in elementary schools. Second, increased parent engagement promoted higher levels of child achievement motivation. These findings suggest that one way that CPC has its long-term benefits is by promoting parents' sustained involvement across the elementary years which, in turn, affects other factors in a cumulative process that promotes children's school success and well-being. Reynolds and Ou (2011) found additional evidence for the family support hypothesis, as parent involvement in school and reduced rates of later child maltreatment mediated the effects of CPC preschool on child educational attainment, crime, and health behaviors in early adulthood. Increased parent involvement in school led to greater school commitment and student achievement, which in turn reduced the incidence of child maltreatment. The generalizability of these results is supported by research from three different programs (Abecedarian Project, Perry Preschool Project, CPC), each of which identified parent involvement as a contributing path from participation in intervention and later educational attainment (Englund et al., 2014).

Further evidence on the importance of family support in fostering well-being comes from home visiting and parenting interventions, including Nurse-Family Partnership (Eckenrode et al., 2010), Family Check-Up, and Parents as Teachers (PAT; Avellar & Supplee, 2013). In a large-scale PAT study, Zigler et al. (2008) found that significant improvements in third-grade achievement for a state sample were initiated by parental home literacy and school readiness skills, both of which were further impacted by preschool participation. This suggests that the effects of early parent engagement programs may operate in multiple ways, including boosting family support for child learning and also increasing child cognitive skills (represented in Fig. 6.2 as cognitive advantage). Other parenting and home visiting programs generally support these findings (Avellar & Supplee, 2013; Sweet & Appelbaum, 2004), though the strongest impacts are for high-need families at relatively high levels of dosage.

6.3.2 Summary of CPC Processes of Influence on Youth and Adult Outcomes

In Fig. 6.3 we summarize the contributions of three of the five hypothesized mechanisms of CPC for youth and adult outcomes. Specifically, we present the percentage contribution of cognitive advantage, family support, and school support to the total indirect (mediated) effect linking CPC preschool to four key adult outcomes (e.g., high school completion, juvenile and early adult arrests, depressive symptoms; see Reynolds and Ou (2011) and Reynolds and Temple (2019) for more details). The figure denotes the extent to which the influence of CPC participation depends on or is mediated by the three hypothesized processes (cognitive advantage, family support, school support). Values for each hypothesis are above and beyond the influence of the motivation construct and social advantage construct that are also included in the 5HM model.

Parent engagement and its influence on children's long-term life course outcomes is considered one dimension of the family support hypothesis. In our analyses, family support was measured by the frequency of teacher and parent ratings from ages 8 to 12 on the item "parents' participation in school." Teacher and parent ratings were used to minimize possible reporter bias. The second measure used was substantiated reports of child abuse and neglect between ages 4 and 12.

For brevity, we excluded motivational advantage and socio-emotional adjustment hypotheses. They are both influential, however. As shown in Fig. 6.3, the

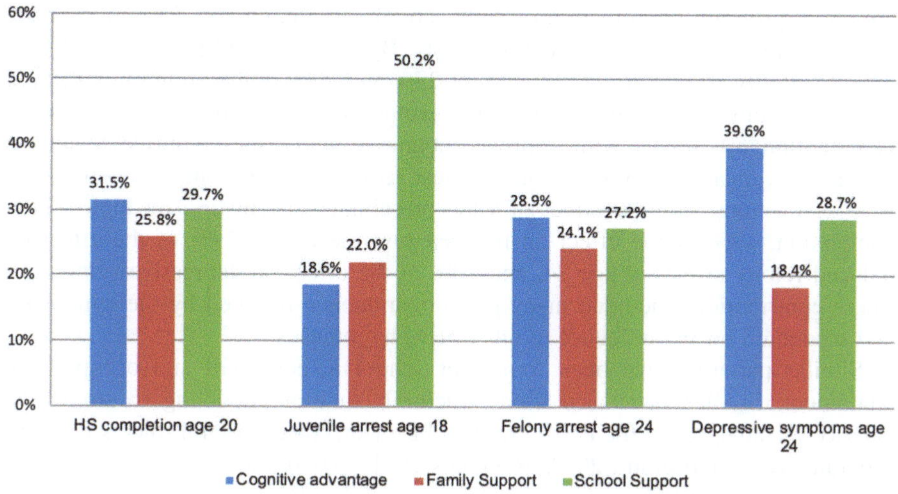

Fig. 6.3 Percentage contributions to total effects of CPC preschool program
Note. The figure summarizes the proportion of the total standardized indirect effect from CPC preschool to long-term outcomes accounted for by cognitive advantage, family support, and school support. Estimates are from LISREL and take into account measurement error and correlated errors. The total indirect effect is the sum of all paths of influence from preschool to outcomes. The indirect effects are categorized by mediator, with the primary emphasis on the mediators that initiated the indirect effect – which were directly and significantly associated with program participation

outcomes are high school completion, juvenile arrest, adult felony arrest, and depressive symptoms at age 24 (see Reynolds & Ou, 2011). The findings are based on structural equation modeling of longitudinal associations in which measurement error, multiple indicators of each process, and alternative specifications are taken into account.

Figure 6.3 summarizes the contributions of three hypotheses to the four life course outcomes. After adjusting for gender, family risk, and the influence of other processes, the family support hypothesis (improved parent involvement in elementary school, reduced maltreatment) accounted for 26% of the total contribution of the effect of CPC attendance on high school completion and 22% of the total contribution on reduced juvenile arrest. In other words, controlling for other hypothesized mechanisms of action, CPC program participation was directly associated with higher levels of parent involvement in elementary school and these higher levels of involvement were significantly linked to school completion and juvenile arrest. Also shown in Fig. 6.3, these same aspects of family support accounted for 24% and 18% of the CPC-related reductions in felony arrest and depressive symptoms in early adulthood, respectively.

The hypothesis that school support may also account for the later benefits of the CPC model was tested using measures of school mobility and attendance in selective enrollment magnet schools. CPC promoted more stable and more supportive subsequent school placements which accounted for 30% of the impact of CPC preschool program participation on high school completion and 50% of the CPC program impact on reduced juvenile arrests. By age 24, CPC promotion of later school stability and quality accounted for 27% and 29% of the program impact on reduced felony arrest and depressive symptoms, respectively. Finally, CPC participation was linked with improved cognitive skills (the cognitive advantage hypothesis), measured by word analysis test scores at age 6, which accounted for 32% of the total indirect effect of CPC preschool participation on high school completion, 19% of the effect on reduced juvenile arrest, 29% of the effect on reduced felony arrests at age 24, and 40% of the effect on depressive symptoms. These contributions included many paths of influence initiated by the hypothesis and accounted for the influence of other 5HM hypotheses.

Similar patterns have been found for school achievement and occupational attainment. Studies have also used structural equation modeling to strengthen validity. Re-analyses of the Perry Preschool Project, Abecedarian Project, and CPC programs (Englund et al., 2014; Reynolds et al., 2010), which included matched measures and sequences of each process (i.e., family support, school support, cognitive advantage), revealed that the processes accounted for a majority of the observed impacts on educational attainment and health behaviors at age 21. The studies also showed that classroom socio-emotional adjustment helped transmit the effects of cognitive advantage. Cognitive advantage contributed more to long-term effects for the Perry Preschool Project and Abecedarian Program, whereas family support and school support influences were larger for CPC.

Overall, these findings indicate the substantial contributions of parent involvement and other intervening factors to the long-run effects of the CPC program. The extent to which other family support measures, ranging from expectations to monitoring and parenting practices, yield similar findings warrants further investigation.

6.3.3 Economic Impact of the CPC Program

To illustrate the economic implications of our intervention effects, a cost-benefit analysis of the CPC program showed that for every dollar invested in the preschool component, $10.15 was returned to society at large through government savings on remedial education and justice system treatment, which increases economic well-being (e.g., higher income and tax revenues; Reynolds et al., 2011). Extrapolating from Fig. 6.3, $2.90 of these economic benefits (over 28%) can be attributed to the family support component of the CPC model or about $15,000 per participant (in discounted 2017 dollars). This estimate is conservative to the extent that parental engagement has synergistic effects with other components of the program. Cognitive advantage as well as school support experiences in the elementary grades also contribute substantially (see Fig. 6.3) to many outcomes and these likely reflect additional components of the CPC model in addition to the family engagement components. Through an intensive family support component in preschool centers

(Reynolds, 2000; Sullivan, 1971), CPC enhances the capacity of parents to positively influence their own and their children's well-being. These benefits are major contributors to long-term and sustained program effects on a wide variety of life course outcomes.

6.4 Future Directions in Research on Parent Engagement and Long-Term Child Outcomes

6.4.1 Understanding Developmental Cycles and Cascades

Parent engagement plays a key role in a cycle of achievement and motivation throughout elementary school. Existing research has begun to document some of these associations, but additional research is needed to fully understand its developmental role. For example, Hayakawa et al. (2013) utilized path analyses for participants in the CLS to examine associations between early parent school engagement, student motivation and achievement, and later parent engagement. Early parent school engagement was related to higher achievement in kindergarten, which led to more motivation for the student to do well in school, which then led to more parent engagement in later elementary school. This study speaks to the need to initiate parent engagement at an early age, so this cycle of achievement and motivation can begin early in a student's academic career.

Parent engagement also interacts with and predicts longer-term academic outcomes in the CLS, such as chronic absenteeism and attending a 2- or 4-year college. Attendance in school is a key factor in a child's academic achievement and attainment. Chronic absenteeism, defined as missing 10% or more days of school in a given school year (e.g., Van Eck et al., 2017) is associated with reduced achievement in eighth grade and reduced probability of four-year high school graduation (Smerillo et al., 2018). Data from the CLS showed that parent engagement during grades one to three was associated with a reduced probability of chronic absenteeism in both the middle grades (grades 4–6) (marginal effect = −2.2%, $p < 0.05$), and during the first 2 years of high school (marginal effect = −7.1%, $p < 0.01$), even after controlling for the association of baseline family characteristics, achievement, and several other school related factors.

In addition, the association between chronic absenteeism and graduation was moderated by levels of parent engagement. Smerillo et al. (2018) found that participants with below-average parental school engagement between grades 1 and 3 had stronger negative associations between early middle school chronic absenteeism and graduating high school with a diploma in 4 years than participants with above-average parental school engagement. Ou and Reynolds (2014) found that parent school engagement between grades 1 and 6 was associated with attending college, such that a 1-point higher teacher-rated parent school involvement score was associated with a 44% higher likelihood of attending a 4-year college (and 33%

higher odds of attending a 2-year college). This finding is especially notable as parent school involvement predicted greater odds of attending college above and beyond parent expectations regarding the number of years of education and the test scores their child would obtain. These findings suggest a dynamic role for parent engagement in student pathways toward academic success that should be a focus of further research.

Recent work with the CLS has begun to examine long-term health and health behavior outcomes and their relation to early parent school engagement. Hayakawa et al. (2016) examined the pathway between early childhood education, kindergarten through third-grade parent engagement, adolescent problem behaviors, and age 22–24 substance abuse. The authors found that early childhood education led to increased parent school engagement and more positive parent expectations concerning their child's educational attainment, which then led to fewer problem behaviors, finally leading to a decreased likelihood of substance abuse in early adulthood. This study highlights developmental cascades that emerge over an extended time span between early childhood and adulthood, linking early parent engagement with reductions in later substance abuse. Additionally, higher parent school involvement in grades 1 through 4 was associated with a reduced odds of lifetime smoking by age 22–24, after controlling for demographic and risk variables (Reynolds et al., 2019a). These studies highlight the potential pathways through which early parent engagement may contribute to better health in early adulthood. Future research should continue to address this association longitudinally and understand the cascading developmental processes.

6.4.2 Measurement Issues in the Study of Parent Engagement

In investigating differences by source of report, Reynolds (1992) examined differences in sources of reporter for parent involvement. The author found that there were weak correlations between teacher, parent, and child ratings of parent involvement. Furthermore, teacher ratings of parent involvement at school had the strongest relation with achievement. Hence, future research should attend carefully to the source of data on parent engagement and further explore the correlates of teacher versus parent ratings.

Recently, researchers with the CLS examined correlations between a parent's attitudes about their child's education, their expectations about how far their child would go in school, and parent involvement at home from grades 4 through 6 (see Table 6.3). A parent's school involvement from grades 1 to 3 was very weakly correlated with their home involvement at grades 4 through 6 ($r = 0.02$). School parent involvement also had the most robust correlations with outcomes such as college attendance, high school completion, and reading achievement than the other parenting variables. The low-to-medium correlations between all of the parent attitudes, behaviors, and expectations implies that domain *does* matter in the parent

Table 6.3 Correlations of parent engagement measures with measures of educational progress and attainment

Measures	1	2	3	4	5	6	7	8	9
1. School parent involvement, grades 1–3	–								
2. Parent involvement at home, grades 4–6	0.02	–							
3. Parent expectations, grades 4–6	0.19*	0.30*	–						
4. Parent attitudes toward education, grades 4–6	0.16*	0.33*	0.23*	–					
5. Parent satisfaction with child's elementary schooling	0.13*	0.11*	0.13*	0.29*	–				
6. Chronic absence, grades 4–6	−0.13*	0.01	−0.08*	−0.01	−0.04	–			
7. Reading achievement score, grade 8	0.38*	0.01	0.29*	0.13*	0.18*	−0.13*	–		
8. High school chronic absence, grade 10	−0.20*	−0.02	−0.09*	−0.07*	−0.04	0.14*	−0.17*	–	
9. High school completion by age 21	0.24*	< −0.01	0.17*	0.16*	0.02	−0.14*	0.34*	−0.41*	–
10. Attended any 4-year college	0.28*	< −0.01	0.21*	0.05	0.15*	−0.12*	0.35*	−0.32*	0.31*

Note. $^{*}p < 0.05$

involvement literature, and school parental involvement in particular has a specific role in academic success later in life.

In other research conducted by the CLS, parent involvement predicted academic success and socio-emotional adjustment in first grade (Reynolds, 1999) as well as increased reading achievement, lower grade retention, and fewer years in special education by age 14 (Miedel & Reynolds, 1999). Parent involvement in school activities also significantly predicted school achievement across two successive school years, academic growth from year 1 to year 2, and growth in reading achievement from kindergarten through ninth grade. Further analyses demonstrated that parent involvement was also significantly related to high school completion and lower levels of juvenile delinquency (Graue et al., 2004; Reynolds et al., 2009). These findings suggest that, even in schools serving disadvantaged areas, children's early school success can be enhanced by providing opportunities for parents to be involved in school and in children's education.

6.4.3 Parent Engagement as a School-Level Versus Family-Level Variable

In addition to considering parent engagement as an individual difference within families, the CPC studies have assessed parent engagement at the school (or site) level. Interestingly, CPC parent engagement at the site level was associated with early academic outcomes in kindergarten and was the only program factor out of others examined (i.e., instructional approach, size of site) that predicted child outcomes. Lower income levels within a school district were also linked with poorer school and social outcomes. These findings also suggest a value in future research in measuring parent engagement at both the school level and the individual parent level, given potential differences in the predictive associations of these two aspects of parent engagement.

6.4.4 Understanding Links between Parent Engagement and Parent Academic Expectations

Many other studies support the positive and significant link between measures of parental involvement and children's school success. A meta-analysis of 25 studies by Fan and Chen (2001) found that parent expectations or aspirations had the largest effect size (ES = 0.40) in relation to measures of academic achievement with parental supervision at home (ES = 0.09) having the smallest effect size. Effect sizes between parent involvement and academic achievement were also larger for global (i.e., GPA) as compared to subject-specific academic achievement measures. Parental commitment and volunteer behavior have smaller positive influences (Fan & Chen, 2001). Parental contact and supervision tend to have small but negative influences on achievement outcomes. It is likely that children receiving more supervision and contact with the school were more in need of such supervision and contact possibly because of prior problematic behavior or academic achievement.

Parent involvement also has been found to positively influence motivational outcomes such as academic self-concept, attributions for academic achievements, and self-regulation as well as high school dropout and truancy behaviors (Barger et al., 2019; Gonzalez-Pienda et al., 2002; Hill & Tyson, 2009). In reports from National Educational Longitudinal Study (NELS; Keith et al., 1993; Singh et al., 1995), parent expectations or aspirations for children's education were most consistently associated with eighth-grade achievement even after controlling for the influence of SES and ethnicity (Fan & Chen, 2001; Reynolds et al., 2017). Moreover, the association between parental expectations and achievement was strongest for higher SES students. Relatively few studies have examined the relation between involvement and children's social and emotional learning, though a recent meta-analysis of school-family interventions by Sheridan et al. (2019) showed sizable impacts of interventions on a variety of socio-emotional competencies. Consistent with the CPC studies reviewed here, meta-analytic impacts were also found to be larger for ethnic minorities (Sheridan et al., 2019). Differential effects over time and continuing studies of impacts by SES and ethnicity are warranted, especially given the high priority on reducing achievement and health disparities among low-income and minority populations.

6.5 Conclusion and Future Research Directions

In conclusion, longitudinal research on CPC and many other programs demonstrate how parent engagement and family support services contribute to children's school readiness, academic achievement, and well-being over time. Impacts are both direct and complex and indicate that parents provide not only a fundamental context for supporting children's learning but that their behavior on behalf of children's well-being is a mechanism supporting long-term effects. This is consistent with Bronfenbrenner's original belief of the importance of parent involvement for sustaining gains as children progress through elementary school. How parental involvement and engagement contribute to life course well-being into adulthood deserves to be a major focus of future research, as the mechanisms of linkages to outcomes found in CPC studies can be examined for generalizability.

The findings reviewed in the chapter have two major implications for enhancing the effects of early childhood programs. First, as is the case for Head Start and the CPC program, increased funding for family support staff and services is warranted for state and local programs (Meloy et al., 2019). Given the importance of leadership in organizing and implementing services, parent engagement coordinators, family liaisons, and home visitors deserve to be more fully integrated with the educational mission. Dedicated school staff are needed to support family engagement in the provision of home support for child learning, participation in school and center activities, community engagement and referral, and opportunities to further parent education and job training. A menu-system approach (choices among a variety of activities, strategies, and supports) to family support as found in the CPC program model is consistent with the most effective programs and also can be tailored to the needs and interests of individual families (Reynolds et al., 2017).

Second, family support and parent engagement efforts deserve further attention as key elements supporting the effectiveness of early childhood programs through preschool and over the transition into elementary grades. The evidence presented in this chapter, this volume, and in the larger field demonstrates the positive contributions that families make to the effectiveness of early education programs. Including family support services as formal elements in early childhood education effectiveness frameworks could lead to an increase in the programming and resources available to support families as new programs are developed and scaled for wide implementation. Family support services are a key element of effectiveness in many frameworks (Ramey & Ramey, 1998; Reynolds et al., 2017; Zigler et al., 2006), but are not so designated in the 10 effectiveness elements of state prekindergarten programs (National Institute for Early Education Research [NIEER, 2018] or in philanthropic guides (Bill and Melinda Gates Foundation, 2015). Although more research is needed to document the most effective approaches for involving parents and enhancing educational benefits for different children, the overall benefits of family support and engagement to early childhood programs and the communities they serve are clear. In addition to increasing the priority on family engagement, financial resources to ensure a strong and well-implemented system of services is essential to effectiveness, especially as programs continue to advance to scale.

References

Avellar, S. A., & Supplee, L. H. (2013). Effectiveness of home visiting in improving child health and reducing child maltreatment. *Pediatrics, 132*(Supplement 2), S90–S97.

Barger, M. M., Kim, E. M., Kuncel, N. R., & Pomerantz, E. M. (2019). The relation between parents' involvement in children's schooling and children's adjustment: A meta-analysis. *Psychological Bulletin, 145*(9), 855.

Bill & Melinda Gates Foundation. (2015). *Early learning: High-quality pre-kindergarten.* Seattle: Author.

Bronfenbrenner, U. (1974). Is early intervention effective? *Day Care and Early Education, 44*, 15–18.

Chicago Longitudinal Study. (2005). *User's guide*. (ver. 7). Minneapolis: University of Minnesota.

Consortium for Longitudinal Studies. (1983). *As the twig is bent...Lasting effects of preschool programs*. Hillsdale: Lawrence Erlbaum Associates.

Eckenrode, J., Campa, M., et al. (2010). Long-term effects of prenatal and infancy nurse home visitation on the life course of youths: 19-year follow-up of a randomized trial. *Archives of Pediatrics and Adolescent Medicine, 164*, 9–16.

Englund, M. M., White, B., Reynolds, A. J., Schweinhart, L. J., & Campbell, F. A. (2014). Health outcomes of early childhood interventions: A 3-study analysis. In A. J. Reynolds et al. (Eds.), *Health and education in early childhood.* New York: Cambridge University Press.

Fan, X., & Chen, M. (2001). Parental involvement and students' academic achievement: A meta-analysis. *Educational Psychology Review, 13*(1), 1–22.

Farrington, D. P., & Welsh, B. C. (2007). *Saving children from a life of crime*. Oxford: New York.

Gonzalez-Pienda, J. A., Nunez, J. C., Gonzalez-Pumariega, S., Alvarez, L., Roces, C., & Garcia, M. (2002). A structural equation model of parental involvement, motivational and aptitude characteristics, and academic achievement. *The Journal of Experimental Education , 70*(3), 257–287.

Graue, E., Clements, M. A., Reynolds, A. J., & Niles, M. D. (2004). More than teacher directed or child initiated: Preschool curriculum type, parent involvement, and children's outcomes in the child-parent centers. *Education Policy Analysis Archives, 12*, 72.

Hayakawa, M., & Reynolds, A. (2016). Strategies for scaling up: Promoting parent involvement through family-school-community partnerships. *Voices in Urban Education, 44*, 45–52.

Hayakawa, M., Englund, M. M., Warner-Richter, M. N., & Reynolds, A. J. (2013). The longitudinal process of early parent involvement on student achievement: A path analysis. *National Head Start Association Dialog, 16*, 103–126.

Hayakawa, M., Giovanelli, A., Englund, M. M., & Reynolds, A. J. (2016). Not just academics: Paths of longitudinal effects from parent involvement to substance abuse in emerging adulthood. *The Journal of Adolescent Health, 58*(4), 433–439.

Hill, N. E., & Tyson, D. F. (2009). Parental involvement in middle school: A meta-analytic assessment of the strategies that promote achievement. *Developmental Psychology, 45*(3), 740–763.

Jeynes, W. H. (2007). The relationship between parental involvement and urban secondary school student academic achievement. *Urban Education, 41*(1), 82–110.

Joo, Y. S., Magnuson, K., Duncan, G. J., Schindler, H. S., Yoshikawa, H., & Ziol-Guest, K. M. (2019). What works in early childhood education programs? A meta–analysis of preschool enhancement programs. *Early Education and Development, 31*, 1–26.

Keith, T. Z., Troutman, G. C., Trivette, P. S., Keith, P. B., Bickley, P. G., & Singh, K. (1993). Does parental involvement affect eighth-grade student achievement? Structural analysis of national data. *School Psychology Review, 22*(3), 474–496.

Meloy, B., Gardner, M., Wechsler, M., & Kirp, D. (2019). What can we learn from state-of- the-art early childhood education programs? In *Sustaining early childhood learning gains: Program, school, and family influences* (pp. 101–132). Cambridge: Cambridge University Press.

Miedel, W. T., & Reynolds, A. J. (1999). Parent involvement in early intervention for disadvantaged children: Does it matter?. *Journal of School Psychology, 37*(4), 379–402.

National Institute for Early Education Research. (2018). *The state of preschool 2017: State preschool yearbook*. New Brunswick: Graduate School of Education, Rutgers University.

O'Connell, M. E., Boat, T., & Warner, K. E. (Eds.). (2009). *Preventing mental, emotional, and behavioral disorders among young people: Progress and possibilities*. Washington: NAP.

Ou, S., & Reynolds, A. J. (2010). Mechanisms of effects of an early intervention program on educational attainment: A gender subgroup analysis. *Children & Youth Services Review, 32*(8), 1064–1076.

Ou, S. & Reynolds, A. J. (2014). Early determinants of postsecondary education participation and degree attainment: findings from an inner-city minority cohort. *Education and Urban Society, 46*(4), 474–504.

Ramey, C. T., & Ramey, S. L. (1998). Early intervention and early experience. *American Psychologist, 53*(2), 109–120.

Reynolds, A. J. (1992). Comparing measures of parental involvement and their effects on academic achievement. *Early Childhood Research Quarterly, 7*, 441–462.

Reynolds, A. J., & Gill, S. (1994). The role of parental perspectives in the school adjustment of innercity black children. *Journal of Youth and Adolescence, 23*(6), 671–694.

Reynolds, A. J. (1999). Educational success in high-risk settings: Contributions of the Chicago Longitudinal Study. *Journal of School Psychology, 37*(4), 345–354.

Reynolds, A. J. (2000). *Success in early intervention: The Chicago Child-Parent Centers*. Lincoln: University of Nebraska Press.

Reynolds, A. J., & Ou, S. (2011). Paths of effects from preschool to adult well-being: A confirmatory analysis of the Child-Parent Center Program. *Child Development, 82*, 555–582.

Reynolds, A. J., & Shlafer, R. J. (2010). Parent involvement in early education. In S. L. Christenson & A. L. Reschly (Eds.), *Handbook of school-family partnerships* (pp. 158–174). New York: Routledge.

Reynolds, A. J., & Temple, J. A. (Eds.). (2019). *Sustaining early childhood learning gains: Program, school, and family influences*. New York: Cambridge University Press.

Reynolds, A. J., Temple, J. A., Robertson, D. L., & Mann, E. A. (2001). Long-term effects of an early childhood intervention on educational achievement and juvenile arrest- A 15-year follow-up of low-income children in public schools. *Journal of American Medical Association, 285*(18), 2339–2346.

Reynolds, A. J., Ou, S., & Topitzes, J. (2004). Paths of effects of early childhood intervention on educational attainment and juvenile arrest: A confirmatory analysis of the Chicago Child-Parent Centers. *Child Development, 75*(5), 1299–1328.

Reynolds, A. J., Chen, C., & Herbers, J. (2009). *School mobility and educational success: A research synthesis and evidence on prevention.* Washington: National Research Council.

Reynolds, A. J., Englund, M., Ou, S., et al. (2010). Paths of effects of preschool participation to educational attainment at age 21: A 3-study analysis. In A. J. Reynolds et al. (Eds.), *Childhood programs & practices in the first decade of life.* New York: Cambridge.

Reynolds, A. J., Temple, J. A., White, B. A., Ou, S., & Robertson, D. L. (2011). Age-26 cost- benefit analysis of the Child-Parent Center program. *Child Development, 82*, 782–804.

Reynolds, A. J., Richardson, B. A., Hayakawa, M., Lease, E. M., Warner-Richter, M., et al. (2014). Association of a full-day vs. part-day preschool intervention with school readiness, attendance, and parent involvement. *The Journal of the American Medical Association, 312*(20), 2126.

Reynolds, A. J., Hayakawa, M., Candee, A. J., & Englund, M. M. (2016a). *CPC P-3 program manual: Child-parent center preschool-3rd grade program.* Minneapolis: University of Minnesota, Human Capital Research Collaborative.

Reynolds, A. J., Richardson, B. A., Hayakawa, M., Englund, M. M., & Ou, S. R. (2016b). Multi-site expansion of an early childhood intervention and school readiness. *Pediatrics, 138*(1), e20154587.

Reynolds, A. J., Ou, S., Mondi, C., & Hayakawa, M. (2017). Processes of early interventions to adult well-being. *Child Development, 88*(2), 378–387.

Reynolds, A. J., Ou, S., & Temple, J. A. (2018). A preschool to 3rd grade preventive intervention and educational attainment at 35 years of age. *JAMA Pediatrics, 172*(3), 247–256.

Reynolds, A. J., Margo, S. W., Ou, S., & Eales, L. (2019a). Are parent involvement and school quality associated with adult smoking behaviors? Findings from an urban early childhood cohort. *Preventive Medicine, 127*, 105768. Open Access.

Reynolds, A. J., Ou, S., Mondi, C. F., & Giovanelli, A. (2019b). Reducing poverty and inequality through preschool-to-third-grade prevention services. *American Psychologist, 74*(6), 653–672.

Reynolds, A. J., Vaisarova, J., Lee, S., Richardson, B., & Eales, L. (2019c). *Parent involvement: Evidence from the Midwest Child-Parent Center Expansion* (Brief report). Minneapolis: Human Capital Research Collaborative.

Schweinhart, L. J., Montie, J., Xiang, Z., Barnett, W. S., et al. (2005). *Lifetime effects: The high/scope Perry preschool study through age 40.* Ypsilanti: High/Scope.

Seefeldt, C., Denton, K., Galper, A., & Younoszai, T. (1998). Former Head Start parents' characteristics, perceptions of school climate, and involvement in their children's education. *The Elementary School Journal, 98*(4), 339–349.

Sheridan, S. M., Smith, T. E., Kim, E. M., et al. (2019). A meta-analysis of family-school interventions and children's socio-emotional functioning: Moderators and components of efficacy. *Review of Educational Research, 89*(2), 296–332.

Singh, K., Bickley, P. G., Keith, T. Z., Keith, P. B., Trivette, P., & Anderson, E. (1995). The effects of four components of parental involvement on eighth-grade student achievement: Structural analysis of NELS-88 data. *School Psychology Review, 24*(2), 299–317.

Smerillo, N. E., Reynolds, A. J., Temple, J. A., & Ou, S. R. (2018). Chronic absence, eighth- grade achievement, and high school attainment in the Chicago Longitudinal Study. *Journal of School Psychology, 67*, 163–178.

Sullivan, L. M. (1971). *Let us not underestimate the children.* Glenview: Scott, Foreman.

Sweet, M. A., & Appelbaum, M. I. (2004). Is home visiting an effective strategy: A meta-analytic review of home visiting programs for families with young children. *Child Development, 75*, 1435–1456.

Van Eck, K., Johnson, S. R., Bettencourt, A., & Johnson, S. L. (2017). How school climate relates to chronic absence: A multi–level latent profile analysis. *Journal of School Psychology, 61*, 89–102.

Varshney, N., Lee, S., Temple, J. A., & Reynolds, A. J. (2020). Does early childhood education enhance parental school involvement in second grade?: Evidence from Midwest Child-Parent Center Program. *Children and Youth Services Review*, 117, 105317.

Zigler, E., Gilliam, W. S., & Jones, S. M. (2006). *A vision for universal preschool education*. New York: Cambridge University Press.

Zigler, E., Pfannenstiel, J. C., & Seitz, V. (2008). The parents as teachers program and school success: A replication and extension. *Journal of Primary Prevention, 29*(2), 103–120.

Chapter 7
Parent-School Partnerships: Accounting for Parents Facing Economic Hardship and Social Marginalization

Katherine A. Magnuson

Abstract The research presented in this volume demonstrates that carefully designed partnerships hold the potential to improve parents' support for their children's learning and children's outcomes. This chapter considers one possible reason that these kinds of partnerships may be more effective than other parent involvement efforts: thoughtful partnerships require attention to and respect for the contexts and perspectives of families who are economically disadvantaged and often from communities of color. Partnerships provide space for schools to more fully account for how low income and economic scarcity as well as systemic racism and white supremacy affect parents and their interactions with schools and other service organizations. Continued efforts to build partnerships that are grounded in parents' lived experiences with economic hardship and systemic marginalization may hold promise for further innovation.

Keywords Parent-school partnerships · Economic disadvantage · Social marginalization · Family engagement · Parenting · Early childhood education · School practices · Teaching · Child learning outcomes

7.1 Introduction

This volume pulls together research on five models of parent-engagement programming designed to improve children's school readiness and early elementary school transitions. These projects are impressive undertakings representing many years of rigorous and dedicated research. The work encompasses the design and implementation of programmatic approaches to engaging and partnering with parents and the meticulous evaluation of outcomes from these programs. For this reason, there is

K. A. Magnuson (✉)
School of Social Work, University of Wisconsin-Madison, Madison, WI, USA
e-mail: kmagnuson@wisc.edu

© Springer Nature Switzerland AG 2022

K. L. Bierman, S. M. Sheridan (eds.), *Family-School Partnerships During the Early School Years*, Research on Family-School Partnerships,
https://doi.org/10.1007/978-3-030-74617-9_7

much that the fields of early childhood education (ECE) and prevention can learn from these endeavors. When read together these chapters provide important insights about how schools and communities attempt to partner with families who are vulnerable. The work described in the chapters also raises questions about the need for continued innovation in program design and delivery that may be needed to build effective parent-school partnerships and move educational systems closer to the equitable institutions they hope to be, serving the learning needs of all children.

In this chapter, I briefly review evidence that suggests that, despite the importance of parenting for children's development, most parent involvement efforts embedded in early childhood education programs do not create better learning outcomes for vulnerable children. However, the positive outcomes of some partnership programs provide an important counterbalance to these findings. Carefully designed partnerships have the potential to improve parents' support for their children's learning and boost children's school outcomes. I explore one possible reason that partnerships may be more effective than other efforts: thoughtful partnerships require knowledge of and respect for the contexts experienced by families who are economically disadvantaged and often from communities of color. Partnerships thus provide space for schools to more fully account for how economic scarcity as well as systemic racism and white supremacy affects parents and their interactions with schools and other service organizations. Continued efforts to build partnerships that are grounded in parents' lived experiences with economic hardship and systemic marginalization may support further innovations that improve program design and impact, promoting lasting change in children's school trajectories.

7.2 What Has Been Learned About the Impact of Parent Involvement in the Early School Years on Children's Learning Outcomes?

Concerns about disparities in children's school readiness across income and racial and ethnic groups have long fueled policymakers' and educators' efforts to reduce early inequalities and promote school readiness skills. A primary mechanism for doing so has been the provision of formal ECE programs such as Head Start and public funded prekindergarten programs. Many evaluations have found that these programs generate important, but modest improvements in students' school readiness (Duncan & Magnuson, 2013; Yoshikawa et al., 2013) and long-run outcomes (McCoy et al., 2017). This had led some scholars and advocates to conclude that this strategy alone is insufficient to yield the outcomes needed to make real progress on improving disadvantaged children's short- and long-run outcomes (Shonkoff & Fisher, 2013).

The science of early childhood development has always afforded parents and parent-child relationships a central role in shaping children's early learning and development. Why are parents important? Because young children spend more time in their homes and in interactions with their parents than in any other settings. As such, parents shape or at least influence nearly all aspects of a child's environment. This is demonstrated clearly in research findings on parenting which show that parental patterns of interaction and the socialization context they create are strong predictors of many aspects of children's early skills including language, emotion-regulation, executive function skills, as well as early academic skills (National Academies of Sciences, Engineering, and Medicine, 2016). In the early years of life, children gain new skills, knowledge, and capacities with seemingly blinding speed, and the ability of parents to scaffold their children's learning with cognitively stimulating interactions and sensitive and responsive emotional support contributes to their healthy development (National Academies of Sciences, Engineering, and Medicine, 2016; Shonkoff & Fisher, 2013).

Given this broad understanding of the foundational role that parents play in early development, efforts to reach parents through ECE programs serving children from disadvantaged families are not new (Teti et al., 2017). Indeed, from its initial conception in the 1960s and reflecting its funding as a community action program, Head Start programs were designed to support, engage, and empower parents (Gibbs et al., 2013; Zigler & Styfco, 1994). Likewise, the now-famous Perry Preschool program from the 1960s also had a strong parenting component with weekly home visits conducted by teachers (Zigler & Styfco, 1994).

As ECE models have evolved over time and broadened their reach, efforts to involve parents in children's early schooling have become increasingly diverse in both scope and mode of engagement. Currently, this focus on family involvement is reflected in the National Association for the Education of Young Children's standard around "families." The standard identifies the important ECE program goal of building trusting relationships that foster family involvement in children's learning and participation in the early learning program. Multiple strategies are suggested to develop these relationships including; (1) talking with parents about their family as well as adapting learning content to reflect family backgrounds; (2) regularly communicating with parents about the child and classroom activities; and (3) encouraging parents' involvement in all aspects of the program.[1] A similar set of suggestions is provided by the federal Head Start program guidelines, with the addition of; (4) creating structured services to ensure communication; and (5) forming collaborations with families that identify "needs, interests, strengths, goals, and services and resources that support family well-being, including family safety, health, and economic stability."[2]

Given the current emphasis on recognizing parents' strengths and building relationships, the wide range of activities that teachers and ECE programs conduct to engage with parents is perhaps to be expected. Formal practices include, for example, having parents volunteer in the classroom, conducting parent workshops,

---

[1] See https://eclkc.ohs.acf.hhs.gov/policy/45-cfr-chap-xiii/1302-50-family-engagement

[2] Seehttps://eclkc.ohs.acf.hhs.gov/policy/45-cfr-chap-xiii/1302-subpart-e-family-community-engagement-program-services

scheduling teacher home visits, hosting parent discussion sessions, and regularly scheduling school-based parent-teacher conferences. More informally, teachers may encourage children to share classwork or other materials with their parents, and they may tell parents what children are learning or how positive behavior is being supported in the classroom. Teachers may also send home educational materials to be used in the home, such as a book with suggestions about how parents can extend their children's reading to other learning opportunities.

Though effort to increase parents' involvement is common in these settings and is represented in early learning standards in the field, systematic reviews of rigorous evidence do not suggest that it boosts the impact of early learning programs on children's outcomes. Indeed, evidence indicates that, on average, children are no more academically successful when early childhood programs include practices intended to improve parenting when compared with programs that do not explicitly do so (Grindal et al., 2016; Magnuson & Schindler, 2016). Of course, that does not mean that these efforts are not valuable or that they do not affect other types of outcomes, such as improving parent-teacher communication.

For many readers, the finding that parent involvement activities do not impact children's learning outcomes may seem counterintuitive. How could involving parents not matter? It's important to note that it may be hard to estimate the added value of parent activities from those of a broader early learning program. In addition, parent involvement efforts vary quite a bit in scope, intensity, and the effectiveness of implementation. Moreover, even if some programs do not have explicit parent involvement activities formalized in their program model, it does not necessarily mean that parents are absent from the programs or have poor communication or relationships with teachers. Yet, systematic analyses and reviews including many evaluation studies that compare early childhood program models with and without explicit parenting activities provide a clear takeaway: adding some form of parent-related support, service, or practice won't necessarily yield a more effective early learning program, as measured by children's academic or socio-emotional outcomes (Grindal et al., 2016). Based on this accumulated evidence, it is hard to conclude that programs should look to increasing parent involvement or engagement in ECE settings as a good approach to improving the learning outcomes of children from disadvantaged families.

Yet the programs included in this volume make a strong and compelling case that some intensive and intentional partnerships with parents, especially low-income and disadvantaged families, are effective. This conclusion is also supported by evidence that considers family-school partnerships for families with older children (Smith et al., 2020). Indeed all of the programs described in this volume provide proof of this concept—when efforts are well designed and resourced, and when parents are approached as partners, when the contexts of their lives are taken into account, programs can leverage parent efforts to improve the impact of ECE, enhancing learning for the most vulnerable children.

7.3 What Explains the Success of Family-School Partnership Programs? Design That Accounts for Families' Lives

Approaching parents as partners requires programs and teachers to build a fuller knowledge and understanding of families' lives, but it also requires them to use this knowledge to design their programming. This is critical, particularly when parents have low incomes and are economically disadvantaged, and from communities of color. To be successful, partnership programs should be designed based on what is known about how low income and economic scarcity, as well as systemic racism and white supremacy, affects parents and their interactions with schools and other service organizations. In the chapters in this book, the attention to the role of economic hardship is sometimes mentioned, but it's role is not always clear with respect to the design of the partnership programs. Efforts to unpack the success of these partnership models require making explicit how circumstances of racism, poverty, and economic vulnerability affect parents and how the partnership model takes these factors into account when working with parents.

Taking into account the impact of economic hardships and racism on parents and family life does not require schools and early learning centers to adopt a deficit perspective. It is possible to recognize the toll that social and economic structures take on families and seek to support them in parenting at the same time. Indeed, evidence is quite clear that low-income parents have many strengths and capabilities, even as they face enormous challenges in providing safe and nurturing care for their families. However, research on parenting documents clear links between low income and, on average, lower rates of stimulating and cognitively enriching parent-child interactions and activities (Magnuson & Duncan, 2018). In addition, low-income parents are, on average, less emotionally responsive, consistent and supportive in interactions with their children than more affluent parents (see Magnuson & Duncan, 2018). These average differences are the target of many parenting and partnership programs, including those included in this volume. But simply knowing that these differences exist or even that these differences matter for children's learning is not sufficient to building a successful partnership program. It is also important to understand the economic and social contexts that low-income parents face and how they contribute to these differences in parenting.

What factors do parent partnership programs need to take into account in families' lives? Major institutional and demographic shifts have shaped the current context of low-income parents (for a review of these trends, see Magnuson & Duncan, 2019). Parents now face more difficult employment prospects, with low-skill work that pays low wages and provides few opportunities for advancement. As the service sector grows, many jobs require parents to work non-standard hours including evenings or weekends; those working in retail often have rotating shifts or just-in-time scheduling, which may complicate family routines and lead to uncertainty in income (Lambert et al., 2019). In addition, whereas low-income parents may have access to in-kind welfare benefits, including childcare and health insurance, they are also more dependent on employment to qualify for these benefits. Parents who struggle to get or maintain employment receive much less (Tach & Edin, 2017). Thus, families' economic fortunes largely depend on parents' earnings. Finally, patterns of family formation and stability have also changed, with family instability contributing to complex family constellations. Increasingly, low-income children do not live with both of their biological parents but instead split time across different households, have nonresident parents, and have nonbiological parent figures in their household (Berger & Carlson, 2020). All of these trends have major implications for how low-income parents organize their family lives and how they interact with school settings.

Despite ongoing hardship, most parents and families work hard to meet their children's needs. Studies of low-income families document that parents spend considerable time and energy ensuring that they have enough money and resources to cover household essentials. Unable to make ends meet simply on what they earn from employment, low-income parents use a variety of economic survival techniques. These can include engaging in informal work, borrowing from family and friends, making use of public assistance programs, visiting food banks, and more generally looking for ways to keep their costs lower by shopping at bargain stores or forgoing needed purchases (Abraham & Houseman, 2019; Morduch & Schneider, 2017). Unexpected expenses for car repairs or health problems and the loss of wages or other forms of expected income can have devastating economic consequences for families on limited budgets. Seeking out public supports, which provide needed assistance, can be stigmatizing.

Efforts to stretch their money and care for their families take a toll on parents' well-being. According to the Family Stress Perspective (Masarik & Conger, 2017), economic hardship as well as other stressful life events create high levels of psychological distress, contributing to depressive and hostile feelings. Being nurturing, rewarding, attentive, and involved with a child requires concentration, patience, and other cognitive and emotional resources that may be difficult to muster under conditions of psychological distress. Parents' psychological distress, in turn, is linked with parenting practices that are, on average, more punitive, harsh, inconsistent, and detached, as well as less nurturing, stimulating, and responsive to children's needs (McLoyd et al., 2014). Certainly not all low-income parents experience psychological distress in ways that compromise the quality of their parenting, but it is evident that economic hardship creates a stressful context that often has harmful effects on parents' mental health in a way that reduces their ability to provide warm, sensitive, and responsive care to their children.

Research from neuroscience, psychology, and behavioral economics points to a core set of cognitive skills that underlie adults' abilities to parent effectively (see Gennetian et al., 2019; Kalil & Ryan, 2020; Sanders et al., 2019). Executive functioning and self-regulation skills are important for paying attention and responding appropriately to children's cues, remaining calm in the face of children's behavioral challenges, planning and carrying out family routines, and shifting course when things go unexpectedly. These skills are employed regularly as parents create stable, healthy environments and build nurturing relationships. When adults effectively employ these skills, they are also supporting the development of children's self-regulation and executive function skills that children will then carry into adulthood (Bridgett et al., 2017; Luthar & Eisenberg, 2017).

Unfortunately, research finds that conditions of poverty and scarcity have cognitive consequences; they reduce cognitive bandwidth, even in the absence of impacts on mental health. Cognitive capabilities, including executive functioning and self-regulation skills are limited and often exhausted by the many daily tasks that require stressed adults to make complicated decisions and evaluate consequential trade-offs. Economic and family contexts that require parents to deploy much of their finite attention skills to handle pressing daily tasks increase the likelihood that subsequent decisions will favor more impulsive and counterproductive choices or that some planning and decision making are left undone. As a result, problems that need urgent attention get solved, but do so at the cost of parents' capacity to tackle other perhaps equally important but less urgent issues. For example, in times of financial distress, paying rent or figuring out how to buy groceries can take up a disproportionate amount of a parent's attention and cognitive load. In turn, parents may neglect other longer-term goals, even if these goals may ultimately be very beneficial to their families and children (Shah et al., 2012). Finally, low-income parents may experience many daily tasks through an economic lens because their concerns about money are pervasive and hard to suppress (Shah et al., 2018).

Scarcity and the resulting reduction in cognitive bandwidth increases the likelihood that low-income parents' decision making will be driven by two types of cognitive biases that are described in detail by Kalil and Ryan (2020) and Gennetian et al. (2019). First, parents may prioritize the present, placing more weight on short-term problems as well as short-term rewards than long-term planning. Second, when cognitive resources are depleted, parents may rely on automaticity or habituated responses. This automaticity means that the parents' reactions and interactions with their children often happen without much planning, reflection, or consideration. To the extent that parents want to change their parenting strategies, the automaticity that arises under cognitive load will work against them.

7.4 How Do Family-School Partnership Programs Attend to the Contexts of Low-Income Families?

If the goal of parent engagement is to increase parents use of high-quality parenting strategies that support children's learning and healthy development, the implications of the constraints associated with economic scarcity are quite clear. Programs need to not only provide relevant information and strategies for parents, but they must start from a point of design that takes into account the challenging economic and life experiences that low-income parents face and how both stress and cognitive load might be present in families lives (Gennetian et al., 2019). The family partnership programs described in this volume addressed these concerns in some ways, although the chapters did not all explicitly talk about how they were designed with these issues in mind.

It is clear in all of these interventions that ongoing relationships with parents are central to the program models and relationships are critical to ensure that the program is supportive rather than focused narrowly on program task completion. These programs focus on building supportive and trusting relationships between program staff and parents, the foundation of which is authenticity and respectful relationships. The importance of this approach has also been recognized in community-based parenting programs (Axford et al., 2012). Without the foundation of a positive authentic relationship, some parents are likely to be unwilling to engage with the program, either because they face barriers to participation that go unrecognized or because they have experiences feeling judged or belittled by prior service providers (Hill et al., 2020; Mytton et al., 2014) . Working to get to know parents provides educators or program staff with the opportunity to build trust, to problem-solve barriers to participation, as well as to make parents feel heard and valued. It is notable that all of the programs described in this volume discuss affirming parents' and children's skills in some way. Affirming parents is known to make them more open to receiving and using support (Hill et al., 2020). Building relationships is not easy and requires staff to have both strong interpersonal skills and sufficient time and resources to support relationship building. This, of course, has implications for the cost of the program and the scaling-up of the programs as mentioned by Bierman and Sheridan (this volume).

Also noteworthy are the efforts of the parent-school partnership programs included in this volume to provide programming in ways that are accessible to families. This is done, for example, by scheduling group meetings at a variety of times in ParentCorps or by meeting with parents in individual sessions at home in REDI-P and Getting Ready programs. In general, inflexible program schedules represent one of the key reasons that parents say they do not participate in parenting programs. For families that already are juggling a large range of complicated and important tasks to care for their family, asking them to add another activity that requires additional planning and problem-solving may be too much. Working with families to find solutions to challenges of accessibility including issues related to work schedules, transportation, and childcare is critical to engaging and maintaining parents' participation.

In ParentCorps and in the Family Check-Up program, the facilitators who work with parents have a mental health or counseling background rather than an early education background. This may be important given the connection between poverty and psychological distress among parents. More specifically, the staff who are working with parents in these two programs are trained in motivational interviewing. Motivational interviewing is a counseling technique that is designed to explore goals and reduce ambivalence or resistance to behavioral changes that will help meet these goals (Magill & Hallgren, 2019). In this way, it directly works against the problems that cognitive load and scarcity may create for parents. The emphasis is on starting with a recognition that parents have worthy goals, but that that they also face challenges in implementing steps that will move them forward. The focus on building motivation holds the promise of reducing the divergence between goals for their children, and how their parenting supports those goals. A slightly less formal process of mutual goal setting with parents and planning a course of action to support children's development is also part of the Getting Ready program. Taken together, these partnership features underscore the importance of capitalizing on parents' desired goals and helping them develop concrete, specific, and actionable plans that are feasible and realistic given their circumstances.

As part of the goal setting and planning processes, several programs underscore the importance of reflection for parents, including Getting Ready, ParentCorps, and Family Check-Up. Indeed, for parents who face significant cognitive demands and a shortage of attention, the dedicated time to pause and consider their parenting may be particularly important to enabling behavioral changes. Few families, but especially low-income families, have time to do this type of reflection and discussion on their own, but reflection is an important part of behavioral change efforts across fields of prevention research.

Common across several programs is a focus on helping families build sustainable family routines. Given potentially complicated work schedules and family complexity, family routines may be especially hard to build in the absence of intentional planning. Family routines provide a foundation for positive behaviors by giving children clear expectations and predictable transitions that support self-regulation and reduce problem behaviors (Ferretti & Bub, 2017). Having established routines that are pre-set also has the potential to reduce cognitive load by removing daily uncertainty and decision points. As such, for parents under stress and experiencing cognitive load, the scaffolding of family activities might support positive parenting behaviors because they become planned into the family's life. Two of the programs described in this volume differ in the extent to which they engage parents in deciding what content to focus on: ParentCorps uses a curriculum to guide group sessions, and Family Check-Up uses a needs assessment as the basis for parents' goal-setting work.

The REDI-P program also takes an approach that reduces parents' barriers to uptake by using a strategy that potentially reduces parents' cognitive load. In the REDI-P program, parents are provided with specific learning materials and curriculum guides designed to help them build children's early learning skills. Parents are also engaged in home visits on a regular basis that support implementation, encourage personal parental goal-setting and reflection, and build the use of other parenting skills that support children's positive behavior and self-regulation. It is interesting that the greatest short-term gains in children's school readiness were linked to the use of these materials, compared with parent engagement. Why might that be? It takes intentionality and work to scaffold children's learning in play activities. Providing parents with a template and set of materials reduces the amount of mental work that they must exert to figure out how to implement parenting strategies. It reduces the need for them to remember what they are supposed to be doing, and to an extent even how they are supposed to be doing it. Providing key activities, including materials with concrete prompts and suggestions, as well as plans for implementing and adapting the activities provides a specific and clear set of learning routines that scaffold children's learning. Packaging the activities and materials and providing support for their use drastically reduces the burden on parents to provide their children with developmentally appropriate learning activities. Moreover, staff feedback, provided in the context of a supportive relationship, provides the opportunity to positively reinforce parents for their efforts and tailor the program to improve the quality of the activities for specific families.

Finally, the Child-Parent Center (CPC) and in Family Check-Up programs make an effort to connect parents with other community services that may be helpful to families. What this means in practical terms is not well explained in the chapters in this volume, and more explicit attention to this component of the interventions might be helpful. Research on parenting education for low-income mothers of older children finds that mothers experience poverty as a barrier to being able to parent effectively. Yet, parenting education programs often do not address issues related to the social and structural context of economic hardship directly. Cucchiara et al. (2019) note that this perpetuates the illusion that good parenting should be unaffected by poverty and economic need. However, their research shows that when families are hungry or on the verge of homelessness, these conditions of poverty make it hard to focus on other parenting issues. In CPC and Family Check-Up, efforts to connect parents with services that directly impact family's economic conditions might increase the effectiveness of the programs.

In summary, for parent-school partnerships to be effective they need not only consider the research base identifying the parenting strategies that support children's early learning but also need to consider research evidence documenting the ways that disadvantage and social marginalization affect parents, specifically through increasing stress and cognitive load. Although improving communication and targeting key aspects of parenting that are specific and known to support children's learning are critical to the success of a parenting program, the efforts can be more effective by building in some other key design elements that are important given the contexts of low-income parents' lives. Ensuring that staff have the skills and resources to build authentic relationships with parents and training in mental health may be critical features of effective programs. In addition, attending to the accessibility of program services, and including a specific emphasis on parent goal setting, building parent motivation for actionable plans, and planning family routines and reflection may all play important roles in fostering engagement and promoting positive growth.

7.5 How Do Family-School Partnership Programs Change Teacher and School Practices?

While all programs in this volume ask parents to engage in a partnership, they differ in the extent to which the schools and teachers commit to the partnership and a process of institutional change. In the Getting Ready, ParentCorps, and CPC programs in which the parents are engaged directly with the school and teachers, the school and teachers are also targets of change. While it may seem like a minor issue to focus on who is "doing" the work of the partnership, in it signifies a strong and potentially important divergence among programs. Programs extend along a continuum from working to support parents in a change process to partnering with parents in a collaborative change process. Programs that are further along this partnership continuum recognize that it is not just parents that need improvement to support children, but school and teacher practices are in need of improvement as well. A full partnership model takes into account that schools may not be experienced by parents as equal or welcome partners in their children's education.

Low-income parents may feel stigmatized and marginalized because of their economic and social position (Russell et al., 2008), which is often not shared by their children's teachers. Indeed, low-income parents and parents of color experience implicit and explicit bias in interactions with teachers. It turns out, despite their training, teachers are no less likely to have racial biases than other adults—explicit and implicit (Starck et al., 2020). Given the pervasive nature of white supremacy, it is hardly surprising that teachers have the same racial attitudes as found in other adults. Yet, education research also documents that teachers treat students differently depending on their race, and this differential treatment contributes to racial disparities in achievement and discipline (Warikoo et al., 2016). Moreover, the consequences of teachers' racial biases are evident in preschool programs, as research suggests that teachers have biased expectations for the behavior of black boys and negative views of disadvantaged parents (Gilliam et al., 2016; Neitzel, 2018).

The importance of research on racial biases among teachers and school staff is also relevant for children in immigrant families, as it suggests that cultural and ethnic biases may be operating as well. As the United States becomes more ethnically diverse, it is not reasonable to expect that teachers will know about all of the home cultures of children in their classrooms, nor that they will be unbiased towards them. Teachers' nativist biases can likewise create challenge experiences for children and families in schools, although their experiences may vary as a function of the different ethnic group stereotypes regarding potential for success in schools (Blanchard & Muller, 2015).

In the ParentCorps, CPC, and Getting Ready programs, it is understood that teachers may need additional supports and training in order to work well with parents and to support children's learning in the classroom. Indeed, this kind of support seems critical to helping teachers build effective partnerships with parents, as both parties have a responsibility to work on improving children's experiences as they transition into formal schooling. An explicit program focus on schools and teachers makes transparent the need for teachers and school settings to improve their own perceptions and understanding of children and families, as well as their teaching practices.

Building in training and ongoing coaching to work towards improved teacher skills and practices in working with families is an important achievable step to building more equitable, culturally relevant and effective schools. Of course, improved parent-teacher relationships will not undo all the systemic racism and white supremacy found in the public education system. Yet, family-school partnerships that formalize schools' roles in the partnership have the potential to provide teachers with tools that may reduce biased perceptions, increase their ability to form positive relationships with families, and improve their classroom teaching practices.

7.6 Conclusion

The family-school partnership programs described in this volume, along with the rigorous research conducted to evaluate their impacts on families and child learning outcomes are important because they point to the promise of such approaches. Both the scaling of these existing programs and the innovation and development of new partnership programs will benefit from such research and push the field forward. I suggest that, in working to better understand why these models have succeeded, it is of value to make explicit connections with broader literatures on the context of family lives in poverty, how poverty affects parenting practices, as well as how families experience classism, racism, and nativism. Attending to these critically important considerations will potentially make important contributions to understanding the success of these programs and refining and improving these programs in the future.

References

Abraham, K. G., & Houseman, S. N. (2019). Making ends meet: The role of informal work in supplementing Americans' income. *RSF: The Russell Sage Foundation Journal of the Social Sciences, 5*(5), 110–131.

Axford, N., Lehtonen, M., Kaoukji, D., Tobin, K., & Berry, V. (2012). Engaging parents in parenting programs: Lessons from research and practice. *Children and Youth Services Review, 34*(10), 2061–2071.

Berger, L. M., & Carlson, M. J. (2020). Family policy and complex contemporary families: A decade in review and implications for the next decade of research and policy practice. *Journal of Marriage and Family, 82*(1), 478–507.

Blanchard, S., & Muller, C. (2015). Gatekeepers of the American dream: How teachers' perceptions shape the academic outcomes of immigrant and language-minority students. *Social Science Research, 51*, 262–275.

Bridgett, D. J., Kanya, M. J., Rutherford, H. J., & Mayes, L. C. (2017). Maternal executive functioning as a mechanism in the intergenerational transmission of parenting: Preliminary evidence. *Journal of Family Psychology, 31*(1), 19–29.

Cucchiara, M., Cassar, E., & Clark, M. (2019). "I Just Need a Job!" Behavioral solutions, structural problems, and the hidden curriculum of parenting education. *Sociology of Education, 92*(4), 326–345.

Duncan, G. J., & Magnuson, K. (2013). Investing in preschool programs. *Journal of Economic Perspectives, 27*(2), 109–132.

Ferretti, L. K., & Bub, K. L. (2017). Family routines and school readiness during the transition to kindergarten. *Early Education and Development, 28*(1), 59–77.

Gennetian, L. A., Marti, M., Kennedy, J. L., Kim, J. H., & Duch, H. (2019). Supporting parent engagement in a school readiness program: Experimental evidence applying insights from behavioral economics. *Journal of Applied Developmental Psychology, 62*, 1–10.

Gibbs, C., Ludwig, J., & Miller, D. L. (2013). Head start origins and impacts. In M. J. Bailey & S. Danziger (Eds.), *Legacies of the war on poverty* (pp. 39–65). New York: Russell Sage Foundation Press.

Gilliam, W. S., Maupin, A. N., Reyes, C. R., Accavitti, M., & Shic, F. (2016). *Do early educators' implicit biases regarding sex and race relate to behavior expectations and recom-*

mendations of preschool expulsions and suspensions? Yale University Child Study Center. http://ziglercenter.yale.edu/publications/Preschool%20Implicit%20Bias%20Policy%20 Brief_final_9_26_276766_5379_v1.pdf.

Grindal, T., Bowne, J. B., Yoshikawa, H., Schindler, H. S., Duncan, G. J., Magnuson, K., & Shonkoff, J. P. (2016). The added impact of parenting education in early childhood education programs: A meta-analysis. *Children and Youth Services Review, 70*, 238–249.

Hill, Z., Spiegel, M., & Gennetian, L. A. (2020). Pride-based self-affirmations and parenting programs. *Frontiers in Psychology, 11*, e910.

Kalil, A., & Ryan, R. (2020). Parenting practices and socioeconomic gaps in childhood outcomes. *The Future of Children, 30*, 29–54.

Lambert, S. J., Henly, J. R., & Kim, J. (2019). Precarious work schedules as a source of economic insecurity and institutional distrust. *RSF: The Russell Sage Foundation Journal of the Social Sciences, 5*(4), 218–257.

Luthar, S. S., & Eisenberg, N. (2017). Resilient adaptation among at-risk children: Harnessing science toward maximizing salutary environments. *Child Development, 88*, 337–349.

Magill, M., & Hallgren, K. A. (2019). Mechanisms of behavior change in motivational interviewing: Do we understand how MI works? *Current Opinion in Psychology, 30*, 1–5.

Magnuson, K. A., & Duncan, G. J. (2019). Parents in poverty. In M. Bornstein (Ed.), Handbook of parenting. *volume 4 social conditions and applied parenting (pp* 301–328). Routledge.

Magnuson, K., & Duncan, G. (2018). Parents in poverty. In M. Bornstein (Ed.), *Handbook of parenting, volume 4: Social conditions and applied parenting* (3rd ed., pp. 95–121). Mahwah: Lawrence Erlbaum Associates.

Magnuson, K., & Schindler, H. S. (2016). Parent programs in pre-K through third grade. *The Future of Children, 26*, 207–221.

Masarik, A. S., & Conger, R. D. (2017). Stress and child development: A review of the family stress model. *Current Opinion in Psychology, 13*, 85–90.

McLoyd, V., Mistry, R. S., & Hardaway, C. R. (2014). Poverty and children's development: Familial processes as mediating influences. In E. T. Gershoff, R. S. Mistry, & D. A. Crosby (Eds.), *Societal contexts of child development: Pathways of influence and implications for practice and policy* (pp. 109–124). New York: Oxford University Press.

McCoy, D. C., Yoshikawa, H., Ziol-Guest, K. M., Duncan, G. J., Schindler, H. S., Magnuson, K., ... & Shonkoff, J. P. (2017). Impacts of early childhood education on medium-and long-term educational outcomes. *Educational Researcher, 46*(8), 474-487.

Morduch, J., & Schneider, R. (2017). *The financial diaries: How American families cope in a world of uncertainty*. Princeton: Princeton University Press.

Mytton, J., Ingram, J., Manns, S., & Thomas, J. (2014). Facilitators and barriers to engagement in parenting programs: A qualitative systematic review. *Health Education & Behavior, 41*(2), 127–137.

National Academies of Sciences, Engineering, and Medicine. (2016). *Parenting matters: Supporting parents of children ages 0–8*. Washington, DC: The National Academies Press. https://www.nap.edu/catalog/21868/parenting-matters-supporting-parents-of-children-ages-0-8.

Neitzel, J. (2018). Research to practice: Understanding the role of implicit bias in early childhood disciplinary practices. *Journal of Early Childhood Teacher Education, 39*(3), 232–242.

Russell, M., Harris, B., & Gockel, A. (2008). Parenting in poverty: Perspectives of high-risk parents. *Journal of Children and Poverty, 14*(1), 83–98.

Sanders, M. R., Turner, K. M., & Metzler, C. W. (2019). Applying self-regulation principles in the delivery of parenting interventions. *Clinical Child and Family Psychology Review, 22*(1), 24–42.

Shah, A. K., Mullainathan, S., & Shafir, E. (2012). Some consequences of having too little. *Science, 338*, 682–685.

Shah, A. K., Zhao, J., Mullainathan, S., & Shafir, E. (2018). Money in the mental lives of the poor. *Social Cognition, 36*(1), 4–19.

Shonkoff, J. P., & Fisher, P. A. (2013). Rethinking evidence-based practice and two-generation programs to create the future of early childhood policy. *Development and Psychopathology, 25*, 1635–1653.

Smith, T. E., Sheridan, S. M., Kim, E. M., Park, S., & Beretvas, S. N. (2020). The effects of family-school partnership interventions on academic and social-emotional functioning: A meta-analysis exploring what works for whom. *Educational Psychology Review, 32*(2), 511–544.

Starck, J. G., Riddle, T., Sinclair, S., & Warikoo, N. (2020). Teachers are people too: Examining the racial bias of teachers compared to other American adults. *Educational Researcher, 49*, 273–284.

Tach, L., & Edin, K. (2017). The social safety net after welfare reform: Recent developments and consequences for household dynamics. *Annual Review of Sociology, 43*, 541–561.

Teti, D. M., Cole, P. M., Cabrera, N., Goodman, S. H., & McLoyd, V. C. (2017). Supporting parents: How six decades of parenting research can inform policy and best practice. *Social Policy Report, 30*(5), 1–34. Society for Research in Child Development.

Warikoo, N., Sinclair, S., Fei, J., & Jacoby-Senghor, D. (2016). Examining racial bias in education: A new approach. *Educational Researcher, 45*(9), 508–514.

Yoshikawa, H., Weiland, C., Brooks-Gunn, J., Burchinal, M. R., Espinosa, L. M., Gormley, W. T., … Zaslow, M. J. (2013). *Investing in our future: The evidence base on preschool education*. Washington, DC: Society for Research in Child Development.

Zigler, E., & Styfco, S. J. (1994). Is the Perry preschool better than head start? Yes and no. *Early Childhood Research Quarterly, 9*(3–4), 269–287.

Chapter 8
Unleashing the Power of Family Engagement to Achieve Impact and Equity for All

Rachel M. Abenavoli, Jessica A. Siegel, and Pamela A. Morris

Abstract The chapters in this impressive volume demonstrate the power and promise of family engagement interventions, theoretically grounded and strategically timed at the transition to school, for promoting children's learning and development. In this commentary, we reflect on the tremendous progress the family engagement field has made in identifying effective programs and practices, varied in their approach, format, and intensity. The next frontier is deploying and sustaining effective approaches at scale to extend the reach of program benefits beyond participants of specific research trials to families across diverse contexts and socioeconomic, racial-ethnic, and linguistic backgrounds. Drawing on insights from diffusion of innovation theory, public health, and research-practice partnership frameworks, we discuss the critical need for, and challenges in, "getting to scale," and argue that greater attention to issues of reach, sustainability, and system-level institutionalization is needed to advance the next generation of family engagement research and practice. With a strong empirical base and consensus around the importance of scaling and sustaining effective approaches, the field is poised to realize the full potential of family engagement interventions for reducing inequities and achieving population-level impact.

Keywords Family engagement · Intervention · Transition to school · School practices · Sustainability · Intervention diffusion · Intervention scaling · Innovation theory · Research-practice partnerships

---

R. M. Abenavoli (✉)
Institute of Human Development and Social Change, Steinhardt School of Culture, Education, and Human Development, New York University, New York, NY, USA
e-mail: rachel.abenavoli@nyu.edu

J. A. Siegel
Psychology and Social Intervention Program, New York University, New York, NY, USA
e-mail: siegej04@nyu.edu

P. A. Morris
Department of Applied Psychology, Steinhardt School of Culture, Education, and Human Development, New York University, New York, NY, USA
e-mail: pamela.morris@nyu.edu

© Springer Nature Switzerland AG 2022

K. L. Bierman, S. M. Sheridan (eds.), *Family-School Partnerships During the Early School Years*, Research on Family-School Partnerships,
https://doi.org/10.1007/978-3-030-74617-9_8

8.1 Commentary

Socioeconomic and racial-ethnic disparities in learning are early-emerging and persist over time as a result of income inequality, structural racism, and inequitable access to high-quality health and educational resources (Carneiro & Heckman, 2003). These early disparities are cause for concern because children's skills at the transition to school lay the foundation for their academic, social-emotional, and behavioral adjustment over time (Cunha & Heckman, 2007; Duncan et al., 2007; Jones et al., 2015). Whereas early inequities interfere with healthy learning and development, supportive and stimulating interactions at home and at school, along with strong connections between family and school contexts, enhance learning for all children and may have the greatest impacts among children experiencing disadvantage (Shonkoff, 2011; Yoshikawa et al., 2013). This rich volume demonstrates the potential of family engagement strategies timed with children's transition to formal schooling for addressing these educational inequities.

The chapters in this volume describe five distinct approaches to engaging families that have been shown to be effective in prior research and that are strategically timed to support families at the transition to kindergarten. As Bierman and Sheridan (Chap. 1) point out, these five exemplar programs are quite varied in their approaches. They include individualized and group-based models, curricular and strategy-focused models, home-visiting and school-based models, more intensive and less intensive models, clinician-facilitated and ECE staff-facilitated models, models developed for specific settings or populations, and models emphasizing unique dimensions of family engagement to different extents (e.g., engagement at home, engagement at school, or family-teacher relationships). Despite this variation, evidence from rigorous experimental and quasi-experimental trials indicates that strategic, theoretically grounded, and well-implemented structural and relational enhancements to ECE programs to promote family-school partnerships can improve children's language, academic, social-emotional, and behavioral development in the early school years (and in some cases, well beyond that). These exemplar programs also boast positive impacts for families on parenting strategies and knowledge that could inform later child-focused decision-making (e.g., parenting skills in FCU-Kindergarten; home language and literacy activities in REDI-P; warmth and sensitivity in Getting Ready; knowledge of evidence-based practices in ParentCorps; positive attitudes and intentions regarding engagement in Child-Parent Centers).

With this, the next challenge facing the family engagement field is deploying and sustaining effective approaches at scale to extend the reach of program benefits beyond families in these specific research trials to those being served in other early educational contexts and who come from diverse backgrounds and live in other community settings. And the time is ripe for this work, with access to ECE having increased dramatically in the last few decades (Barnett et al., 2016; Child Trends Databank, 2019; Friedman-Krauss et al., 2018), and policies and standards relating to school-family partnerships also growing. For example, supporting family engagement is a cornerstone of the federally funded Head Start programs, and the vast majority of states encourage or require K-12 school districts to implement formal plans or policies to address family engagement (Chriqui et al., 2018). These forces demonstrate increased support, momentum, and (perhaps) opportunity to reach more children and families through family-school partnerships than ever before.

Yet, as the authors of this volume acknowledge, the extent to which these varied models are ready to meet this opportunity remains an open question. The program developers and research teams that are part of this volume have made enormous progress in developing these programs and building evaluation evidence for each of them, yet questions remain as to whether these program models will be fully successful as they "scale up" to larger populations and "scale out" to new contexts or new delivery systems (Aarons et al., 2017). To briefly summarize where each program is currently with regard to this question:

- Research-based, Developmentally Informed Parent (REDI-P) has been evaluated in one RCT in Pennsylvania with children from 24 Head Start centers who have been followed longitudinally.
- Getting Ready has been tested in two RCTs in Nebraska, one in 19 Head Start sites and one in 62 Head Start and other publicly funded pre-K programs.
- The kindergarten adaptation of the Family Check-Up (FCU) program has been tested in one RCT in 5 elementary schools in the Pacific Northwest; several other FCU adaptations have been tested in a variety of settings (e.g., schools, community mental health centers, pediatric primary care, treatment settings) and across families with children spanning ages 2–17.
- ParentCorps has been tested in two RCTs in New York City, the first with families from 8 schools and the second with families from 10 schools; ongoing trials are underway in 180 New York City school-based and center-based programs, as well as with sites in other geographic locations (Texas, Michigan).
- The Child-Parent Center (CPC) model has been tested in two large, longitudinal quasi-experimental studies, first in Chicago-based CPC centers in the 1980s, and more recently across 26 schools in 4 Midwestern cities.

In short, each program is the sum of a large and extensive (and impressive) research and program development base, but together, they have not yet provided the field with sufficient information to support implementation on a national level.

The authors and editors of this volume identified a number of challenges and high-priority directions for future research related to scaling and sustaining the five family engagement models – carefully articulating a path forward to "get to scale." Program intensity, dosage, and cost were among the most commonly cited barriers to scaling effective approaches. Authors also noted the need to identify more efficient and cost-effective delivery formats (e.g., online), to clarify programs' "active ingredients" and mechanisms of change to inform further refinement and adaptation, and to study (and potentially adapt) programs across a range of settings and culturally and linguistically diverse children and families.

In the sections that follow, our goal is to build on the insights already shared and offer additional, complementary perspectives to advance the next generation of family engagement research and real-world practice. First, we step back and describe the long-standing challenge of scaling social programs and discuss the need for new models to address this challenge. Next, we present three frameworks that approach the issue of scale from different angles, which serve to reinforce critical points by chapter authors and raise additional challenges, questions, and opportunities for consideration. We conclude with remaining questions and next steps for the field as we work to realize the potential of evidence-based family engagement programs and move the dial on educational outcomes and persistent inequities in the United States.

8.2 Bridging Research, Practice, and Policy: An Old Challenge

The challenge of bridging research, practice, and policy is not new or unique to the family engagement literature. Scholars across the fields of medicine, public health, prevention, psychology, and education have long lamented the fact that practice and policy in the real world do not necessarily reflect the latest science. Much of the research over the last few decades on testing and scaling programs has been guided by the Institute of Medicine's (IOM; Mrazek & Haggerty, 1994) framework, which suggests that successful scale-up is the culmination of a linear progression through efficacy, effectiveness, and dissemination research stages (Flay et al., 2005). Programs are first developed and tested in tightly controlled efficacy trials; efficacious programs are then implemented and evaluated "under real-world conditions" with larger and more diverse samples, and effective programs are then scaled for broad dissemination in the third and final stage. Efficacy and – to a lesser extent – effectiveness trials in the tradition of this model have identified a number of evidence-based interventions, including interventions designed to support families during early childhood, now catalogued in registries across multiple disciplines (e.g., SAMHSA's National Registry of Evidence-based Programs and Practices, the Institute of Education Science's What Works Clearinghouse, Child Trends' What Works/LINKS database, Blueprints for Healthy Youth Development).

Despite this important progress, major public investment and decades of research have not achieved population-level impact and equity in health, education, and well-being (Shonkoff, 2017), leading scholars to challenge existing research paradigms and call for new ways of developing, testing, scaling, and sustaining scientific innovations (Dodge, 2018; Haskins et al., 2019; Tseng et al., 2017). In the field of public health, Glasgow and colleagues (Glasgow & Emmons, 2007; Glasgow et al., 2003) argue that characteristics of programs, settings, and research interact in ways that slow the translation of research to practice at scale. For example, programs that are tested and successful in efficacy trials are typically characterized by their high intensity and cost, complexity, standardization, and delivery by highly trained and closely supervised implementers (including the original program developers). In contrast, programs that are successful at scale are more often characterized by their feasibility and low cost, the ease with which they can be implemented by a diverse workforce, their customizability and relevance to local contexts, and their broad appeal and reach. This is in part because target settings – and the local decision-makers, policy leaders, and practitioners within those settings – are guided by a set of values, policies, priorities, incentives, and unique needs of the community that may differ from or compete with scientific innovations to be scaled. Policymakers face fixed, limited resources (e.g., time, money, staff) or other constraints that might make it difficult to scale evidence-based programs and practices as originally designed; however, research findings typically provide little guidance regarding how to choose and/or adapt program models to make them more relevant for and accessible to the local context without harming program integrity or how to allocate resources while maximizing impact. Other characteristics of the existing research base and the typical research process also make it difficult for policymakers and practitioners to apply that research at scale, including the (non)representativeness of participants and sites (who are motivated to participate in research), the emphasis on internal validity over external validity in much experimental work, and limited information about aspects of implementation (besides dosage and quality) that are critically important to the success of programs at scale, including cost, reach, and sustainability of implementation once the research concludes.

8.3 Frameworks for Scaling and Sustaining Programs and Practices

Given the limitations of the traditional IOM model, and the continued disconnect between research and practice, other models are needed to significantly advance the next generation of policy-relevant research on social programs. We highlight three perspectives below that address the challenge of scaling and sustaining programs in different ways: (a) diffusion of innovation frameworks, (b) population-level frameworks, and (c) partnership frameworks. We highlight these three not because they are the only useful frameworks, but because they offer unique perspectives, useful insights, and instructive examples that illuminate opportunities for the family engagement field, which we highlight throughout.

8.3.1 Diffusion of Innovation Framework

Conceptual Foundations The diffusion of innovation framework describes how innovations – for example, evidence-based programs or practices – are communicated through social systems and come to be adopted, implemented, and institutionalized in those systems (Rogers, 2003; Rohrbach et al., 1993). According to diffusion theories, characteristics of innovations (actual and perceived) have the largest influence on the decision to adopt an innovation and the institutionalization (or sustained use by organizations and/or individuals) of that innovation. Key characteristics that contribute to the rate and success of diffusion include an innovation's (a) feasibility versus complexity of implementation, (b) compatibility or fit with the needs and values among local organizations and individuals, and (c) relative advantage or added value over current practice and relative to the cost of change. Programs and practices are also more likely to be adopted and sustained when they produce strong, clear benefits that can be readily tested ("trialability") and observed ("observability"; Dingfelder & Mandell, 2011; Rogers, 2003). In addition, because people and contexts are dynamic, what "fits" in the early phase of diffusion may not be relevant in later years, so sustained use of innovations requires that they be adapted and reinvented over time (Murray, 2009).

In addition to characteristics of the innovations themselves, communication channels and the messages prospective users receive about the innovation contribute to the adoption, implementation, and institutionalization of that innovation. Formal (e.g., mass media) and informal (e.g., interpersonal networks) communication channels may facilitate diffusion by increasing awareness of the innovation and endorsement of the innovation by early adopters and opinion leaders within the system (Murray, 2009; Rogers, 2003). In addition, the presence of a "champion" for the innovation facilitates institutionalization, as does support from other key stakeholders (Scheirer, 2005).

Lessons and Questions for the Family Engagement Field Diffusion theory underscores the importance of feasibility, flexibility, and fit and suggests that these factors are critical to widespread and sustained diffusion of family engagement programs because they ensure that programs are (and stay) relevant and practical in local contexts at both the setting level (e.g., school systems, superintendents) and individual level (teachers, families). As several authors of this volume noted, however, many programs are (to varying degrees) intensive, complex, and standardized and involve implementation by highly trained facilitators. As a group, because they are timed strategically at the transition to school, the five models in this volume are less intensive (and therefore potentially more scalable) than more comprehensive, holistic approaches that characterize models for families with younger children. Even so, the high intensity and dosage of some programs, in particular, might limit their feasibility at scale. Sheridan and colleagues (Chap. 3), for example, note that the duration of the Getting Ready intervention (2 years) may make the program too burdensome and costly to scale as originally designed. Bierman and colleagues (Chap. 2) make a similar observation about the number of individual home visits (16) in the REDI-P program that span the pre-K and kindergarten years, and they also describe findings suggesting that it may be possible to reduce the number of visits, particularly for families above a certain threshold of risk, without reducing benefits for families and children. In contrast to higher-intensity programs, models that are less intensive and more flexible like FCU-Kindergarten (in-take interview and assessment, followed by 2–3 individualized sessions) also produce positive impacts and may be more readily scalable.

Thus, for some of the family engagement programs in this volume, ahead lies the challenge of "scaling back" these programs to "scale up." Identifying active ingredients or well-defined kernels (Embry & Biglan, 2008; Jones & Bouffard, 2012), as well as precisely articulating and testing mechanisms of change, can inform program refinement and adaptation during the process of scaling by revealing which components should be retained, which require refinement, and which could be eliminated in order to optimize intervention impact and efficiency (Sheridan et al., Chap. 2: Bierman et al., Chap. 3). Dawson-McClure and colleagues (Chap. 4) discuss their experimental approach for addressing the question of intensity, which involves testing the complete, more intensive ParentCorps program relative to a less intensive model in which ECE staff are trained in family engagement best practices (Thrive Professional Learning), a model developed and tested in close partnership with district leaders for the explicit purpose of scaling. Forthcoming results will uncover whether the less intensive program model yields benefits that are comparable to the more intensive program model. If results indicate that the more intensive model adds value, researchers and policymakers can consider the relative advantage in light of the added costs.

When it comes to the feasibility versus complexity of the family engagement programs in this volume, it is worth highlighting at least two other dimensions along which programs vary and which may contribute to their scalability: (a) their use of a manualized approach versus a strategy-based approach and (b) the supports needed to ensure high-quality implementation by program facilitators. REDI-P and ParentCorps are manualized approaches, FCU-Kindergarten and Getting Ready are strategy-based approaches, and CPC focuses on structural changes and principles of family engagement. There is some debate in the field as to whether manualized or strategy-based approaches are more effective for ensuring and supporting high-quality implementation (Jones & Bouffard, 2012). Manualized or curricular approaches are expected to increase fidelity to core intervention components across diverse facilitators and participants, but there is a tradeoff between standardization and flexibility. In contrast, strategy-based approaches may be more flexible and customizable, but this leaves more room for variability across implementers and may not provide enough scaffolding for newer implementers. To the extent manualized approaches are perceived as overly cumbersome by potential adopters (relative to the expected benefits), this may hinder the rate or extent of diffusion at scale. Intersecting the manual-vs-strategies question is one of implementation supports: strategy-based programs may require more highly skilled professionals (e.g., FCU-Kindergarten), while manualized programs may allow for greater staffing flexibility (e.g., REDI-P). A critical question for the field, then, is which approach, combined with which set of supports, best optimizes tradeoffs to achieve high-quality implementation (and, thus, impact) even when delivered at scale. Effective approaches may differ across contexts and different stages in the diffusion process (e.g., initial adoption versus sustained use).

In addition to the feasibility with which a program can be adopted, implemented, and sustained over time, compatibility, or fit, with local settings is critical. Most of the family engagement models in this volume are individualized approaches that can be customized somewhat to address the unique needs and values of individual families. This responsiveness to individual families may increase program relevance and facilitate widespread diffusion and sustained use. However, there is a clear need to assess the cultural and linguistic relevance of existing models before scaling more broadly (National Academies of Sciences, Engineering, and Medicine, 2016; Sheridan et al., Chap. 2; Dawson-McClure et al., Chap. 4; Stormshak et al., Chap. 5). Indeed, descriptive family engagement research documents important cultural differences in the nature and meaning of different types of engagement at school, home, and across the two contexts (Hill & Taylor, 2004). While common elements and mechanisms exist, what "family engagement" looks like among white families may be different than how high-quality family engagement is represented among families of color and other marginalized groups. The FCU-Kindergarten model has been adapted (at older ages) for use with Native American families, and the ParentCorps model, which has been implemented in schools serving high proportions of Black families, has been adapted over time to include an explicit emphasis on race and racism. With the exception of FCU, most models have been implemented to date in a specific setting (REDI-P in Pennsylvania, Getting Ready in Nebraska, CPC in four Midwestern cities, and ParentCorps in New York City). The extent to which the relevance and impact of individual programs generalize to other settings is not yet known, though it is promising that family engagement programs, as a class of interventions, have been successful across a range of geographic locations and socioeconomic and racial-ethnic groups.

In addition to issues of complexity, flexibility, and relevance, several authors raised the need to develop and test more efficient delivery methods to reduce costs, including web-based or other technology-enhanced platforms (e.g., REDI-P and Getting Ready); a web-based adaptation of FCU for middle school is in development. Other strategies that leverage technology and existing communication channels (e.g., texting-based behavioral nudges) might also enhance awareness and reach of programs, participation, retention, and ongoing use of targeted practices outside of intervention sessions (Hall & Bierman, 2015).

As noted throughout this discussion, characteristics of family engagement programs, and the channels through which they are communicated, are expected to influence both their initial adoption *and* institutionalization. Most programs represented in the volume have followed children longitudinally and documented persistent benefits into later elementary school (or adulthood, for CPC) – evidence which highlights the power of family engagement programs and their potential to combat the problem of fading ECE impacts. However, the extent to which schools, centers, and teachers continue to use family engagement programs and practices beyond the first or second implementation year is not known. How do dosage, fidelity, and implementation quality change over time? What level of supports are needed (or not needed) as programs are implemented over time, implementers become more experienced, and sites experience turnover among staff or leadership? To what extent are program models implemented as originally designed versus adapted or streamlined? What characteristics of programs or of the local context facilitate sustained use? Longitudinal follow-up of settings and implementers is an important direction for future research and will provide critical evidence regarding which program models are both scalable and sustainable, and under what conditions.

8.3.2 Population-Level Framework

Conceptual Foundations Researchers and policymakers across multiple fields generally agree that the goal of widespread program dissemination and institutionalization is improving outcomes and reducing inequities to the greatest extent possible, among as many people and settings as possible. At its furthest logical extension, this would mean achieving population-level impact and equity (Dodge, 2018; Fagan et al., 2019; Haskins et al., 2019; Shonkoff, 2017). Despite this stated goal, our research agendas and research questions often focus specifically on the task of taking programs to scale (e.g., "What will it take to scale this program while maintaining implementation quality?") rather than the ultimate goal (e.g., "How can we achieve impact and equity in this population?"). The subtle shift from focusing on scale to focusing on population impact is sorely needed, as achieving population impact requires scaling, but scaling does not necessarily achieve population impact.

Population-level impact is a function of the magnitude of program impact, the quality of implementation, *and* the extent of program reach; all three metrics are critical for judging the success of a program at scale (Dodge, 2018; Glasgow & Emmons, 2007). In the experimental research literature, however, greater attention has been paid to the magnitude of impact and less to reach. Relatedly, greater attention has been paid to internal validity – necessary for demonstrating impacts, to be sure – and less attention has been paid to external validity and generalizability, though this information is just as critical when attempting to bring innovations to scale (Glasgow & Emmons, 2007). Furthermore, population-level frameworks highlight the need to center equity in conversations about scale and to look beyond main effects and examine differential program reach, relevance, and impact. Of critical importance is to avoid reinforcing the very inequities the programs seek to address (Chaudry et al., 2018). That is, as they move from tightly controlled settings to scale, programs might have the unintended consequence of reinforcing inequities, rather than reducing them, if they do not reach the families, individuals, or communities who need it most and may stand to benefit the most; if aspects of implementation (e.g., adherence, quality) are weaker for those families or communities; or if the program does not lead to benefits for them. This might be the case if the program is not relevant to their needs, is not culturally appropriate, or requires a level of resources, background knowledge, or prior skill in order to experience or maximize benefits.

Given both the importance and the challenge of broad reach and equitable access, population-level frameworks highlight the importance of leveraging (or building) systems to support the broad dissemination and use of evidence-based programs and practices (Dodge, 2018; Fagan et al., 2019). A recent report by the National

Academies of Sciences also highlights the potential opportunities for scaling effective parenting interventions using existing systems and platforms (e.g., healthcare, public education, other community services). Using these existing systems and services as both points of entry and avenues for ongoing support would extend both the reach and sustainability of effective programming (National Academies of Sciences, Engineering, and Medicine, 2016). Where comprehensive, universal systems do not already exist, as in the case of the fragmented "nonsystem" of early childhood education (Barnett & Hustedt, 2011), scholars have called for new systems of care that can universally track, triage, and tailor tiered supports to children and families (Dodge, 2018; Shonkoff, 2017).

As an example of this type of approach, Family Connects (Dodge & Goodman, 2019) leverages the healthcare system for population reach. In Family Connects, a trained nurse meets with every family immediately following the birth of their child at the hospital, conducts a needs assessment with each family at subsequent home visits, and, based on that assessment, connects families to services in the community. Data and monitoring are key here: psychosocial and educational records are stored in a unified data system to facilitate monitoring and links to services in the community. In a randomized controlled trial in Durham, North Carolina, Family Connects reached 80% of the intended population with at least one intervention session, and the program was shown to increase access to community services, improve parenting, and reduce serious injuries among infants (Dodge et al., 2014).

Lessons and Questions for the Family Engagement Field Population-level frameworks illuminate just how critical it is to maximize the *reach* of family engagement programs in a target setting, not only the magnitude of their impact, if our goal is to achieve impact and equity at the population level. Implementation quality is of course necessary for producing meaningful impacts at scale, and nearly all chapters in this volume described intentional, robust strategies for supporting implementation quality and carefully measuring it. But in order to move the dial on family and child outcomes at the population level, there is a need for as much care and attention to be given to measuring reach in the target setting and developing strategies to maximize penetration. Documenting the proportion of sites (schools, centers) that adopt family engagement programs or opt in to research on those programs in the first place, and the extent to which those sites do or do not represent the broader target population, is a useful starting point. Relevant questions for participating sites include (a) what proportion of families choose not to participate in family engagement studies or programs, (b) does participation differ systematically for historically marginalized groups (e.g., low-income families, families of color, families speaking languages other than English, diverse family forms and configurations), and (c) what are barriers to participation? Also, once enrolled, who stays engaged and who benefits? On this last question, there is some indication that, among those who volunteer to participate in research, sustained participation over time in REDI-P was greater among white families compared to families of color (Bierman et al., Chap. 3), and impacts of Getting Ready were greater for parents with more education compared to parents with a GED or less than a high school education (Sheridan et al., Chap. 2). These patterns are important to track and address, as systematic gaps in participation or benefits may be replicated or magnified at scale. This highlights a critical need to examine and address potential barriers to participation, which might include refining program content to increase relevance, adapting delivery times or methods to increase reach, or developing other strategies to support equitable access.

A population-level impact framework highlights the value of studying existing setting- and systems-level supports and barriers, tapping into existing systems to maximize the reach and impact of family engagement programs at scale, and developing new systems to provide new opportunities for supporting families. The family engagement programs represented in this volume have been implemented and tested in a variety of settings, including Head Start programs (REDI-P, Getting Ready), public schools (CPC, ParentCorps, FCU), and other center-based programs (ParentCorps, in progress). This setting diversity indicates the promise of family engagement approaches, broadly, across varied contexts. A unique challenge facing family engagement programs at the transition to school is the fragmented and decentralized nature of ECE in the United States (Barnett & Hustedt, 2011). Prior to kindergarten entry children may attend ECE programs that vary in terms of their organization, structure, focus, and quality, and others may be cared for in less formal settings including family childcare or home care. While public schooling represents a system with near universal reach, children in the United States do not typically enter this system until kindergarten. No parallel system exists for supporting and tracking children from birth to age 5, and ECE systems, when they exist, are still typically disconnected from K-12 public school systems. To strengthen horizontal alignment (across ECE programs) and vertical alignment (as children age), scholars have called for coordinated systems of care from birth to age 5 (Dodge, 2018) and alignment across pre-K to third grade (Bogard & Takanishi, 2005; Reynolds & Temple, 2008).

Family engagement program developers and researchers have navigated this challenge in different ways, focusing on the time period before the transition to kindergarten (Getting Ready, ParentCorps), after the transition to kindergarten (FCU-Kindergarten), spanning the pre-K to kindergarten transition (REDI-P), or creating structural and programmatic alignment across pre-K to third grade (CPC). Bierman and colleagues (Chap. 3) note a challenge of supporting families across the transition from pre-K to kindergarten. In the REDI-P trial, children dispersed from just over 20 Head Start programs to nearly 70 elementary schools for kindergarten. This makes institutionalization challenging, creating pragmatic difficulties in intervention program management and staffing. It may also weaken the potential for long-term impacts to the extent some programs work by building communities of families that support each other and reinforce key practices over time (Dawson-McClure et al., Chap. 4). Open questions remain about the most effective approach for delivering or institutionalizing family engagement programs across the critical transition to school or the extent to which increasing access to publicly funded pre-K in the United States will provide new opportunities for embedding family engagement programs within those new systems.

8.3.3 Partnership Frameworks

Conceptual Foundations To narrow the gap between research and practice, some scholars have emphasized the need for more effective dissemination of science in the real world; underlying this focus is an assumption that increasing policymakers' and practitioners' knowledge about and access to existing research will result in greater use of that research. In contrast, partnership frameworks suggest that the gap between research and practice is not simply a knowledge gap and in fact may stem from a more fundamental disconnect between what and how research is conducted and what and how practice and policy unfold in the real world. Scholars have called for partnered research in health, community psychology, and education to investigate problems of practice and identify potential solutions that are mindful of local needs, priorities, and constraints (Coburn & Penuel, 2016; Israel et al., 1998; Tseng et al., 2017).

In contrast to primarily unidirectional models of science that prioritize the pathway *from* research *to* practice, partnership frameworks underscore the necessity and mutual value of a bidirectional approach (Coburn & Penuel, 2016; Tseng et al., 2017). Strong connections between researchers, decision makers, and members of the community can speed the translation of science to practice. Perhaps even more importantly, partnerships can also increase opportunities for rigorous research within large-scale systems and strengthen the practical applicability of the research design and thereby increase the subsequent public value of the scientific findings. By involving many stakeholders at multiple levels of the system with different perspectives and types of expertise, partnerships increase the relevance of research and the likelihood that it will be used, yield benefits, and become embedded in the system for ongoing use. Research and practice/policy partners collaborate across all phases of the research process by jointly articulating research agendas, developing or adapting intervention models, identifying methods for rigorously answering policy-relevant questions, and interpreting and sharing actionable evidence with all involved parties. Through this process, potential solutions to problems of practice address high-priority problems of practice while navigating constraints and capitalizing on opportunities within the system. Research-practice partnerships typically are guided by the dual aims of addressing specific priorities of practice and policy partners *and* contributing to a broader field of research, though this can be challenging given a tension between addressing problems of local (and perhaps immediate) importance and addressing problems that are generalizable to other settings or politically sensitive.

Another key feature of research-practice partnerships is their longevity. Instead of coming together to conduct an isolated research project, partnerships typically form with a broader mission. Solving complex problems requires sustained commitment of the partnership that is built on trust and regular communication and can withstand member turnover, leadership changes, and policy shifts. Long-term collaboration allows partners to remain connected beyond the initial installation of an innovation; it allows them to work together to monitor, study, refine, and strengthen innovations over time to maximize benefits for end users.

Lessons and Questions for the Family Engagement Field Research conducted in partnership with local decision makers and community members offers a way to address some of the challenges of scaling and sustaining programs highlighted by diffusion of innovation theory, population-level impact frameworks, and the authors of this volume. For example, involving practice and policy partners during program development and refinement can strengthen and sustain the compatibility of programs in a local, dynamic context. Policy partners who understand priorities, constraints, and opportunities for supporting family engagement can help researchers and program developers find ways to fit within existing systems or create new processes so that program implementation is feasible and efficient. With a deep understanding of and commitment to the target population, practice and policy partners can also strengthen the quality of family engagement research by emphasizing issues of relevance, external validity, and rigor of research at scale (and therefore its likelihood of scaled and sustained use). By articulating a shared research agenda and co-developing infrastructure for ongoing data collection, research and policy partners can monitor and strengthen program reach and implementation quality, continually assess and reassess the benefits and costs, and adapt programming over time to maximize impact.

Several authors of this volume describe their approach for engaging community stakeholders – including schools, teachers, and families – in developing programs and note the potential for partnerships to support scaling efforts. Dawson-McClure and colleagues describe their collaborative approach with the New York City Department of Education to develop, scale, implement, and evaluate an adaptation of ParentCorps that involves professional development for pre-K teachers. By working in partnership with district leaders, this team has developed a tiered system of supports, ranging from more intensive targeted supports to less intensive universal supports, to maximize the reach of family engagement strategies across New York City's universal pre-K system, which serves about 70,000 children in over 1800 public school and center-based sites each year. Findings from this work will reveal key lessons involving successful family engagement approaches at scale, and relative costs and benefits of more or less intensive adaptations within a single system, and may suggest a promising process (i.e., partnering with district leaders) by which to scale and sustain evidence-based family engagement programs and practices.

8.4 Next Steps for the Family Engagement Field: A Call for Population Impact

The chapters in this volume demonstrate that supporting family engagement at the transition to school can and does have large and lasting benefits and has the potential to narrow early-emerging and persistent learning disparities between higher- and lower-income children, between white children and children of color, and between more advantaged children and their less advantaged peers. Positive impacts have been documented across a range of approaches – including individualized and group-based models, home-based and school-based models, manualized and strategy-based models, and models of varying intensity and complexity – highlighting considerable success for this field to this point. The authors who led this work are to be commended for the substantial progress they have made in this field over the last two decades, showing that family engagement strategies can be designed to "work" for children and families at risk is no small feat. As the authors of these chapters note, however, most programs are at the early stages of scaling and real-world implementation; as such, achieving population impact and equity through family engagement is an aspiration but not yet a reality for our nation's children and families.

Drawing on a few insights from our discussion above, different paths to scale might exist for the five model family engagement programs in this volume. For example, because the FCU program is an individualized, flexible, and relatively low-cost model with a "lighter footprint," this model can be (and has been) easily adapted for use in different systems and with different populations. For more intensive programs (e.g., REDI-P, Getting Ready), the best path to scale may be the use of alternative, more cost-efficient delivery methods (e.g., web-based platforms) and/or reducing program intensity, given evidence that this might be done without reducing impacts. Partnering with local districts to translate multicomponent, intensive approaches into tiered systems of universal and targeted supports (as in the case of ParentCorps) or making structural changes to school settings (as in the case of CPC) represent other avenues for institutionalizing family engagement approaches.

Across models, several authors noted a need for information about active ingredients, cost, thresholds of implementation quality, and generalizability for diverse groups. To this we add several additional future research needs: (1) providing information on reach within the target population (overall and differential across key subgroups), (2) examining population-level impact beyond study participants, and (3) exploring the extent, quality, and nature of sustained use of family engagement programs and practices (by settings, schools, etc.) over time, after the initial research on short-term effects has concluded. In addition, there is a need to study, leverage, and strengthen systems to improve the reach of family engagement programs and practices, facilitate their institutionalization, and monitor and strengthen implementation, reach, and impact over time. This will require innovative solutions for navigating the currently fragmented ECE system and bridging the disconnect between ECE and K-12 systems. Partnering with practice/policy leaders may unearth barriers and opportunities for scale and sustained programming, as well as support ongoing research and evaluation as programs are implemented and potentially adapted in evolving systems and with new cohorts of families.

As we close, we refer again to the goal of supporting family engagement at scale, which is to leverage the research base built over the last few decades to improve children's learning and reduce learning inequities to the greatest extent possible. We typically consider scaling as the "problem" of a particular program or research team. Yet, perhaps the greatest progress will be made not by focusing attention and resources on the next stage of any one of these particular programs nor by building new approaches and the requisite evidence base (given how many successful approaches this group of researchers and others have identified here), but by supporting a coordinated strategy and an overarching learning agenda for embedding family engagement strategies into the kindergarten transition, across all school districts in the United States. It is now time to think beyond the next follow-up study and/or the next reanalysis of the existing data and begin to work more effectively together – across research teams, program developers, and policymakers – to institutionalize the learning from *all* of these approaches and embed family engagement as a "way of doing business" into our national school system (Sheridan et al., Chap. 2). In short, how do we make "family engagement" in school part of every kindergartener's experience, much the way that circle time and recess are? How do we help every school district in the United States recognize that engaging families at this transition to formal schooling can have profound impacts on how children start their educational experience, regardless of the specific approach they choose? Once we answer that question, we will be one step closer to doing right by our nation's children – by clearing the path for their families to be engaged in their children's educational success.

References

Aarons, G. A., Sklar, M., Mustanski, B., Benbow, N., & Brown, C. H. (2017). "Scaling-out" evidence-based interventions to new populations or new health care delivery systems. *Implementation Science, 12*, 111.

Barnett, W. S., & Hustedt, J. T. (2011). *Improving public financing for early learning programs* (Preschool policy brief, 23). New Brunswick: National Institute for Early Education Research.

Barnett, W. S., Friedman-Krauss, A. H., Gomez, R. E., Horowitz, M., Weisenfeld, G. G., & Squires, J. H. (2016). *The state of preschool 2015: State preschool yearbook*. New Brunswick: National Institute for Early Education Research.

Bogard, K., & Takanishi, R. (2005). PK-3: An aligned and coordinated approach to education for children 3 to 8 years old. *Social Policy Report, 19*(3), 3–23.

Carneiro, P., & Heckman, J. J. (2003). Human capital policy. In J. J. Heckman, A. B. Krueger, & B. M. Friedman (Eds.), *Inequality in America: What role for human capital policies?* Cambridge, MA: MIT Press.

Chaudry, A., Morrissey, T., Weiland, C., & Yoshikawa, H. (2018). *Cradle to kindergarten: A new plan to combat inequality*. New York: Russell Sage.

Child Trends Databank. (2019). *Preschool and prekindergarten.* Available at: https://www.childtrends.org/?indicators=preschool-and-prekindergarten

Chriqui, J., Stuart-Cassel, V., Piekarz-Porter, E., Temkin, D., Lao, K., Steed, H., … Gabriel, A. (2018). *Using state policy to create healthy schools coverage of the whole school, whole community, whole child framework in state statutes and regulations school year 2017–2018.* Bethesda: Child Trends.

Coburn, C. E., & Penuel, W. R. (2016). Research-practice partnerships in education: Outcomes, dynamics, and open questions. *Educational Researcher, 45*(1), 48–54.

Cunha, F., & Heckman, J. (2007). The technology of skill formation. *American Economic Review, 97*, 31–47.

Dingfelder, H. E., & Mandell, D. S. (2011). Bridging the research-to-practice gap in autism intervention: An application of diffusion of innovation theory. *Journal of Autism and Developmental Disorders, 41*, 597–609.

Dodge, K. A. (2018). Toward population impact from early childhood psychological interventions. *American Psychologist, 73*, 1117–1129.

Dodge, K. A., & Goodman, W. B. (2019). Universal reach at birth. *The Future of Children, 29*(1), 41–60.

Dodge, K. A., Goodman, W. B., Murphy, R. A., O'Donnell, K., Sato, J., & Guptill, S. (2014). Implementation and randomized controlled trial evaluation of universal postnatal nurse home visiting. *American Journal of Public Health, 104*(S1), S136–S143.

Duncan, G. J., Dowsett, C. J., Claessens, A., Magnuson, K., Huston, A. C., Klebanov, P., … Japel, C. (2007). School readiness and later achievement. *Developmental Psychology, 43*, 1428–1446.

Embry, D. D., & Biglan, A. (2008). Evidence-based kernels: Fundamental units of behavioral influence. *Clinical Child and Family Psychology Review, 11*, 75–113.

Fagan, A. A., Bumbarger, B. K., Barth, R. P., Bradshaw, C. P., Cooper, B. R., Supplee, L. H., & Walker, D. K. (2019). Scaling up evidence-based interventions in US public systems to prevent behavioral health problems: Challenges and opportunities. *Prevention Science, 20*, 1147–1168.

Flay, B. R., Biglan, A., Boruch, R. F., Castro, F. G., Gottfredson, D., Kellam, S., … Ji, P. (2005). Standards of evidence: Criteria for efficacy, effectiveness and dissemination. *Prevention Science, 6*, 151–175.

Friedman-Krauss, A. H., Barnett, W. S., Weisenfeld, G. G., Kasmin, R., DiCrecchio, N., & Horowitz, M. (2018). *The state of preschool 2017: State preschool yearbook.* New Brunswick: National Institute for Early Education Research.

Glasgow, R. E., & Emmons, K. (2007). How can we increase translation of research into practice? Types of evidence needed. *Annual Review of Public Health, 28*, 413–433.

Glasgow, R. E., Lichtenstein, E., & Marcus, A. C. (2003). Why don't we see more translation of health promotion research to practice? Rethinking the efficacy-to-effectiveness transition. *American Journal of Public Health, 93*, 1261–1267.

Hall, C. M., & Bierman, K. L. (2015). Technology-assisted interventions for parents of young children: Emerging practices, current research, and future directions. *Early Childhood Research Quarterly, 33*, 21–32.

Haskins, R., Dodge, K. A., & Daro, D. (2019, Spring). *Achieving broad-scale impacts for social programs* (The future of children, policy brief). Princeton: Princeton University.

Hill, N. E., & Taylor, L. C. (2004). Parental school involvement and children's academic achievement: Pragmatics and issues. *Current Directions in Psychological Science, 13*, 161–164.

Israel, B. A., Schulz, A. J., Parker, E. A., & Becker, A. B. (1998). Review of community-based research: Assessing partnership approaches to improve public health. *Annual Review of Public Health, 19*, 173–202.

Jones, S. M., & Bouffard, S. M. (2012). Social and emotional learning in schools: From programs to strategies. *Social Policy Report, 26*(4), 1–33.

Jones, D., Greenberg, M. T., & Crowley, D. M. (2015). Early social-emotional functioning and public health: The relationship between kindergarten social competence and future wellness. *American Journal of Public Health, 105*, 2283–2290.

Mrazek, P. J., & Haggerty, R. J. (Eds.). (1994). *Reducing risks for mental disorders: Frontiers for preventive intervention research*. Washington, DC: National Academy Press.

Murray, C. E. (2009). Diffusion of innovation theory: A bridge for the research–practice gap in counseling. *Journal of Counseling & Development, 87*, 108–116.

National Academies of Sciences, Engineering, and Medicine. (2016). *Parenting matters: Supporting parents of children ages 0–8*. Washington, DC: National Academies Press.

Reynolds, A. J., & Temple, J. A. (2008). Cost-effective early childhood development programs from preschool through third grade. *Annual Review of Clinical Psychology, 4*, 109–139.

Rogers, E. M. (2003). *Diffusion of innovations* (5th ed.). New York: Free Press.

Rohrbach, L. A., Graham, J. W., & Hansen, W. B. (1993). Diffusion of a school-based substance abuse prevention program: Predictors of program implementation. *Preventive Medicine, 22*, 237–260.

Scheirer, M. (2005). Is sustainability possible? A review and commentary on empirical studies of program sustainability. *American Journal of Evaluation, 26*, 320–347.

Shonkoff, J. P. (2011). Protecting brains, not simply stimulating minds. *Science, 333*, 982–983.

Shonkoff, J. P. (2017). Rethinking the definition of evidence-based interventions to promote early childhood development. *Pediatrics, 140*(6), e20173136.

Tseng, V., Easton, J. Q., & Supplee, L. H. (2017). Research-practice partnerships: Building two-way streets of engagement. *Social Policy Report, 30*, 1–17.

Yoshikawa, H., Weiland, C., Brooks-Gunn, J., Burchinal, M. R., Espinosa, L. M., Gormley, W., … Zaslow, M. J. (2013). *Investing in our future: The evidence base on preschool education*. New York: Foundation for Child Development, Society for Research in Child Development.

Index

© Springer Nature Switzerland AG 2022

K. L. Bierman, S. M. Sheridan (eds.), *Family-School Partnerships During the Early School Years*, Research on Family-School Partnerships,
https://doi.org/10.1007/978-3-030-74617-9

Q

R

MIX
Papier aus verantwortungsvollen Quellen
Paper from responsible sources
FSC® C105338

If you have any concerns about our products,
you can contact us on
ProductSafety@springernature.com

In case Publisher is established outside the EU,
the EU authorized representative is:
Springer Nature Customer Service Center GmbH
Europaplatz 3, 69115 Heidelberg, Germany

Printed by Libri Plureos GmbH
in Hamburg, Germany